G000058252

LESS STRESS MORE SUCCESS

Home Economics
Revision

Mary Anne Halton

GILL EDUCATION

Gill Education

Hume Avenue

Park West

Dublin 12

www.gilleducation.ie

Gill Education is an imprint of M.H. Gill & Co.

© Mary Anne Halton 2018

ISBN 978 07171 83562

Design by Liz White Designs

The paper used in this book is made from the wood pulp of managed forests.
For every tree felled, at least one tree is planted, thereby renewing natural resources.

At the time of going to press, all web addresses were active and contained information relevant to the topics in this book. Gill Education does not, however, accept responsibility for the content or views contained on these websites. Content, views and addresses may change beyond the publisher or author's control. Students should always be supervised when reviewing websites.

For permission to reproduce photographs, the author and publisher gratefully acknowledge the following:

© Alamy: 53, 69, 158, 159T, 160; Courtesy of Bord Bia: 83, 95, 138; Courtesy of Bord Iascaigh Mhara (BIM): 139; Courtesy of BSI: 258; Courtesy of Enterprise Ireland: 139; Courtesy of Excellence Ireland Quality Association (EIQA): 258; Courtesy of Food Safety Authority of Ireland: 139; Courtesy of Glanbia: 108, 159B; Courtesy of Guaranteed Irish: 258; Courtesy of Irish Organic Association: 114L; © iStock: 140, 141, 181, 235, 245, 258L; Courtesy of Killowen Farm: 105; Courtesy of National Standards Authority of Ireland (NSAI): 258T, 258B; Courtesy of Organic Trust: 114R; Courtesy of safefood: 54; Courtesy of Teagasc: 139; Courtesy of The Soil Association: 114C.

The author and publisher have made every effort to trace all copyright holders, but if any have been inadvertently overlooked we would be pleased to make the necessary arrangement at the first opportunity.

CONTENTS

Electives

- Revise your chosen elective on **www.moresuccess.ie**:
  - **Elective 1:** Home Design and Management
  - **Elective 2:** Textiles, Fashion and Design
  - **Elective 3:** Social Studies
- **Chapter 3:** Extra revision on **Food Studies** builds your confidence in this extensive topic

Just search for Home Economics Leaving Cert and look under 'Additional Resources'.

Introduction and Exam Guidelines

This book covers the **key topics** of the **compulsory Core** area for your Leaving Certificate Home Economics: Scientific and Social examination. Extra material is provided online at **www.moresuccess.ie**:

- **Chapter 3:** Food Studies
  - – Extension 1: Methods of Cooking
  - – Extension 2: Soups, Sauces and Pastry
- **Elective 1:** Home Design and Management
- **Elective 2:** Textiles, Fashion and Design
- **Elective 3:** Social Studies

How to use this book

Each chapter/section includes:

- **Learning Intentions:** what you will learn/revise

- Topics

- **Higher level** material identified

- **Links** between topics LINKS

- **Exam focus** with hints for the exam

- **Key points** with information to note

- Tables integrating the topics

- **Sample answers** to exam questions with **summaries** of key points.

The syllabus and the exam

Structure of the syllabus

The exam is offered at two levels, **Higher** and **Ordinary**. The syllabus is divided into a **core** section and a choice of three **electives**.

Syllabus	What is in this section?
Mandatory core topics – study *all* the core topics (80%) **All students must submit Food Studies Coursework Journals	1. Food Studies (45%) 2. Resource Management and Consumer Studies (25%) 3. Social Studies (10%)
Electives – choose *one* of the three topics (20%) **Elective 2 (Textiles) has a practical coursework element	Elective 1: Home Design and Management OR Elective 2: Textiles, Fashion and Design OR Elective 3: Social Studies

How Home Economics is examined

If you choose **Elective 1: Home Design and Management** *or* **Elective 3: Social Studies,** the exam consists of:

- a written examination (80%)
- Food Studies coursework with a journal (20%)

If you choose **Elective 2: Textiles, Fashion and Design,** the exam consists of:

- a written examination (70%)
- Food Studies coursework with a journal (20%)
- Textiles, Fashion and Design Elective coursework (10%)

How the exam is marked

Marks are allocated to each component as follows:

- Candidates choosing **Home Design and Management** *or* **Social Studies Elective:**

Component of exam	Marks	Percentage
Written paper	320	80
Food Studies coursework	80	20
Total	**400**	**100**

- Candidates choosing **Textiles, Fashion and Design Elective:**

Component of exam	Marks	Percentage
Written paper	280	70
Food Studies coursework	80	20
Textiles, Fashion and Design Elective coursework	40	10
Total	**400**	**100**

Structure, marking and timing of the exam paper

There are **three** sections in the exam paper: Section A, Section B and Section C (the elective). You have 2 hours and 30 minutes to complete the exam paper. The sections are structured and marked for Higher Level *and* Ordinary Level papers as follows:

Section	Requirements	Marks	Total marks	Time allocated
Section A (short questions)	Answer **10** out of 12 questions	6 marks per question	60 marks	25–30 minutes
Section B (long questions): Question 1	Question 1 is **compulsory**	80 marks	80 marks	30–35 minutes
Section B: Questions 2, 3, 4, 5	Answer any **two** questions from 2, 3, 4 and 5	50 marks *each*	100 marks	20 minutes × 2 = 40 minutes
Section C Electives 1 and 3	Answer a *and* b **or** c	80 marks	80 marks	30–35 minutes
Section C Elective 2 (Textiles)	Answer a *and* b **or** c	40 marks	40 marks	30–35 minutes

Do not forget to allow time for:

1. Reading through the paper before you start writing. Take ten minutes to read the questions and decide which questions you will answer. Underline key words and phrases.

2. Reading through your work at the end. Take 5–10 minutes to read over your work and make additions or adjustments.

Make sure you complete **all** parts of the written exam.

The above timings are only a guideline. Practise answering questions within the times suggested in the table. **Budget your time carefully!**

Guidelines for each section

- **Section A**
  - Short, concise answers.
  - Answer the questions in the spaces provided in the exam booklet.
  - Hand the booklet to the superintendent.

- **Section B**
  - Question 1 is *compulsory*.
  - All questions in this section begin with a statement. Read them carefully.
  - You will be asked to read and analyse tables, charts and pie diagrams in the questions and draw conclusions where appropriate.

- **Section C – The Electives**
  - Candidates *must answer* (a) *and either* (b) *or* (c).
  - Part (a) is compulsory.

Key words

Look out for these key words in questions. Make sure you understand what they mean.

Characteristics: Qualities.

Compare: Show the similarities or differences between two items; you could use a table to illustrate your answer.

Define: Give the exact meaning of a word or phrase. Use examples if necessary to make your definitions clear.

Describe: Give the description in bullet/point form. Use a clearly labelled diagram to illustrate answers.

Discuss: Give a detailed description. Use a series of points.

Enumerate: List key points with a short explanation of each.

Evaluate: Refer to the positive and negative points.

Explain: Give a detailed account, with examples, and a diagram if appropriate.

Illustrate: Use a diagram to explain a point.

List: List the key points – a detailed explanation is not needed.

Name: One or two words; no details are necessary.

Outline: Give one or two sentences on each point.

Principle: Describe how something works or the reason for something.

Properties: The characteristics of something, e.g. a nutrient.

Suggest: State your answer in a few words.

Other key words and phrases:

- identify
- indicate
- give an account
- write
- summarise
- factors
- sources
- uses

> *exam focus*
>
> *Remember:* Home Economics involves **integration of topics** within questions. Sections B and C demonstrate this key principle. Learn all **linked material** when revising topics.

> *exam focus*
>
> As you revise, make a list of all the key words, key terms and phrases for the topics, and any relevant sample/past exam questions.

Effective revision – setting smart goals

The best way to approach sections/topics is to:

- Make a revision time plan.
- Read the material carefully.
- Make notes as you revise (make these *visual*: do not simply copy notes from your class work/textbooks).
- Make tables of key information.

- Draw spider/web diagrams or mind maps for *each* topic.
- Revise linked material in each topic.
- Attempt past exam questions on each topic.

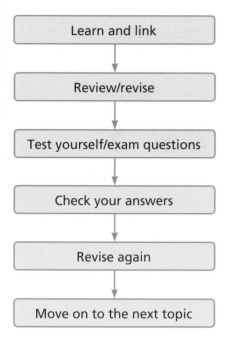

| Learn and link |
| Review/revise |
| Test yourself/exam questions |
| Check your answers |
| Revise again |
| Move on to the next topic |

Tick (✓) each topic when you have read, learned and tested yourself.

Essential skills:
1. Recognising **key words** in questions.
2. **Analysing** case studies, charts and tables of information, labels and symbols and drawing conclusions.
3. **Sketching** and **labelling** diagrams to illustrate an answer.
4. **Checking** and *knowing* the latest legislation/updates.

Final preparation for the written exam

1. Revise the complete course.
2. Note what to learn for Higher and Ordinary levels.
3. Be familiar with the layout of the exam paper.
4. Know how many questions you have to answer and how much time is needed to answer them.
5. Know which are the compulsory questions.
6. Know how the questions are marked.
7. Practise answering questions from past papers. Check possible solutions on www.examinations.ie. It is important to read the advice given in the Chief Inspector's Reports.

Guidelines on the day

1. Stay calm. Make sure you have pens, pencils, etc.
2. **Listen** to instructions given by superintendent.
3. Write your **exam number** in the box on the answer paper.

4. **Read** all questions and **highlight**/underline *key words*.

5. Mark the *compulsory* questions and choose which other questions you will answer.

6. Keep rigidly to your *time plan*.

7. Attempt *all* questions in Section A.

8. In Sections B and C, write neat *headings*, answer in *point form* and *elaborate* as appropriate.

9. *Attempt all parts*/sub-sections of a question. *Never* leave a section of a question unanswered: you could lose valuable marks.

10. *Label* all diagrams/sketches fully and clearly.

11. *Answer each new question on a new page.* Leave space at the end of each question in case you want to add more information when you read through your answers at the end of the exam.

12. Write *menus* in a box and use the correct *format*.

13. *Do not leave until the exam is finished.* Use all the time available to answer questions fully and to read over the questions and answers before the end.

exam focus

- **Use relevant** terminology/vocabulary.
- **Do not waffle** or write essay-style answers.
- **Do not repeat** information.

Study/revision plan

Overview of school year:

- Term 1 (September to December)
- Term 2a (December to Mock exams)
- Term 2b (Mock exams to Easter)
- Term 3 (Easter to Leaving Certificate exams)

Deadlines

Write down the dates/times for each of these:

- Submit Food Journal _____
- Christmas exam _____
- Mock exam _____
- Leaving Certificate exam _____

Your teacher will give you deadlines for homework (written and learning), classwork and revision. ***Listen* and take all the advice given**. Pay attention in class.

Check what has been covered: The LLR–PQR method of revision

Tick (✓) each core topic when you have learned it (**L**) in class, checked the links (**L**), revised it once (**R1**), practised answering exam questions (**PQ**) and revised it for a second time (**R2**). At the end is a column to help identify where **help or advice is needed.**

Topic	Learned (L)	LINKS (L)	Revised (R1)	Practised questions (PQ)	Revised (R2)	Do I need to ask for help?
Food choices						
Protein						
Carbohydrates						
Lipids						
Vitamins						
Minerals						
Water						
Energy						
Dietary guidelines						
Dietary requirements						
The Irish diet						
The Irish food industry						
Food commodities						
Meal management and planning						
Food preparation and cooking						
Food processing and packaging						
Food additives						
Food legislation						
Food spoilage						
Food safety and hygiene						

Topic	Learned (L)	LINKS (L)	Revised (R1)	Practised questions (PQ)	Revised (R2)	Do I need to ask for help?
Family resource management						
Components of management						
Attributes affecting management						
Management of household resources						
Household technology						
Textiles						
Consumer studies						
Consumer choices						
Consumer responsibility						
Consumer protection						
The family in society						
Sociological concepts						
Defining the family						
Family structures						
Family functions						
Marriage						
Family: a caring unit						
Family law						

Note: Similar checklists for electives can be downloaded from GillExplore.ie.

Week	Revision	LINKS – examples	Links and/or revision – examples
1	Food choice, protein, dietary guidelines, vegetarian diets	Meat, poultry, eggs, food preparation and cooking (meal management and planning), the Irish diet	Components of management, consumer choice
2	Lipids, dietary requirements, energy requirements, obesity, CHD, diabetes	Fats, oils, storage of lipid foods, food additives, food preparation and cooking methods	Consumer choice
3	Carbohydrates, dietary requirements, energy, coeliac disease, diabetes, obesity	Cereals, fruits vegetables, food preparation and cooking (sauce making, pastry making)	Management of household finances, consumer choices
4	Vitamins, minerals, dietary guidelines	The Irish diet, food additives, nutritional supplements	Household technology, consumer studies
5	Food profiles, alternative protein foods	The Irish food industry, food processing and packaging	Family resource management
6	Microbiology, food spoilage and preservation	Food preparation and cooking (yeast), food safety and hygiene, HACCP	Consumer responsibility, consumer protection
7	Aesthetic awareness of food	Food agencies and food legislation	Housing
8	Resource management	*Revise any topics not covered*	Textiles
9	The family	Family resource management	Family resource management
10	Marriage	The family, functions and legislation	
11	Family as a caring unit	Food requirements of different family members Meal management and planning	Family resource management, household financial management, housing
12	Elective 1 or 2 or 3 – *List the topics*		
13	Elective 1 or 2 or 3 – *List the topics*		

- **Revise exam questions** alongside topics. **Practise** past exam papers with each topic.
- Always check the **linked topics** so that you are prepared for **integrated** exam questions.
- Check the **compulsory questions** and note the integration of specific topics in these questions.
- Note what has to be learned for **Higher Level** and **Ordinary Level**.
- Check for **updates** on topics so that you are familiar with the latest information.
- Read and **practise exam questions** for the different topics/sections.

And finally: good luck!

Core Topics

1 Food Science and Nutrition

aims To learn and revise:
- Food choices
- Nutrients
- Water

Food choices

Factors affecting food choices:

1. Specific countries, cultural beliefs and traditions.
2. Availability, convenience and access to food.
3. Nutritional awareness and health status.
4. Sensory aspects and food presentation.
5. Financial resources.
6. Eating patterns, lifestyle and preferences.
7. Cookery and health TV programmes.
8. Advertising and marketing campaigns.

LINKS
- Individual dietary requirements (p. 55)
- The Irish diet (p. 75)
- Meal management and planning (p. 123)

Nutrients

Macronutrients	Micronutrients
● Protein	● Vitamins
● Lipids (fats/oils)	– fat-soluble
● Carbohydrates	– water-soluble
	● Minerals

exam focus

Nutrients may be included in questions on dietary requirements, food commodities, methods of cooking or methods of processing.

exam focus

You must *understand* and *be able to explain* what is meant by these **nutritional terms**:

- Macronutrients
- Micronutrients
- Elemental composition
- Chemical formula or equation
- Classification
- Sources
- Properties
- Reference intake

- Biological functions
- Biological value
- Energy value
- Digestion
- Absorption and utilisation of digested nutrients
- Enzymes
- Substrate

Protein

Elemental composition

- Carbon (C), hydrogen (H), oxygen (O) and nitrogen (N).
- Some contain sulphur (S), iron (Fe) and phosphorus (P).

Chemical structure

- Proteins are made up of chains of amino acids.
- Amino acids contain carbon, hydrogen, a variable (R), an amino group (NH_2) and an acidic carboxyl group (COOH).

H (hydrogen)

(variable) R—C—COOH (carboxyl group)

NH_2 (amino group)

Basic amino acid

Practise drawing and labelling the chemical structure of an amino acid.

H

$HSCH_2$—C—COOH (carboxyl group)

NH_2
(amino group)

Cysteine showing the R (variable) group

Essential and non-essential amino acids

- There are 20 common amino acids.
- Eight are essential for adults (these cannot be made by the body).
- Children need these eight plus two more (ten in total).

Essential amino acids	Non-essential amino acids
• Cannot be made by the body • Must be supplied by food	• Can be made by the body
Examples: isoleucine, leucine, lycine, methionine, phenylalanine, threonine, tryptophan, valine *For children:* histidine, arginine	*Examples:* alanine, aspargine, aspartic acid, cysteine, glutamic acid, glutamine, glycine, proline, serine, tyrosine

Peptides and peptide bonds

Amino acids are linked by a peptide bond. A carboxyl group (COOH) of one amino acid combines with an amino group (NH_2) of the next amino acid. A molecule of water (H_2O) is released (condensation) during this process. A dipeptide is formed.

NH_2—C—C   H—N—C—COOH

H   O   H

OH   H   R

R

Removal H_2O → Condensation	Addition H_2O → Hydrolysis

Hydrolysis

During digestion the reverse of the condensation process happens. Peptide bonds are broken by the addition of water, producing single amino acids. This is called hydrolysis.

Practise drawing and labelling a peptide bond/link showing condensation and hydrolysis.

- Two amino acids linked by peptide bond = **dipeptide**.
- Three amino acids linked = **tripeptide**.
- Many amino acids linked = **polypeptide chain**.

LINKS

- Digestion of protein (p. 9)
- Absorption of amino acids/ proteins (p. 10)

Exam question and sample answer

Higher Level 2014, Section B, Q1 (d)

LINK

- Classification of protein (p. 6)

(d) Give a detailed account of protein and refer to:
Classification (simple and conjugated)

(3 groups × 4 marks = 12 marks and 6 points × 2 marks = 12 marks = 24 marks)

Classification	Group	Sub-group	Examples	Food sources
Simple	*Animal*	*(a) Fibrous*	*Collagen, elastin, myosin*	*Connective tissue (meat)*
		(b) Globular	*Myoglobin Lactalbumin Ovalbumin*	*Meat Milk Eggs*
	Plant	*(a) Glutelins*	*Glutenin Oryzenin*	*Wheat Rice*
		(b) Prolamins	*Gliadin Zein*	*Wheat Maize/corn*
Conjugated (protein + non-protein)	*Lipoproteins Phosphoproteins Nucleoproteins Chromoproteins*		*Lecithin Casein Chromosomes Myoglobin*	*Egg yolk Milk Cell nuclei/DNA Meat*

Supplementary value or complementary value   (2 points × 4 marks = 8 marks)

- *Protein foods deficient in one or more amino acids can make up for the deficiency by being combined with foods rich in that amino acid at the same meal.*

- *A full complement of essential amino acids can be provided by serving (a) beans on toast (b) dhal and chapatti or (c) hummus and pitta bread. For example: Beans are high in lysine and low in methionine and toast is low inlysine and high in methionine.*

Structure (primary, secondary and tertiary)   (3 points × 5 marks = 15 marks)

Primary structure:

- *The sequence of amino acids in a polypeptide chain.*

- *The chain is formed by peptide links.*

- *The OH from the carboxyl group of one amino acid joins with the H of an amino group of another amino acid and water (H_2O) is released (condensation reaction).*

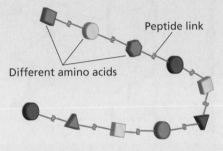

Peptide link

Different amino acids

-Ala-Ser-Val-Tyr-Gly-Val-Ser-Cys-Ile-Ala-Val-Ser-

Secondary structure:

- *Amino acids in polypeptide chains are further folded and cross-linked to create definite shapes and structures.*

- **Disulphide links** *occur when two sulphurs are linked together on a polypeptide chain or across two polypeptide chains e.g. two cysteine amino acids (contain SH group).*

- **Hydrogen bonds** *occur in polypeptide chains when hydrogen in one chain links with oxygen in a nearby chain, e.g. collagen.*

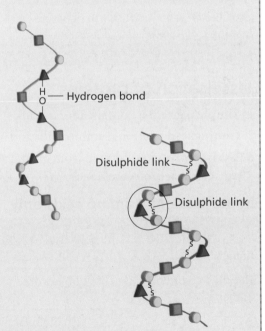

H
O — Hydrogen bond

Disulphide link

Disulphide link

Tertiary structure:

- *Refers to the pattern of folding polypeptide chains into three-dimensional shapes.*

- *Chains are held in place by cross-links and to form fibrous (straight, coiled or zigzag) or globular (ball-shaped) structures.*

> **LINK**
> - Tertiary structure diagrams (p. 6)

Tertiary structure

- Pattern of folding polypeptide chains into three-dimensional shapes.
- Shapes are held in place by cross-links and may be fibrous (straight, coiled or zigzag) or globular (ball-shaped).

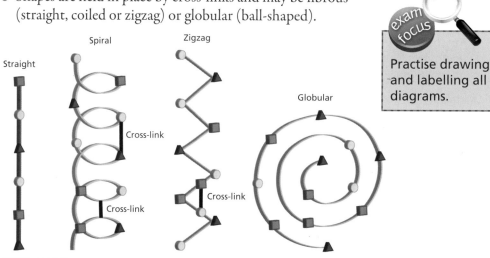

> **exam focus**
>
> Practise drawing and labelling all diagrams.

Fibrous shapes	Globular shapes
Insoluble in water – difficult to denature *Examples:* gluten (wheat), elastin (meat)	Soluble in water – easily denatured *Examples:* myoglobin (meat), haemoglobin (blood)

Classification of proteins

1. **Simple proteins:** contain amino acids.
2. **Conjugated proteins:** amino acids and a non-protein component.
3. **Derived proteins:** formed from chemical/enzymatic actions on the protein itself, e.g. rennin acts on caseinogen.

Simple proteins – amino acids only

Types	Examples		Sources
Animal			
Classified according to shape	HL	(a) Fibrous	Collagen Elastin – connective tissue
		(b) Globular	Albumin – egg white
Plant			
Classified according to solubility	HL	(a) Glutelins: • insoluble in water • soluble in acids and alkalis	Glutenin – wheat Oryzenin – rice
		(b) Prolamins: • insoluble in water • soluble in alcohol	Gliadin – wheat Zein – maize/corn

Conjugated proteins (protein + non-protein molecule)

HL

Types	Examples	Source
Lipoprotein	Lecithin	Egg yolk
Phosphoproteins	Casein	Milk
Chromoproteins	Haemoglobin Myoglobin	Blood Meat
Nucleoproteins	Chromosomes	DNA (Deoxyribonucleic Acid)

Sources of protein – classification

Animal proteins	Plant proteins
Meat, fish, poultry, eggs, milk, cheese	Soya beans, whole cereals, nuts, pulses

Biological value (BV) – classification

- Measures the quality of a protein as a percentage.
- Is determined by how many essential amino acids a food has in proportion to the body's needs.

> **LINK**
> - Food commodities (p. 81)

High biological value (HBV) proteins or complete proteins:
- Contain all the essential amino acids.
- Come mainly from animal sources (*exception*: soya beans – source of HBV protein).

Low biological value (LBV) proteins or incomplete proteins:
- Lack one or more essential amino acids.
- Come mainly from plant sources (*exception*: gelatine – source of LBV protein).

Biological value of foods and distribution of proteins

Foods	Biological value	Distribution of proteins
Eggs	100%	Ovalbumin, vitelin, livetin
Milk	95%	Casein, lactalbumin, lactoglobulin
Meat	80–90%	Elastin, gelatine, collagen, myosin
Fish	80–90%	Actin, myosin, collagen
Soya Beans	74%	Glycinin
Rice	67%	Oryzenin
Wheat	53%	Gluten
Maize	40%	Zein
Gelatine	0%	

Supplementary role of protein

If a protein is deficient in one amino acid the deficiency can be overcome by eating a food rich in that amino acid at the same meal, e.g. beans on toast:

- Beans are **high** in lysine and **low** in methionine.
- Toast is **low** in lysine and **high** in methionine.

LINK

- Vegetarianism (p. 66)

key point

The complementary role of proteins ensures that vegans and vegetarians can get all their essential amino acids from plant-based foods.

Properties of protein

1. Denaturation and coagulation	• Protein chain unfolds and its structure changes – loss in structure cannot be reversed. • Sequence of amino acids is the same. The change may be due to: (a) **Agitation** – mechanical action, e.g. whipping or whisking an egg white (forming a foam) or cream. (b) **Chemicals** – adding acids, alkalis, enzymes, e.g. lemon juice causes milk to curdle. (c) **Heat** – causes protein to coagulate and set, e.g. albumin in eggs. (d) **Enzymes** – rennin coagulates caseinogen to casein.
2. Solubility	Most proteins are insoluble in water. Exceptions: (a) Collagen is soluble in hot water. (b) Albumin (egg white) is soluble in cold water.
3. Maillard reaction (dry heat)	Non-enzymic browning results when an amino acid reacts with carbohydrate in dry heat, e.g. toast, roast potatoes, breads.
4. Elasticity	Gluten (wheat) is very elastic – it allows breads and cakes to rise during baking.
5. Moist heat	During stewing, boiling and steaming, connective tissue changes to gelatine, making foods more digestible.
6. Gel formation	A gel is a semi-solid viscous solution with a three-dimensional network in which molecules of water can become trapped. *Gel formation process:* (a) Gelatine absorbs water and swells to form a gel. (b) When heated the gel becomes liquid and forms a sol. (c) On cooling, the sol sets and becomes solid. *Uses:* jellies, soufflés, cheesecakes

HL

exam focus

Practise drawing and labelling a diagram showing gel formation.

7. Foam formation	• Whisking egg whites causes protein chains to unfold and air bubbles to form, which trap air (foaming).
	• Whisking produces heat, which lightly sets the egg white. Foam will collapse unless heated.
	Uses: meringues, pavlova

LINKS
- Food commodities (p. 81)
- Food preparation and cooking processes (p. 123)

Biological functions of protein

Type	Functions	Deficiency
Structural proteins	• Growth and repair • Production of cells, muscles and skin	• Stunted growth • Delayed healing of wounds
Physiologically active	• Production of antibodies, enzymes, hormones, blood proteins and nucleoproteins	• Illness and infections • Malfunction of body systems and organs
Nutrient proteins	• Provide essential amino acids • Excess converted to energy	• Lack of energy • Marasmus and kwashiorkor

Energy value: 1 g protein = 4 kcal/17 kJ energy.

Reference Intake* – how much protein do I need?

1 g of protein a day is required for each 1 kg of body weight. (Children and adolescents need more for growth and development.)

Group	RI per day
Children	30–50 g
Adolescents	60–80 g
Adults	50–75 g
Pregnant women	70–85 g

Digestion of protein

Hydrolysis and digestion of protein – a summary

Proteins are hydrolysed with the help of protein-splitting enzymes and water.

DEAMINATION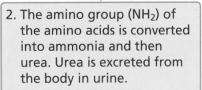

1. Excess proteins are deaminated by the liver.

2. The amino group (NH_2) of the amino acids is converted into ammonia and then urea. Urea is excreted from the body in urine.

3. The carboxyl group (COOH) is oxidised (used for heat and energy). Excess is stored in the body as glycogen (energy source).

* Reference Intake (RI) was previously known as Recommended Daily Allowance (RDA).

Organ/gland	Secretions	Enzymes	Substrates	Products
Stomach	Gastric juice	Pepsin Rennin	Protein Caseinogen	Peptones Casein
Pancreas	Pancreatic juice	Trypsin	Peptones	Peptides
Small intestine (duodenum)	Intestinal juice	Peptidase	Peptides	Amino acids

Absorption of amino acids/proteins

Amino acids are absorbed by the blood vessels in the villi of the small intestine and transported to the liver via the hepatic portal vein.

 ## Utilisation of amino acids

Amino acids in the liver are used to:

- Repair and maintain liver cells.
- Form new cells, repair damaged tissues and make antibodies, enzymes and hormones.

Excess amino acids are deaminated in the liver.

Exam questions and sample answers

Higher Level 2017, Section A, Q1 (6 marks)

Amino acids are the building blocks of proteins. Explain **and** give an example of **each** of the following terms.

- Essential amino acids:
  Cannot be manufactured by the body and must be supplied by the diet. 8 are essential for adults, 10 are essential for children. Examples: Isoleucine, leucine, lysine, methionine, phenylalanine, threonine, tryptophan, valine.

- Non-essential amino acids:
  Can be manufactured by the body and do not need to be supplied by the diet. Examples: alanine, asparagine, aspartic acid, cysteine, glutamic acid, glutamine, glycine, proline, serine, tyrosine.

Higher Level 2016, Section A, Q1 (6 marks)

Name **one** food source of **each** of the proteins listed below.

Proteins	Food source
Casein	*Milk*
Actin	*Meat*
Albumin	*Eggs*

Higher Level 2015, Section A, Q1 (6 marks)

Explain protein **deamination**.

Excess proteins are broken down by the liver. The amino group (NH₂) of the amino acids is converted into ammonia, then urea and excreted by the kidneys as waste product in urine. The carboxyl group (COOH) is oxidised and used to produce heat and energy. Excess is stored in the body as glycogen.

Higher Level 2013, Section A, Q1 (6 marks)

Complete the table below in relation to the **biological functions** of protein.

Type	Biological functions
Structural proteins	*Growth and repair of body cells, skin and muscles.*
Physiologically active proteins	*Production of antibodies, enzymes, hormones, blood proteins.*
Nutrient proteins	*Provide essential amino acids, excess is used for heat and energy.*

Ordinary Level 2017, Section A, Q3 (3 ticks × 2 marks = 6 marks)

Indicate with a tick (✓) which of the protein foods listed below are of high biological value and which are of low biological value.

Protein foods	High biological value	Low biological value
Eggs	✓	
Peas		✓
Fish	✓	

Ordinary Level 2016, Section A, Q1 (3 ticks × 2 marks = 6 marks)

Indicate with a tick (✓) whether each of the following statements is true or false.

	True	False
Protein is the only nutrient that contains nitrogen.	✓	
Excess protein is stored as adipose tissue.	✓	
Protein is necessary for growth of body cells.	✓	

Ordinary Level 2015, Section A, Q2   (6 marks)

Using the words listed, **complete the statements** in relation to the effect of heat on protein foods:

       Maillard reaction   **coagulate**   **opaque**

- Heat causes the protein in eggs to *coagulate*.
- The non-enzymic browning of protein foods is called the *Maillard reaction*.
- Fish flesh changes from translucent to *opaque* during cooking.

Ordinary Level 2013, Section B, Q1 (b), (c)

(b) Give an account of protein under **each** of the following headings:

Composition   (4 points × 1 mark = 4 marks)

- *Protein contains carbon, hydrogen, oxygen and nitrogen.*
- *Protein is the only nutrient that contains nitrogen which is essential for growth.*
- *Small amounts of sulphur, phosphorus and iron.*
- *Elements are arranged into basic units called amino acids.*

Classification   (2 classes × 4 marks = 8 marks)

- **Simple proteins:** *animal and plant source.*
- **Conjugated protein:** *Protein combined with a non-protein unit, e.g. haemoglobin, myoglobin.*
- **Derived proteins:** *formed due to chemical or enzymic action on a protein itself, e.g. high biological value proteins come from animal sources, low biological value proteins come from plant sources.*

Dietary sources   (4 sources × 3 marks = 12 marks)

- **Animal:** *meat, poultry, fish, eggs, milk, cheese (dairy product).*
- **Plant:** *soya beans, TVP, nuts, legumes (peas, beans, lentils).*

exam focus

Include examples from both animal and plant sources – choose **two** sources from each group.

Functions in the body   (2 functions × 4 marks = 8 marks)

- *Growth and repair of body cells.*
- *Formation of muscles, skin and cell membranes.*

(c) Explain the following properties of protein and give an example of each.
                                                    (12 marks)

Denaturation   **Coagulation**

LINK
- p. 8

LINK
- p. 8

Carbohydrates

Photosynthesis – formation of carbohydrates in plants

- Roots absorb water from the soil.
- Leaves absorb carbon dioxide from the air.
- Chlorophyll in leaves converts sunlight into energy.
- Energy from sunlight reacts with water and carbon dioxide to produce glucose and oxygen.

$$6CO_2 \quad + \quad 6H_2O \quad + \quad \text{sunlight} \longrightarrow C_6H_{12}O_6 \quad + \quad 6O_2$$

| carbon dioxide from air | water from soil | energy | glucose stored in plant | oxygen released into air |

Elemental composition

Carbon (C), hydrogen (H) and oxygen (O) in the ratio 1:2:1.

Chemical structure of carbohydrates

- Monosaccharides
- Disaccharides
- Polysaccharides

Higher level students: practise drawing and labelling the chemical structures of carbohydrates. Learn the explanations for each one.

1. Formation of a monosaccharide – hexagonal ring structure.

2. Formation of a disaccharide. (Higher level)

HL

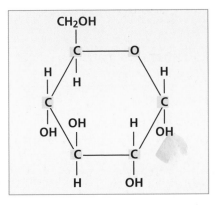

H₂O (condensation reaction as water is lost)

3. Formation of polysaccharides (condensation reaction).

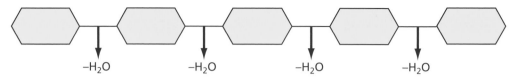

$-H_2O$ $-H_2O$ $-H_2O$ $-H_2O$

Condensation reaction (removal of water):

$$C_6H_{12}O_6 + C_6H_{12}O_6 = C_{12}H_{24}O_{12} - H_2O = C_{12}H_{22}O_{11} + H_2O$$

Classification, chemical formulae, properties and sources

Classification	Chemical formula	Characteristics	Examples and sources
Monosaccharides (*Mono* = one – single unit)	$C_6H_{12}O_6$	Simple sugar unit with a ring structure	Glucose ⟶ fruit Fructose ⟶ honey, fruit Galactose ⟶ milk
Disaccharides (*Di* = two)	$C_{12}H_{22}O_{11}$	Two simple sugars joined together with the removal of H_2O (condensation)	Maltose (glucose + glucose) ⟶ barley Sucrose (glucose + fructose) ⟶ table sugar Lactose (glucose + galactose) ⟶ milk
Polysaccharide (*Poly* = many)	$(C_6H_{10}O_5)n$	● Three or more sugar units joined together ● Chains may be branched or straight	Starch ⟶ cereals, potatoes Glycogen ⟶ meat Cellulose ⟶ skins of fruit/vegetables Pectin ⟶ fruits
Non-starch polysaccharides (NSP)		● Indigestible ● Absorb water ● Aids waste removal	Soluble fibres (gums, pectins) Insoluble fibres (cellulose, lignins)

key point

Gums are found in seaweed, e.g. carrageen, dulse, agar.

Properties of carbohydrates – a summary

LINK
- Food commodities (p. 81)

Sugars

1. Sweetness	Sweet crystalline solids with varying degrees of sweetness enhance flavours
2. Solubility	Sugar is soluble in water Solubility increases if water is heated – forms a syrup when boiled
3. Maillard reaction	Causes non-enzymic browning in dry heat, *Examples:* toast, breads, cakes LINK - Maillard reaction in protein (p. 8)
4. Assists aeration	Whisking or beating sugar with eggs denatures the protein and causes the egg to trap air, resulting in a light mixture *Uses:* egg sponges, cakes
5. Caramelisation	Happens between 104°C and 177°C in dry heat *Uses:* crème brûlée
6. Crystallisation	Occurs when excess sugar is added to a liquid already saturated with sugar and crystals form on cooling *Uses:* confectionery
7. Hydrolysis	Disaccharides react with water to produce monosaccharides
8. Inversion (or hydrolysis) of sugar	When sugar reacts with water in the presence of an acid *or* an enzyme (invertase) it converts disaccharides into monosaccharides *Uses:* jam-making
9. Reducing sugars	Acts as a reducing agent by removing oxygen from other substances *Examples:* glucose, fructose

HL

Starch

1. Solubility	Insoluble in cold water
2. Hygroscopic	Absorbs moisture from the air, e.g. biscuits go soft if left exposed
3. Flavour	Starches lack flavour
4. Gelatinisation	*Gelatinisation happens in stages:* (a) Moist heat causes starch grains to swell, burst, absorb moisture and thicken liquids, e.g. sauces (b) As the liquid is heated to initial temperatures of 55–70°C it is absorbed by the starch (c) The starch granules swell and join together to form a sticky paste (d) Temperatures greater than 85°C create a **sol**. *Examples:* sauces, soups (e) On cooling the mixture forms a **gel**

key point

Different starches gelatinise at different temperatures.

5. Dry heat	Starch grains burst and absorb any fat present *Example:* popcorn

key point

Uncooked starch is indigestible; cooking improves its digestibility.

6. Dextrinisation	Heating starchy foods causes foods to brown and polysaccharide chains called pyrodextrins to form *Example:* toast
7. Gel formation	Heating pectin in the presence of an acid and sugar causes its long polysaccharide chains to form a three-dimensional network which traps water molecules. On cooling, this mixture forms a gel *Examples:* jams, jellies

Non-starch polysaccharides (NSP)

1. Gel formation	**Gums** absorb water to form gels
2. Solubility	**Cellulose** is insoluble in water. It absorbs water, creating bulk in the diet
3. Pectin extraction	Protopectin in under-ripe fruit cannot absorb water and form a gel. Adding acid (lemon juice) converts protopectin to pectin. Pectin forms gels in the presence of heat, acids and sugar *Examples:* jams, jellies

LINKS
- Food preservation (p. 182)
- Sauces (Chapter 3, Extension 2, see www.moresuccess.ie)

Biological functions of carbohydrates

Class	Biological functions
Carbohydrates – starches and sugars	1. Cheap source of heat and energy – sugars provide instant energy, starches release energy more slowly 2. Excess is converted into fat: stored as adipose tissue; insulates the body 3. Act as 'protein sparers' 4. Some stored in the liver as an instant energy reserve
Cellulose (NSP or dietary fibre)	1. Prevents bowel diseases by encouraging peristalsis and speeds up waste removal 2. Produces a feeling of fullness, reduces over-eating

Culinary uses of carbohydrates

Sugar

1. **Preservative:** prevents microbial growth (jams, jellies).
2. **Sweetener:** sweetens cakes, desserts, beverages.
3. **Caramelisation:** dry heat caramelises sugar (desserts, cakes).
4. **Fermentation:** activates yeast fermentation (baking, wine, beer).
5. **Aeration:** strengthens whisked egg white proteins.

key point

Sugars are also used for **glazing**, as a **main ingredient** and in **gel formation** when making jams and jellies.

Starch

1. **Thickener:** gravies, sauce and soups.
2. **Hygroscopic:** extends shelf-life of cakes (preservative).
3. **Dextrinisation:** browning of foods.

key point

Starch is also used as a **main ingredient** and in the manufacture of processed foods.

Pectin

Gel formation: pectin acts as a setting agent in jam-making.

Cellulose/fibre

1. Adds **texture** to dishes, e.g. stews.
2. Creates a feeling of **fullness**.

Energy value: 1 g carbohydrate = 17 kJ energy.
Reference Intake (RI) of carbohydrates: depends on level of activity, but deficiency is rare. Sugar should not exceed 30 g per day for adults (WHO).

LINKS
- Food preparation and cooking processes (p. 129)
- Sauces (Chapter 3, Extension 2, see www.moresuccess.ie)
- Food commodities (p. 81)

Dietary targets for NSP intake

Intake of NSP (dietary fibre) should be approximately 25–35 g per day, drawn from a variety of grains, fruits, legumes and vegetables.

LINK
- The Irish diet (p. 75)

Achieving the dietary targets – increasing fibre in the diet

1. Replace processed cereals with wholegrain varieties.
2. Eat high-fibre breakfast cereals, e.g. porridge, or add nuts, seeds and bran.
3. Eat whole fruits/vegetables, preferably raw where possible.
4. Use wholemeal flour for bread and cakes.
5. Eat skins of fruits and vegetables.
6. Increase intake of seeds and nuts in the diet – add to raw and cooked dishes.

Digestion of carbohydrates

Organ/gland	Secretions	Enzymes	Act on/ substrates	Products
Salivary glands (mouth)	Saliva	Salivary amylase	Starch	Maltose
Duodenum/ pancreas	Pancreatic juice in the duodenum	Amylase	Starch	Maltose
Small intestine	Intestinal juice	(a) Maltase (b) Lactase (c) Sucrase	(a) Maltose (b) Lactose (c) Sucrose	Glucose Glucose + galactose Glucose + fructose

Absorption of carbohydrates

1. Monosaccharides are absorbed through the villi of the small intestine into the bloodstream.
2. They are transported to the liver via the portal vein. Fructose and galactose are converted into glucose.

key point

Stomach acid halts the digestion of carbohydrates. Digestion then resumes in the small intestine.

Utilisation of carbohydrates

In the liver:

1. Glucose is oxidised for heat and energy.
2. Glucose is converted into glycogen (energy reserve).
3. Excess is converted to fat and stored as adipose tissue (insulation).

LINK
- Modified diets: diabetes (p. 69)

exam Q

Exam questions and sample answers

Higher Level 2017, Section A, Q2　　　　　　　　　　　　　　(6 marks)

Describe the effect of **gelatinisation** on starch.

When starch is mixed with a liquid and heated, the starch grains swell, burst, absorb moisture and thicken the mixture, a sol. Sols form at temperatures greater than 85°C. Different starches gelatinise at different temperatures.

Give **two** culinary examples of gelatinisation.
- *Roux sauces*
- *Lemon curd*

Higher Level 2015, Section A, Q2 (6 marks)

Complete the table below in relation to carbohydrates.

Class	Examples	Food Source
Monosaccharides	Glucose Fructose Galactose	Fruit Honey, fruit Digested milk
Disaccharides	Maltose Sucrose Lactose	Barley Table sugar Milk
Polysaccharides	Starch Glycogen Cellulose Pectin	Cereals, bread, potatoes Meat Whole cereals, fruit, vegetables Fruits

Higher Level 2014, Section A, Q1 (6 marks)

In relation to carbohydrates, explain **each** of the following properties.

Caramelisation: *When heat is applied to sugar or sugar syrup, it melts, becomes darker in colour (caramel) and has a sticky consistency. It produces a pleasant aroma and taste. Example: crème brûlée.*

Crystallisation: *This occurs when more sugar is added to a liquid already saturated with sugar and on cooling crystals form. The liquid cannot absorb any more sugar. Example: confectionary and sweet making industries.*

Higher Level 2010, Section A, Q2 (6 marks)

Name **three** properties of sugar and state one culinary use of each.

Property	Culinary use
Preservative	Jam-making
Sweetener	Cakes and desserts
Aeration and foam formation	Sponge cakes

Ordinary Level 2017, Section A, Q2 (6 marks)

Name **three** different sources of fibre in the diet.

- *Wholegrain cereals, e.g. brown bread, porridge, nuts.*
- *Brown rice, wholegrain pasta.*
- *Skins of fruits and vegetables, e.g. apples, beans.*

Ordinary Level 2016, Section A, Q2 (6 marks)

Give **one** dietary source of each of the following carbohydrates.

Carbohydrate	Dietary source
Sugar	*Fizzy drinks (also cakes, biscuits, fruit, table sugar, honey, jam)*
Starch	*Rice (also breads, pasta, potatoes, flour, breakfast cereal)*
Fibre	*Vegetables (also fruits, wholegrain cereals and breads, nuts)*

Higher Level 2016, Section B, Q1 (80 marks)

'Current intakes of dietary fibre are generally inadequate in adults with over 80% not meeting the European Food Safety Authority (EFSA) recommendation of 25–30 grams per day. The chart below provides information on the contribution of different foods to dietary fibre intake in Ireland for adults aged 18–64 years and those over 65 years.'

Food	18-64 years		≥ 65 years	
Foods	%	grams	%	grams
Bread and rolls	26	4.8	29	5.4
Vegetables and vegetable dishes	17	3.3	18	3.2
Potatoes and potato products	13	2.2	12	2.0
Fruit and fruit juices	10	2.1	15	3.1
Breakfast cereals	9	2.0	10	2.1
Others	25	4.8	16	3.2
Total	100	19.2	100	19.0

(a) Using the information provided in the chart, comment and elaborate on the contribution of four foods to the intake of dietary fibre with reference to the two categories of people identified above.   (4 points × 6 marks = 24 marks)

You must give four points, then comment and elaborate on each.

Read the 'grams' column to determine the level of contribution of dietary fibre.

Bread and rolls: *Highest contribution to dietary fibre in both groups, 3% higher for the over 65 group than for the 18–64 group, Wholegrain breads/rolls are high in fibre; high fibre intake prevents bowel disorders.*

Vegetables and vegetable dishes: *Second highest dietary fibre contributor for the over 65 year group and third for the 18–64 group, both groups benefit from increased nutritional awareness due to the '5 or more a day'. For vegetarians and vegans, availability of pre-prepared vegetables and salads are useful as they save time and effort. Use in smoothies, salads, casseroles/stews, soups, stir-fries, vegetarian/vegan curries, stir-fries, vegetable burgers and nut roast.*

Potatoes and potato products: *Fourth highest contributor of dietary fibre to 18–64 group and the fifth contributor for the over 65 group, are easy to digest and a useful source of dietary fibre for both groups, widely available throughout the year, affordable, versatile and easy to prepare, e.g. baked, boiled, mashed, in salads. Wide variety available in prepared form, e.g. chipped, wedges, waffles, potato cakes; combined with other products, e.g. shepherd's pie. Chipped potatoes and crisps for snacking are popular among all age groups, however crisps may be high in fat and salt.*

Breakfast cereals: *Provide the lowest dietary fibre contribution to both groups, perhaps both groups choose from the wide variety of low-fibre high sugar ready-to-eat breakfast cereals available rather than making porridge or choosing granola or muesli, or adding extra fibre in the form of dried/fresh fruits, seeds and nuts, people might choose a low-fibre breakfast, e.g. toast, fruit juice, tea instead of opting for whole cereals, brown bread or whole fruit for breakfast.*

(b) Suggest **three** strategies to increase the intake of dietary fibre in order to meet the European Food Safety Authority (EFSA) recommendation.

(3 points × 4 marks = 12 marks)

1. **Breakfast:** *Choose high fibre breakfast cereals with a minimum of 3 g fibre per 100 g of cereal e.g. porridge (9 g per 100 g), increase fibre with the addition of bran, dried fruit, nuts and seeds, choose wholemeal bread or toast, include fresh fruit (2 g of fibre approx.).*

2. **Brown rice/pasta:** *Replace white rice/pasta with brown varieties.*

3. **Vegetables:** *Increase the fibre content of dishes with the addition of extra vegetables in curries, lasagne, stews and soups, choose extra vegetables/salads for lunch, dinner and for snacks.*

(c) Evaluate the benefits of a diet rich in fibre. (3 points × 5 marks = 15 marks)

- *Reduces constipation as waste passes through the system more quickly.*
- *Reduces risk of haemorrhoids, diverticulitis, IBS, and cancer.*
- *Creates a feeling of fullness, useful in maintaining a healthy weight.*

LINK
- Fibre (p. 17)

(d) Name and give an account of one bowel disease. Refer to symptoms/effects. (9 marks)

LINK
- Bowel disorders (p. 62)

Bowel disease	Account of disease	Symptoms/effects
Constipation	• Stools move too slowly through the large intestine (part of the digestive system). • Too much water is reabsorbed. • Faeces becomes too hard and dry. • Faeces difficult to eliminate from rectum.	• Hard stools/faeces. • Cramps, pain and discomfort. • Fewer bowel movements. • Feeling of not being able to empty stools from rectum. • Can lead to haemorrhoids.

Ordinary Level 2014, Section B, Q1 (b), (c)

(b) Give an account of carbohydrates under **each** of the following headings:

Classification: (3 classes × 3 marks = 9 marks)
- Monosaccharides: simple sugars.
- Disaccharides: double sugars.
- Polysaccharides: complex non-sugars.

Dietary sources: (3 sources × 3 marks = 9 marks)
- Monosaccharides/disaccharides: table sugar, fruit, honey, biscuits.
- Polysaccharides/starch: potatoes, breakfast cereals, rice, pasta, flour.
- Polysaccharides/cellulose: skins of fruit and vegetables, wholegrains, brown bread.

Note the number of points for each section.

Functions in the body: (2 functions × 4 marks = 8 marks)
- Produces heat and energy in the body.
- Prevents bowel disease by speeding up peristalsis and the removal of waste.

Properties: (2 properties × 4 marks = 8 marks)
- Maillard reaction: amino acids and sugars react in the presence of heat, e.g. toast.
- Hydrolysis: disaccharides react with water to produce monosaccharides (digestion).

(c) Outline **three** ways an individual can ensure an adequate intake of fibre in his/her diet. (3 ways × 4 marks = 12 marks)
- Increase daily intake of fruit and vegetables.
- Replace white bread, white rice and pasta with wholegrain varieties.
- Add fresh/dried fruits, seeds and nuts to breakfast cereals and savoury dishes.

Always keep the current dietary guidelines in mind.

Lipids

Elemental composition

Carbon (C), hydrogen (H) and oxygen (O).

Chemical structure of a triglyceride

- A triglyceride is formed when **one** molecule of glycerol combines with **three** fatty acids.
- Glycerol is a trihydric alcohol with **three** hydroxyl groups (OH).
- A fatty acid (R=COOH) molecule attaches itself to each OH group with the elimination of three molecules of water (condensation).

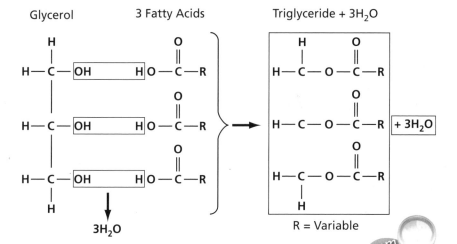

Glycerol   3 Fatty Acids   Triglyceride + 3H₂O

3H₂O

R = Variable

Classification of fatty acids

1. Saturated fatty acids.
2. Monounsaturated fatty acids. *l one*
3. Polyunsaturated fatty acids (PUFAs). *many*

1. Saturated fatty acids

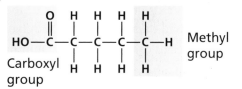

Carboxyl group   Methyl group

Structure	Properties (form and melting point)	Sources and examples
• Fully saturated with hydrogen atoms • **No** double bonds, carbon atoms linked by single bonds	• Solid at room temperature • High melting point	• *Sources:* dairy produce (butter, cheese, milk), egg yolk, meat, fats, hard margarines • *Examples:* stearic acid (meat), butyric acid (butter)

2. Monounsaturated fatty acids
   (one double bond)

Carboxyl group

$$HO-\overset{\overset{\displaystyle O}{\|}}{C}-\overset{\overset{\displaystyle H}{|}}{\underset{\underset{\displaystyle H}{|}}{C}}-\overset{\displaystyle H}{C}=\overset{\displaystyle H}{C}-\overset{\overset{\displaystyle H}{|}}{\underset{\underset{\displaystyle H}{|}}{C}}-H$$

Methyl group

Structure	Properties	Sources and examples
• Carbon chain **not** saturated with hydrogen atoms • Bonds are incomplete • One double bond between carbon atoms	• Liquid/soft at room temperature • Lower melting point • Lowers cholesterol	• Plants • Olive oil (oleic acid)

3. Polyunsaturated fatty acids
   (two or more double bonds)

Carboxyl group

$$HO-\overset{\overset{\displaystyle O}{\|}}{C}=\overset{\overset{\displaystyle H}{}}{\underset{\underset{\displaystyle H}{|}}{C}}-\overset{\overset{\displaystyle H}{|}}{C}-\overset{\displaystyle H}{C}=\overset{\displaystyle H}{C}-\overset{\overset{\displaystyle H}{|}}{\underset{\underset{\displaystyle H}{|}}{C}}-H$$

Methyl group

Structure	Properties	Sources and examples
• Carbon atoms **not** saturated with hydrogen atoms • **More than one** double bond	• Liquid/soft at room temperature • Lower melting point • Lowers cholesterol	• *Plant sources:* corn oil, vegetable oils, nuts, seeds • *Examples:* linoleic acid (two double bonds); linolenic acid (three double bonds); arachidonic acid (four double bonds)

Essential fatty acids

What are fatty acids?

1. Fatty acids are long chains of hydrocarbons.
2. A fatty acid has a **methyl group** (CH_3) at one end and a **carboxyl group** (COOH) at the other end.

HL **Cis fatty acids:** hydrogen atoms are located on the same side as a double bond causing a bend in the chain.
Sources: foods containing some fat or oil.

$$-\overset{\overset{\displaystyle H}{|}}{\underset{\underset{\displaystyle H}{|}}{C}}-\overset{\displaystyle H}{C}=\overset{\displaystyle H}{C}-\overset{\overset{\displaystyle H}{|}}{\underset{\underset{\displaystyle H}{|}}{C}}-$$

Trans fatty acids: hydrogen atoms are located at opposite sides of the double bond, molecules are rigid.
Sources: hard margarines, fried foods, processed foods.

$$-\overset{\overset{\displaystyle H}{|}}{\underset{\underset{\displaystyle H}{|}}{C}}-\overset{\overset{\displaystyle H}{|}}{C}=\overset{\displaystyle H}{C}-\overset{\overset{\displaystyle H}{|}}{\underset{\underset{\displaystyle H}{|}}{C}}-$$

Significance of trans fatty acids in the diet:

1. May contribute to increased risk of CHD.
2. Raise levels of **LDL** (bad cholesterol).
3. High levels reduce levels of **HDL** (good cholesterol).

Omega-3 polyunsaturated fatty acids:

1. Omega-3 is determined by the position of the double bond.
2. A double bond is between the third and fourth carbon atoms.

Benefits: Help lower blood fat levels; reduce risk of blood clots, strokes and coronary heart disease (CHD); and improve brain function.

Sources: Oily fish, nuts, seeds and soya beans.

key point

Cis fatty acids are converted to trans fatty acids during cooking and processing.

key point

LDL = low-density lipoprotein (bad cholesterol)

HDL = high-density lipoprotein (good cholesterol)

key point

Omega-3 fatty acids are known as EPA (eicosapentaenoic) and DHA (docosahexaenoic).

$$HO-\underset{\underset{H}{|}}{\overset{\overset{O}{\|}}{C}}-\underset{\underset{H}{|}}{\overset{\overset{H}{|}}{C}}-\overset{\overset{H}{|}}{C}=\overset{\overset{H}{|}}{C}-\underset{\underset{H}{|}}{\overset{\overset{H}{|}}{C}}-\underset{\underset{H}{|}}{\overset{\overset{H}{|}}{C}}-\overset{\overset{H}{|}}{C}=\overset{\overset{H}{|}}{C}-\underset{\underset{H}{|}}{\overset{\overset{H}{|}}{C}}-\underset{\underset{H}{|}}{\overset{\overset{H}{|}}{C}}-H$$

Functions of essential fatty acids

1. To build healthy cell membranes.
2. To reduce risk of CHD.
3. To counteract the effects of cholesterol in arteries.

Classification, sources and degree of saturation of lipids

Class	Sources	Degree of saturation
Animal	Dairy produce e.g. cheese, butter, egg yolk; meat, meat fats	Mainly saturated
Plant/vegetable	Avocado, cereals, olive oil, nuts, soya beans	Unsaturated except for some margarines
Marine	Oily fish, e.g. mackerel, salmon, trout; fish oils from cod, halibut, etc.	Fish contain omega-3 polyunsaturated fatty acids (EPA and DHA)

(HL) Distribution of fatty acids in foods – some examples

	Saturated fatty acids	Monounsaturated fatty acids	Polyunsaturated fatty acids
Vegetable			
Olive oil	10%	20%	66%
Sunflower oil	13%	74%	8%
Soft tub margarine	17%	47%	31%
Block margarine	19%	59%	18%
Animal/marine			
Tuna	27%	26%	37%
Chicken fat	30%	45%	21%
Butter	62%	29%	4%

Properties of hard fats and oils

1. Fats are **solid** and oils are **liquid** at room temperature.
2. **Solubility:** insoluble in water, soluble in solvents.
3. **Absorb flavours** if left uncovered, e.g. from onions.
4. **Effects of heat:**
   - *melting point* – solid fats melt between 30°C and 40°C
   - *smoke point* – overheating causes glycerol and fatty acids to separate. Glycerol changes to acrolein and a blue haze or smoke rises (fats 200°C, oils 250°C)
   - *flash point*: can burst into flames (fats 310°C, oils 325°C).

5. **Rancidity:** spoilage of lipids happens in two ways:
   - *oxidative rancidity* occurs when oxygen in the air reacts with the carbon atoms of a double bond in an unsaturated carbon chain
   - *hydrolytic rancidity* is caused when enzymes or microbes react in a lipid, breaking it down into glycerol and fatty acids, e.g. food in a freezer.
6. **Hydrogenation:** occurs when hydrogen is added to an unsaturated fatty acid in the presence of a nickel catalyst, converting it into a saturated fat, e.g. margarine.

$$-C=C- \Rightarrow -C-C-$$

7. **Plasticity:** relates to whether the lipid is solid, liquid or spreadable. Allows for shape and structure and is determined by the degree of saturation: the more unsaturated fatty acids present, the softer the lipid.

8. **Emulsions:** form when two immiscible liquids are forced together to form a solution. There are two types of emulsion:
   - Oil in water (mayonnaise).
   - Water in oil (butter).

Emulsions may be permanent or temporary:
   - *Permanent emulsions* are formed in the presence of an emulsifier, e.g. lecithin in egg yolk in mayonnaise
   - *Temporary emulsions* are formed when oil and vinegar are shaken together, e.g. French dressing.

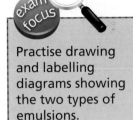

Practise drawing and labelling diagrams showing the two types of emulsions.

Working principle of an emulsifier:
The hydrophilic end (water-loving) attaches itself to the water molecule. The hydrophobic (water-hating) end attaches itself to the fat/oil molecule. The mixture stabilises.

Examples of emulsions in foods:
   (a) *Lecithin* in mayonnaise (oil-in-water emulsion).
   (b) *Casein* in butter (water-in-oil emulsion).
   (c) *Casein, lecithin and GMS* in margarine.

LINK
   - Food additives (p. 161)

9. **Stabilisers:** maintain the emulsions in cakes, ice cream and salad cream, preventing the ingredients separating out, e.g. gelatine, gum, pectin, carrageen.

Biological functions of lipids

1. Concentrated source of heat and energy.
2. Excess forms adipose tissue, insulates the body.
3. Protect delicate organs, e.g. kidneys, heart.
4. Source of fat-soluble vitamins (A, D, E and K).
5. Source of essential fatty acids.

Unsaturated lipids may have a role in preventing CHD. Phospholipids are part of cell membranes.

Energy value: 1 g lipid = 9 kcal/37 kJ energy.

Associated dietary disorders

1. Obesity
2. Coronary heart disease
3. High blood pressure
4. High cholesterol
5. Stroke

Reference Intake (RI) of lipids (adults)
   - Total fat = less than 70 g per day
   - Saturated fat for women = less than 20 g per day
   - Saturated fat for men = less than 30 g per day

Culinary functions of lipids

1. Improves flavour of food e.g. oil infused with herbs.
2. Involved in emulsification e.g. mayonnaise.

3. Creates different textures e.g. flakiness in pastries.

4. Involved in heat transfer during cooking e.g. frying.

Digestion of lipids – a summary

Organ/gland	Secretions	Enzymes	Acts on/substrates	Products
Liver	Bile	Bile salts	Large fat globules	Emulsified fats
Pancreas	Pancreatic juice	Pancreatic lipase	Lipids	Glycerol and fatty acids
Small intestine	Intestinal juice	Intestinal lipase	Lipids	Glycerol and fatty acids

Absorption of lipids

1. Glycerol and fatty acids are absorbed into the lacteals of the villi of the small intestine.

2. Digested lipids are transported by the lymph to the bloodstream via the left subclavian vein.

 ## Utilisation of lipids

1. Oxidised in the liver and muscles to produce heat and energy, and form cell membranes.

2. Excess is stored as adipose tissue (insulation) or around delicate organs, e.g. kidneys, and as an energy reserve.

Exam questions and sample answers

 Higher Level 2016, Section A, Q2 (6 marks)

(a) State **one** function of omega 3 fatty acids in the diet.
 Omega 3 fatty acids reduces risks of coronary heart disease, strokes and formation of clots.

(b) Name **two** different food sources of omega 3 fatty acids.
 - *Oily fish e.g. salmon*
 - *Soya beans*

Higher Level 2015, Section A, Q4 (6 marks)

In relation to lipids, explain **each** of the following terms:

Smoke point:
 Fats reach smoke point at 200°C and oils at 250°C. Heating beyond the smoke point results in lipids breaking down. Glycerol changes to acrolein and produces a blue haze and an acrid smell.

Flash point:

Fats suddenly burst into flames at 310°C and oils at 325°C. Used for frying and sautéing foods. Lipids continue to decompose beyond these temperatures.

Higher Level 2013, Section A, Q2   (6 marks)

In relation to lipids, explain **each** of the following terms:

Oxidative rancidity:

Occurs when unsaturated fatty acids and oxygen in the air react. Oxygen combines with the carbon atoms at the double bond in an unsaturated carbon chain. It results in a rancid smell due to the production of aldehydes and ketones.

Hydrolytic rancidity:

Occurs when enzymes (lipase) or microbes react in lipids/fats and breaks them down into glycerol and fatty acids giving a rancid smell and unpleasant taste to foods.

Ordinary Level 2017, Section A, Q1   (6 marks)

Indicate with a tick (✓) whether **each** of the following statements is true or false.

	True	False
Lipids (fats) are made up of fatty acids and glycerol	✓	
Lipids (fats) contain the element nitrogen		✓
Omega 3 fatty acids help reduce the risk of heart disease	✓	

Ordinary Level 2014, Section A, Q1   (6 marks)

Indicate with a tick (✓) whether **each** of the following statements is true or false.

	True	False
Fats contain the element nitrogen		✓
Essential fatty acids are made in the body		✓
Omega 3 fatty acids are found in oily fish	✓	

Higher Level 2013, Section B, Q1 (c), (d)

(c) Outline the significance of fatty acids in the diet.

(2 points × 4 marks = 8 marks)

Essential fatty acids cannot be manufactured within the body, must come from the diet. Unsaturated fatty acids reduce LDL (bad cholesterol) and increase HDL (good cholesterol) and counteract the hardening effects of cholesterol on blood vessels. Reduce the risk of heart disease. Saturated fatty acids increase levels of LDL cholesterol, reduce HDL levels (good cholesterol) and increase risk of coronary heart disease.

(d) Describe the structure of **each** of the following:

(3 points × 4 marks = 12 marks)

	Structure
Cis fatty acids	Occur when hydrogen atoms on either side of a double bond are on the same side of the carbon chain, either above or below. Molecules are flexible and some are liquid at room temperature.
Trans fatty acids	Hydrogen atoms are on opposite sides of the double bond making the fat molecule inflexible and straight and solid at room temperature.
Omega 3 fatty acids	These are polyunsaturated fatty acids where the double bond is located between the 3rd and 4th carbon atom on the carbon chain to the left of the methyl end (CH3, on the right hand side).

Ordinary Level 2016, Section B, Q1 (a)–(d)   (80 marks)

'Saturated fat has a bad reputation in recent years, but it might not be entirely deserved. Foods such as milk that are high is SFA [saturated fatty acids] and high in calcium don't seem to raise harmful cholesterol levels' *(Paula Mee, The Irish Times, July 2015)*

The table **below** shows the nutritional content of two pre-prepared meals.

Pre-prepared meal	Ingredients	Nutritional information (per serving)	
Fisherman's pie	Potato, cod, cream, milk, butter, cheese, onion, peas, salt.	Energy	392 kcal
		Fat	18.4 g
		Carbohydrates	37.9 g
		Fibre	3.1 g
		Protein	17.2 g
		Salt	1.9 g
Chicken curry with rice	White rice, chicken, apple, onion, curry powder, garlic, tomato puree, flour, salt.	Energy	524 kcal
		Fat	8.0 g
		Carbohydrates	88.0 g
		Fibre	4.8 g
		Protein	22.0 g
		Salt	1.7 g

(a) Using the information presented in the table **above**, state which of the pre-prepared meals you would recommend for a young person involved in sport.

Explain **three** reasons for your choice.   (20 marks)

Fisherman's pie   (name = 2 marks, reasons = 3 × 6 marks; total = 20 marks)

- White fish is low in saturated fats which prevents the build-up of cholesterol.
- Fat and low GI carbohydrates will sustain energy during sporting activities.
- Contains fibre to prevent constipation and salt for hydration.
- HBV protein supports growth and repair and recovery from training.

(b) Give an account of lipids (fats) under each of the following headings:

Classification: (2 classes × 4 marks = 8 marks)

Class	Examples
According to source	Animal (mainly saturated) Plant (mainly unsaturated) Marine (mainly polyunsaturated)
According to degree of saturation	Unsaturated, monounsaturated, polyunsaturated

Functions in the body: (2 functions × 4 marks = 8 marks)

- Supply fat-soluble vitamins A, D, E and K and essential fatty acids.
- Provide heat and energy.
- Others: protect delicate organs, delays feeling of hunger, increases transmission of nerve impulses.

Dietary sources: (4 sources × 3 marks = 12 marks)
Meat, eggs, milk, dairy products (cheese), avocados, vegetable and nut oils

(c) Outline **three** ways an individual can reduce his/her intake of fat.

                                                          (3 ways × 4 marks = 12 marks)

- Replace full-fat produce with low-fat varieties, e.g. choose low-fat spreads instead of butter.
- Reduce intake of red meat, cheddar cheese, butter, cakes, pastries and biscuits.
- Steam, grill or poach instead of frying foods, e.g. poached eggs, steamed fish.

(d) Discuss **four** ways consumers can be environmentally aware when shopping and buying food for the family.   (4 ways × 5 marks = 20 marks)

- Buy fruit and vegetables loose, avoid packaged goods.
- Select foods and products in recycled packaging, e.g. cereals, eggs.
- Buy products in biodegradable packaging and reusable containers.
- Look out for ECO and Fairtrade labels.

Vitamins

Classification of vitamins

Fat-soluble vitamins	Water-soluble vitamins
Vitamin A (retinol; beta-carotene) Vitamin D (cholecalciferol; ergocalciferol) Vitamin E (tocopherol) Vitamin K (naphthoquinone)	Vitamin C (ascorbic acid) Vitamin B-group: • B_1 (thiamine) • B_2 (riboflavin) • B_6 (pyrodoxine) • B_{12} (cobalamin) • folic acid (folate) • niacin

LINKS

- The Irish diet (p. 75)
- Fruit (p. 109)
- Vegetables (p. 112)
- Food processing (p. 147)
- Food additives (p. 161)

Questions on vitamins and minerals are asked in Section A and in Section B. Revising the LINKED topics is essential when preparing for these types of integrated questions.

Revise dietary food requirements.

Fat-soluble vitamins

Vitamin A (retinol and beta-carotene)

Vitamin A is available in two forms:

	Sources	Examples
1. Retinol (pure vitamin A)	Animal	Fish, fish oils, butter, liver, fortified milk
2. Beta-carotene (pro-vitamin A converted to retinol in the body)	Fruit and vegetables (brightly coloured)	Dark green leafy vegetables, broccoli, apricots, carrots, tomatoes, peppers

Functions, deficiency, RI and properties of vitamin A

Functions	• Produces rhodopsin to aid night vision • Essential for lining membranes • Aids growth and repair of cells • Needed for healthy hair and skin – beta-carotene acts as an antioxidant
Effects of deficiency	• Night blindness – poor vision due to lack of rhodopsin • Xerophthalmia (dry eyes) • Retarded/stunted growth in children • Dry mucous membranes – rough and dry skin
RI (µg per day)	• Children: 400–500 µg • Adolescents: 600–700 µg • Adults: 600–700 µg • During pregnancy/lactation: 950 µg
Properties	*Retinol:* • Yellow fat-soluble alcohol • Insoluble in water • Heat stable • Reduced by dehydration • Powerful as an antioxidant • Destroyed by exposure to oxygen *Beta-carotene:* • Bright orange or yellow oil • Insoluble in water • Heat stable • Sensitive to dehydration • Powerful antioxidant

Dangers of hypervitaminosis – excess vitamin A

Dry skin, enlarged liver, fatigue, hair loss, headaches, vomiting and even death, risk of birth defects and miscarriage.

Vitamin D – the sunshine vitamin

Vitamin D is available in two forms:

	Sources	Examples
1. Cholecalciferols (Vitamin D_3)	Sunlight	Sunlight converts 7-dehydrocholesterol in the skin to choleocalciferol
	Food	Oily fish, fish oils, eggs, milk, margarine
2. Ergocalciferols (Vitamin D_2)	Fungi, yeasts	Action of the sun converts ergosterol to ergocalciferol

Functions, deficiency, RI and properties of vitamin D

Functions	• Needed for strong bones and teeth • Aids absorption of calcium and phosphorus • Prevents rickets and osteomalacia • Regulates blood calcium levels
Effects of deficiency	• Rickets in children • Osteomalacia (weakness of bones) • Osteoporosis (brittle bones) • Dental caries/decay
RI (µg per day)	• Children: 10 µg • Adolescents: 15 µg • Adults: 10 µg • During pregnancy/lactation: 10 µg
Properties	• A fat-soluble vitamin • Insoluble in water • Stable to heat – cooking, food processing • Stable to acids, alkalis, oxygen

Dangers of hypervitaminosis – excess vitamin D

More common among young children than adults due to a high concentration of calcium in the blood.
Symptoms: nausea, mental confusion, a metallic taste, vomiting and thirst, loss of bone mass.

As of 2010, the HSE advises parents to give their 0–12-month-old infants a daily 5 µg vitamin D3 supplement.

Vitamin E (tocopherols)

Sources	Margarine, egg yolk, wholegrain cereals, spinach, pulses, olive oils, wheat germ, nuts, avocados
Functions	• Acts as an antioxidant – reduces risk of CHD • Destroys free radicals – reduces effects of aging • Protects healthy blood cells from damage – improves clotting of blood • Strengthens the immune system • Helps ease pre-menstrual tension
Deficiency	Rare for the majority of the population
RI (µg/per day)	None
Properties	• Fat-soluble antioxidant • Insoluble in water • Delays rancidity and oxidation • Damaged by alkalis, oxygen and light • Heat stable, stable in acids

Vitamin K (napthoquinones)

There are three forms of vitamin K:

1. Phyllonapthoquinone (from plant sources) – K_1
2. Menanapthoquinone (made by bacteria in the intestine) – K_2
3. Menanapthone (a synthetic form) – K_3

Sources	*Plant:* green vegetables, cereals *Animal:* fish, meat, liver, eggs *Body:* made by bacteria in the gut
Functions	● For synthesis of prothrombin, essential for clotting of blood ● Regulates calcium balance in bones
Effects of deficiency	● Delayed clotting of blood ● Deficiency is rare but may occur in newborn babies due to limited diet and poor gut flora
RI (µg/per day)	None
Properties	● Fat-soluble ● Insoluble in water ● Heat stable, unaffected by cooking ● Destroyed when exposed to sunlight

Water-soluble vitamins

Vitamin C (ascorbic acid)

Sources	*Fruit:* blackcurrants, rosehips, strawberries, citrus fruits *Vegetables:* cabbages, tomatoes, potatoes, green peppers
Functions	● Antioxidant, prevents CHD and some cancers ● Prevents scurvy ● Essential for collagen formation (connective tissue) ● Necessary for strong bones/teeth ● Essential for the absorption of non-haem iron ● Helps white cells fight infections – builds a strong immune system
Effects of deficiency	● Scurvy in severe cases ● Anaemia (poor absorption of iron) ● Slower healing of cuts and wounds ● Bruising and bleeding due to weaker blood vessels and tissues
RI *(mg per day)*	● Children: 45 mg ● Adolescents: 60 mg ● Adults: 60 mg ● During pregnancy/lactation: 80 mg

Properties	• White, water-soluble acidic vitamin with a sharp flavour
	• Destroyed by alkalis, dry or moist heat and enzymes (oxidase)
	• Acts as an antioxidant
	• Destroyed by oxygen and light
	• Affected by metals, e.g. copper, iron, zinc, cooking utensils

Vitamin B complex or B-group vitamins

Vitamin B₁ (thiamine)

Sources	Wholegrain cereals, fortified breakfast cereals, meats, offal, milk, eggs, yeast extract
Functions	• Aids metabolism of carbohydrates and fats (release of energy)
	• Needed for healthy nervous and muscle systems
	• Promotes growth and development in children
	• Necessary for general good health
Effects of deficiency	• Beri-beri in severe cases
	• Lack of energy, depression, irritability, poor concentration
	• Tiredness and muscle cramps
	• Stunted growth in children
Properties	• Water-soluble, white crystalline vitamin
	• Destroyed by high temperatures, dry heat and alkalis
	• 70% destroyed during the milling process

Vitamin B₂ (riboflavin)

Sources	Meat, milk, eggs, breakfast cereals, spinach, offal, yeast extracts
Functions	• Involved in the metabolism of nutrients – proteins, lipids and carbohydrates
	• Necessary for healthy mucous membranes
	• Needed for healthy skin, hair and nails
	• Works with other vitamins to maintain a healthy immune system
Effects of deficiency	• Sore mouth, swollen tongue, cracked lips and skin
	• Eye infections, sensitivity to light
	• Lack of energy, loss of appetite
	• Checked growth, poor general health, body weakness
Properties	• Water-soluble, yellow-orange in colour
	• Destroyed by alkalis, sunlight
	• Unstable at high temperatures

Vitamin B$_6$ (pyridoxine)

Sources	Meat, offal, fish, wheat germ, pulses, green vegetables, bananas, cereals, yeast, nuts
Functions	• Assists metabolism of protein, carbohydrates and fats by acting as a co-enzyme • Aids the formation of blood cells • Required for healthy nervous and immune systems • Promotes healthy skin
Effects of deficiency	• Anaemia, tiredness and fatigue • Convulsions in infants • Worsening of pre-menstrual tension
Properties	• Water-soluble • Generally stable at normal temperatures but destroyed by high temperatures • Destroyed by alkalis, sunlight and oxygen

Vitamin B$_{12}$ (cobalamin)

Sources	Dairy produce, eggs, fish, offal, meats, poultry
Functions	• Aids the formation of the myelin sheath surrounding nerve fibres • Needed for red blood cells • Aids the metabolism of fatty acids and folic acid
Effects of deficiency	• Fatigue, shortness of breath • Pernicious anaemia (non-absorption of vitamin B$_{12}$) • Anxiety and irritability, depression • Degeneration of nerve fibres
RI (µg per day)	• Children: 0.7–1 µg • Adolescents: 1.4 µg • Adults: 1.4 µg • During pregnancy: 1.6 µg • During lactation: 1.9 µg
Properties	• Water-soluble • Heat stable up to 100°C • Destroyed by strong acids, alkalis and sunlight (UV)

key point

As vitamin B$_{12}$ is only found in animal foods, vegans must include foods fortified with this vitamin in their diets.

Folic acid (folate)

Sources	Fortified foods, wholegrain cereals, green leafy vegetables, offal, milk, wheat germ, nuts, supplements
Functions	• Essential for manufacture of DNA and RNA • Protects against neural tube defects, e.g. spina bifida • Assists B_{12} in the formation of red blood cells • Assists protein metabolism • Supports the immune system
Effects of deficiency	• Tiredness and fatigue • Anaemia in young children and pregnant women • Risk of neural tube defects in foetus during pregnancy
RI (µg per day)	• Children: 100–200 µg • Adolescents: 300 µg • Adults: 300 µg • During pregnancy: 500 µg • During lactation: 400 µg
Properties	• Water-soluble • Unaffected by acid environments • Sensitive to alkalis, light and oxygen • Unstable in cooking, easily destroyed

Niacin (nicotinic acid)

Sources	Bread, fortified breakfast cereals, meat , offal, tuna, nuts
Functions	• Assists the metabolism of nutrients • Necessary for a healthy brain and nervous system • Promotes growth and maintenance of healthy skin • Prevents pellagra
Effects of deficiency	• Pellagra (symptoms are the five Ds) • Lack of energy, fatigue and weight loss
Properties	• Water-soluble • Stable to heat, acids and alkalis • 80%–90% lost in milling

Exam questions and sample answers

Higher Level 2016, Section A, Q4 (6 marks) HL

State **three** functions of folic acid (folate).

- *Needed for formation of red blood cells, DNA and RNA.*
- *Essential for development of brain and spinal cord in foetus to reduce risk of neural tube defects, e.g. spina bifida.*
- *Assists metabolism of protein.*

Higher Level 2004, Section A, Q3 (6 marks)

The conditions listed below are caused by a deficiency in the diet of specific vitamins. Identify the vitamin in **each** case.

Conditions	Vitamins
Night blindness	*A*
Rickets	*D*
Lack of Poor clotting of blood	*K*
Anaemia	*C, B$_{12}$, folic acid (folate)*
Beri-beri	*B$_1$ (thiamine)*
Neural tube defects	*Folic acid (folate)*

Ordinary Level 2016, Section A, Q3 (6 marks)

State **two** functions of vitamin A.

- *Production of rhodopsin in retina to aid night vision.*
- *Essential for healthy lining membranes in nose, mouth and throat.*

Name **two** good dietary sources of vitamin A. (Choose from the list below)

- *Retinol: fish, fish liver oils, dairy products, e.g. butter, meat, eggs*
- *Beta-carotene: green leafy vegetables, red peppers, carrots, tomatoes*

Ordinary Level 2015, Section A, Q4 (6 marks)

State **two** functions of vitamin C.

- *Necessary for production of collagen.*
- *Aids the absorption of calcium and iron.*

Name **two** good dietary sources of vitamin C. (Choose from the list below)

- *Fruit: blackcurrants, citrus fruits, e.g. oranges, strawberries, kiwis*
- *Vegetables: green leafy cabbage, broccoli, potatoes, peppers*

Ordinary Level 2013, Section A, Q2 (6 marks)

Use the words listed below to complete the following statements in relation to vitamin A.

hypervitaminosis   **rhodopsin**   **night blindness**

Vitamin A is necessary for the production of *rhodopsin* a pigment in the retina of the eye.

A deficiency of Vitamin A causes *night blindness*.

Hypervitaminosis can occur through over-use of dietary supplements containing vitamin A.

Higher Level 2016, Section B, Q2 (c) (15 marks)

Oily fish and fish liver oils make a significant contribution to a persons' intake of vitamin D. Give an account of vitamin D and refer to type/form, properties and effects of deficiency.

LINKS
- Vitamin D (p. 33)
- Fish (p. 88)

Type/form: (Name = 1 mark + details × 2 marks = 3 marks
- *D3 – cholecalciferol is found mainly in animal foods, e.g. fish, fish oils, eggs, milk, and can be formed by action of sunlight on the skin, which converts 7-dehydrocholesterol in the skin to vitamin D3.*

Properties: (3 × 2 marks = 6 marks)
- *Fat soluble, insoluble in water.*
- *Heat stable, not affected by cooking and preservation.*
- *Stable to acids, alkalis and oxygen.*

Effects of deficiency: (2 points × 3 marks = 6 marks)
- *Osteoporosis in adults increases risks of bone fractures.*
- *Rickets in children results in weak, malformed bones.*

Higher Level 2012, Section B, Q2 (c) (18 marks)

(c) Give an account of vitamin A under each of the following headings:

LINK
- Vitamin A (p. 32)

Biological functions: (3 points × 2 marks = 6 marks)
- *Produces rhodopsin in the retina, which prevents night blindness.*
- *Maintains healthy lining membranes in the eye, nose, mouth and throat.*
- *Assists growth and development in the body.*

Effects of deficiency: (3 points × 2 marks = 6 marks)
- *Night blindness, eyes unable to adapt to reduced light.*
- *Retarded or stunted growth in children.*
- *Xeropthalmia, eye infection.*

Properties: (3 points × 2 marks = 6 marks)
- *Solubility: Fat-soluble vitamin, insoluble in water, soluble in organic solvents.*
- *Effects of heat: heat stable.*
- *Powerful antioxidant.*

Ordinary Level 2017, Section B, Q1 (b), (c)

(b) Give an account of vitamin C under **each** of the following headings:

Dietary sources: (4 sources x 4 marks = 8 marks)
- *Fruits: blackcurrants, citrus fruit*
- *Vegetables: green leafy vegetables, potatoes*

Functions in the body: (2 functions × 4 marks = 8 marks)
- *Needed for the absorption of iron and calcium.*
- *Maintains the immune system by helping to fight infections.*

Effects of deficiency: (1 effect × 4 marks = 4 marks)
- *Scurvy in severe cases of deficiency.*

(c) Vitamin C assists the absorption of nutrients. Name one of these nutrients.

Iron (5 marks)

Ordinary Level 2012, Section B, Q1 (c)

(c) Identify ways of retaining vitamin C when (i) preparing **and** (ii) cooking foods with a high vitamin C content. (Choose any three from points listed below)
(3 ways × 4 marks = 12 marks)

(i) Preparation:
- *Eat foods as fresh as possible and raw if possible.*
- *Prepare just before cooking, using a sharp knife or vegetable peeler.*

(ii) Cooking:
- *Cook for the shortest possible time in the least amount of liquid, in a saucepan with a tightly fitted lid or steam to retain maximum nutrients.*
- *Never add bread soda when cooking vegetables as it destroys vitamin C.*

Minerals

Major mineral elements	Trace mineral elements
Calcium (Ca)*	Iron (Fe)*
Chlorine (Cl)	Chromium (Cr)
Magnesium (Mg)	Cobalt (Co)
Phosphorous (P)	Copper (Cu)
Potassium (K) 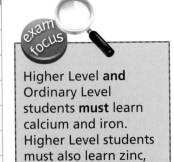 HL	Fluoride (F)
Sodium (Na)	Iodine (I) HL
Sulphur (S)	Manganese (Mn)
	Nickel (Ni)
	Selenium (Se)
	Zinc (Zn) HL

Important for Ordinary and Higher Level.

exam focus

Higher Level **and** Ordinary Level students **must** learn calcium and iron. Higher Level students must also learn zinc, iodine, potassium and sodium.

LINKS
- Dietary and food requirements (p. 54)
- The Irish diet (p. 75)

Calcium

Sources	Calcium-fortified foods, dairy products, green leafy vegetables, tinned fish, seeds, nuts, dried fruit, hard water
Functions	• Aids formation and development of strong bones and teeth • Assists blood clotting • Aids functioning of nerves and muscles • Helps regulate metabolism in cells
Effects of deficiency	• Poor quality teeth, tooth decay • Osteomalacia (softening of bones) in adults • Osteoporosis in young people, adults and older people • Rickets (deformed bones) in children • Muscular spasm/cramps • Abnormal clotting of blood
RI (mg per day)	• Children: 800 mg • Adolescents: 1200 mg • Adults: 800 mg • During pregnancy/lactation: 1200 mg

Absorption of calcium

1. Absorption is **increased** by vitamin D, phosphorus, an acid environment, a diet rich in amino acids, lactose, parathormone and oestrogen.
2. Absorption is **inhibited** by saturated fatty acids, dietary fibre, oxalic acid, phytic acid, lack of acid, vitamin D deficiency, low oestrogen levels in post-menopausal women and incorrect calcium to phosphorus ratio.

Phytic acid binds to calcium and prevents its absorption. *Sources:* cereals and grains.
Oxalates bind to calcium and prevent its absorption. *Sources:* rhubarb and spinach.

Iron

Iron is available in two forms:

1. **Haem** (ferrous iron, Fe^{2+}, organic): soluble and easily absorbed.
2. **Non-haem** (ferric iron, Fe^{3+}, inorganic): insoluble; must be reduced from ferric state to ferrous state in order to be absorbed.

Sources	*Haem iron:* chicken, liver, red meat, meat products
	Non-haem iron: fish, green vegetables, eggs, cereals, pulses
Functions	• Component of haemoglobin in red blood cells • Transports oxygen to the cells (component of myoglobin) • Essential component of enzyme systems (release of energy)
Effects of deficiency (mild/severe)	• Iron deficiency anaemia, reduced levels of haemoglobin • Breathlessness, fatigue, paleness, lack of energy
RI (mg per day)	• Children: 10 mg • Adolescents: 14 mg • Adults: 10–14 mg *(females need higher intake)* • During pregnancy/lactation: 15 mg

Absorption of iron

Absorption of iron depends on its source:

1. **Haem iron:** more absorbable than non-haem iron; absorption is independent of meal composition.
2. **Non-haem iron:** strongly influenced by meal composition; boosted by the presence of vitamin C and meat in a meal, or inhibited by dietary factors.

Absorption is **increased** by:	Absorption is **inhibited** by:	
1. **Combining** haem and non-haem iron sources 2. **Vitamin C** – converts non-haem into haem iron 3. **Hydrochloric acid** in the stomach aids non-haem absorption 4. The **MFP factor** (meat, fish and poultry)	1. **Oxalic acid** (rhubarb) 2. **Phytic acid** (cereals) 3. High **fibre** intake 4. **Tannins** (tea, coffee, cocoa) 5. Meals with only non-haem sources	 All these attach or bind to iron, making it insoluble.

Excess iron may result in:

- **Haemochromatosis:** iron overload caused by a genetic disorder.
- **Haemosiderosis:** iron overload associated with nutritional overload.

HL Zinc

Sources	Meat, meat products, shellfish, bread, milk, cheese, cereals
Functions	• Enzyme and hormone activity • Helps in the healing of wounds • Supports healthy skin • Promotes general good health • Protein and carbohydrate metabolism
Effects of deficiency	• Poor appetite • Slow healing of wounds • Increased risk of infections • Dry, flaky skin
RI (mg per day)	• Children: 4–7 mg • Adolescents: 7–12 mg • Adults: 7–12 mg

Iodine

Sources	Fish, seaweed, iodised salt, meat, milk, eggs
Functions	• Necessary for the production of thyroxine • Regulates metabolism • Regulates growth and development
Effects of deficiency	• Lethargy, tiredness, fatigue, slower metabolism • Goitre (enlargement of the thyroid gland) • Cretinism in children • Risk of miscarriage and stillbirth
RI (µg per day)	• Children: 60–90 µg • Adolescents: 125 µg • Adults: 140 µg

Potassium

HL

Sources	Whole foods, fruits, vegetables, whole grains, fresh meat, fish, milk
Functions	• Controls fluid balance in body tissues • Formation and functioning of body cells • Involved in protein metabolism • Regulates nerve and muscle activity
Effects of deficiency	• Deficiency is rare • Muscular weakness and fatigue in rare cases • Severe depletion can cause cardiac arrest
RI (g per day)	Adults: 3.5 g Children: 0.8–1.2 g

Sodium

Sources	Bread, fish, butter, processed foods, soy sauce, table salt
Functions	• Regulates water balance in the body • Assists muscle functioning • Promotes healthy nerve activity
Effects of deficiency	• Rare due to availability of salt in diet • Low blood pressure • Loss of appetite and weakness, muscular cramps
RI (g per day)	Adults: Less than 6 g salt/2.4 g sodium Children: Less than 4 g salt/1.6 g sodium

Exam questions and sample answers

Higher Level 2017, Section A, Q4 (6 marks)

Complete the following table in relation to anaemia.

Cause	• Low intake of iron-rich foods. • Lack of haemoglobin in red blood cells. • Blood loss due to menstruation.
Effect of deficiency	• Reduced oxygen levels in the blood. • Breathlessness, fatigue/tiredness, pale skin.
Corrective measure	• Increase intake of iron-rich foods (haem and haem iron sources). • Increase intake of vitamin C-rich foods to help absorption. • Reduce intake of excess fibre, phytic and oxalic acid and tannins (inhibit absorption of iron).

Higher Level 2014, Section A, Q3 (6 marks)

Differentiate between the following and give **one** food source of each.

Haem iron: *Ferrous iron (Fe^{2+}), soluble and easily absorbed, unaffected by inhibiting factors.*
Source: *Meat and meat products.*

LINK
• Iron (p. 43)

Non-haem iron: *Ferric iron (Fe^{3+}), cannot be absorbed by the body, must be changed into ferrous iron to be absorbed which is facilitated by vitamin C, absorption also influenced by animal protein, e.g. meat.*
Source: *Green leafy vegetables.*

Higher Level 2012, Section A, Q1 (6 marks)

Give **one** main function of sodium in the diet.

Sodium regulates water balance in the body tissues.

List **two** good dietary sources of sodium.
• *Processed foods, e.g. cheese, instant sauces.*
• *Smoked and cured meats and fish.*

Ordinary Level 2017, Section A, Q4 (6 marks)

List **two** biological functions of calcium.
• *Formation of strong bones and teeth.*
• *Necessary for the functioning of muscles and nerves.*

LINK
• Calcium (p. 42)

Name **two** good dietary sources of calcium.
- Milk and dairy products, e.g. cheese, yoghurt.
- Fortified foods, e.g. flour, white bread.

Higher Level 2015, Section B, Q1 (b), (c)

(b) Poor food choices have contributed to 42% of teenage girls and 23% of teenage boys not getting enough **calcium** in their diet. Give an account of calcium and include reference to: sources, biological functions and factors assisting/inhibiting absorption.

Sources: (3 sources × 2 marks = 6 marks)
- *Milk and dairy products, e.g. cheese and yoghurt.*
- *Dark green leafy vegetables, e.g. cabbage.*
- *Fortified foods, e.g. flour, milk, juices.*

> **LINK**
> - Calcium (p. 42)

Biological functions: (3 functions × 2 marks = 6 marks)
- *Essential for the formation of healthy bones and teeth.*
- *Important in the clotting of blood.*
- *Necessary for the normal functioning of nerves and muscles.*

Factors assisting/inhibiting absorption: (3 factors × 2 marks = 6 marks)
- *Assisting factors: Vitamin D stimulates calcium binding protein and increases levels of absorption; Parathormone controls the level of calcium in the blood; Amino acids combine with calcium salts; Phosphorus combine with calcium and forms calcium phosphate; Acidic environment helps calcium absorption.*

> *exam focus*
>
> Choose one assisting factor, one inhibiting factor and any one other factor.

- *Inhibiting factors: Phytic acid/phytates (cereals, grains) and oxalic acid/oxalates (spinach, rhubarb) bind to calcium preventing its absorption; Dietary fibre binds to calcium preventing its absorption; Excess saturated fats; Over-consumption of fizzy drinks; Tannins prevent absorption.*

(c) Explain:

(i) What is osteoporosis?   (2 points × 3 marks = 6 marks)
Osteoporosis is a disease which causes bones to lose calcium, become thin and porous. Bones become brittle and fracture or break easily.

(ii) The main factors that increase risk of developing osteoporosis.
                                               (3 factors × 4 points = 12 marks)

- *Gender: more common in women, especially after pregnancy due to calcium loss, post-menopausal women as part of the aging process*
- *Heredity: family history of osteoporosis increases risk.*
- *Diet: lack of calcium and inadequate vitamin C in the diet increases risk.*

Ordinary Level 2015, Section B, Q1 (a)–(c)

'Iron deficiency remains a common condition in children, with research suggesting many negative effects on the developing child.' The table below shows the nutritional content of four different meats.

Meat	Protein	Fat	Calcium	Iron	Vitamins
Beef	18.1g	17.1g	7mg	1.9mg	B-group
Chicken	24.8g	5.4g	9mg	0.8mg	B-group
Liver	24.9g	13.7g	14mg	8.8mg	B-group, C, D
Pork	15.8g	29.6g	8mg	0.8mg	B-group

(a) Why, in your opinion, is iron deficiency a common condition in children?

(2 points × 4 marks = 8 marks)

- *Insufficient vitamin C in their diet to help iron absorption.*
- *Children prefer processed foods to meats and vegetables.*

(b) Using the information provided in the table and having regard to current healthy eating guidelines comment on the nutritional value of the different meats. (4 points × 6 marks = 24 marks)

- *All meats contain B-group vitamins which are involved in energy release and production of red blood cells and varying amounts of calcium. Beef has second highest amount of iron which helps prevent anaemia.*
- *Liver has the highest amount of high biological value protein for growth and repair of body cells, calcium for strong bones and teeth, iron to prevent anaemia and vitamins C and D which are lacking in the other meats.*
- *Pork has a high amount of saturated fat, which contributes to coronary heart disease (CHD) and obesity, and has the lowest amount of protein when compared to the other meats.*
- *Chicken has the lowest amount of fat, the second highest amount of HBV protein useful for growth and development in children and the second lowest amount of calcium.*

exam focus

Read the table given very carefully and then plan your answer. Elaborate on relevant points

(c) Give an account of iron under **each** of the following headings:

Dietary sources: (3 sources × 4 marks = 12 marks)
- *Red meat and offal e.g. liver.*
- *Cereals.*
- *Green vegetables.*

Functions in the body: (2 functions × 4 marks = 8 marks)
- *Manufacture of haemoglobin in the blood which carries oxygen around the body.*
- *Involved in production of myoglobin which carries oxygen to muscles.*

Effects of deficiency: (1 effect = 4 marks)
Anaemia, fatigue, lack of energy

Name **one** nutrient that is necessary for the absorption of iron.   (4 marks)
Vitamin C

Water

Composition: 2 hydrogen + 1 oxygen = H_2O (ratio 2:1).

exam focus

Water is in every body cell, organ and secretion. It is essential for life.

Sources, properties, function and RI

Sources	Most foods, beverages (milk, tea, coffee), tap and bottled water, fruit and vegetables
Properties	• Colourless, odourless and tasteless liquid • Boils at 100°C, freezes at 0°C • Neutral pH of 7, neither acid nor alkaline • Three states: solid (ice), liquid, gas (steam) • A solvent: substances dissolve readily in water • Water absorbs and retains heat
Functions	• Component of all body cells and fluids • Assists digestion and absorption of nutrients • Transports nutrients, oxygen, hormones, enzymes in the body • Source of calcium and fluorine • Assists the removal of waste and toxins from the body • Regulates body temperature through perspiration • Refreshing to drink, quenches thirst
RI (litres per day)	2–2·5 litres per day, with 2 litres coming from beverages and 0·5 litres from food

Exam questions and sample answers

Higher Level 2015, Section A, Q3 (6 marks)

Enumerate **three** biological functions of water.

- *Removal of waste and toxins from the body, e.g. via the kidneys.*
- *Regulating body temperature through perspiration.*
- *Essential component of all body cells, tissues and fluids.*

Ordinary Level 2012, Section A, Q3 (6 marks)

List **three** biological functions of water.

- *Quenches thirst and prevents dehydration.*
- *Source of calcium and fluoride in the diet.*
- *Necessary for the breakdown of food during digestion.*

LINK
- Water (p. 49)

2 Diet and Health

aims To learn and revise:

- Energy
- Current dietary guidelines
- Dietary needs of individuals and special groups
- The Irish diet

Energy

Energy is defined as 'the body's ability to do work'.
Sources of energy: proteins, lipids and carbohydrates.

MEASURING ENERGY
Proteins: 1 g = 4 kcal (17 kJ) energy
Lipids: 1 g = 9 kcal (37 kJ) energy
Carbohydrates: 1 g = 4 kcal (17 kJ) energy

The topics in this chapter are examined in **Section A** and **integrated** with nutrients and food commodities in **Section B** of the exam paper.

Factors determining energy requirements

1. Age	Children/teenagers require more energy than adults
2. Body size	Larger bodies require more energy
3. Climate	Less energy is needed in warmer climates
4. Gender	Males have higher energy requirements (higher muscle to fat ratio)
5. Occupation	Sedentary workers require less energy than more active people
6. Physical activity	The greater the physical activity, the higher the energy needs
7. Pregnancy and lactation	More energy required for the foetus to grow and when breast feeding
8. Health status	Less energy needed when ill, more needed to repair physical injuries

Role of energy in the body

Energy is needed for:

1. Chemical and metabolic reactions, including BMR.
2. Physical activities, both voluntary and involuntary.
3. Growth, e.g. during pregnancy, adolescence, childhood.
4. Producing heat and maintaining body temperature.
5. Functioning of all internal organs.

LINK
- Dietary and food requirements (p. 54)

Metabolism is the total number of chemical reactions taking place in the body.

Basal metabolic rate (BMR):

- Is the minimum amount of energy needed to keep the body functioning.
- Is measured when a person is at rest, 10–12 hours after their last meal, during which time no physical activity has taken place.
- **BMR is highest** in growing babies and children, and decreases as one gets older.
- **BMR varies** between individuals due to a variety of factors, e.g. climate, after eating a meal.

Daily energy requirements

	(kcal per day)	
Babies (0–1)	800	
Toddlers (1–4)	1,000–1,400	
Children (5–7)	1,800	
	Female	*Male*
Teenagers	2,300	2,800–3,000
Sedentary adult	2,100	2,700
Active adult	2,500	3,500
Pregnancy/lactation	2,400–2,700	
Older adult	2,000	2,250

To maintain a constant **energy balance (intake/output):**

$$\underset{\text{(food)}}{\text{Energy intake}} = \underset{\text{(physical activity)}}{\text{Energy output}}$$

LINKS

- Meal management and planning (p. 123)
- Energy value (protein, carbohydrates and lipids) (pp. 9, 17, 27)

Factors controlling food intake

Physiological factors	• Hunger (desire to find food) • Satiety (fullness) • Hypothalamus (centre of control in the brain)
Psychological factors	• Appetite (desire to eat) • Dislike of a particular food • Stress • Mood
External factors	• Cultural preferences • Stimuli from food/foods • Social occasion • Time of day

Dietary guidelines

The health of the Irish population is monitored by the Department of Health supported by the HSE, National Nutritional Surveillance Centre, Health Promotion Unit, the Irish Nutrition and Dietetic Institute, Food Safety Authority of Ireland and Safefood.

The purpose of the nutritional guidelines is to:

- Encourage people to improve their eating habits and improve their health.
- Encourage people to take more exercise.
- Reduce diet-related diseases in Ireland, e.g. childhood obesity, heart disease, bowel disorders.

Check for changes in the above departments and agencies.

Current nutritional guidelines

1. Eat a wide variety of foods from the five main food groups.
2. Use the **Food Pyramid** to guide the number and size of servings.
3. Increase fibre intake to 30 g per day, e.g. whole grains, fruits, vegetables.
4. Choose calcium and iron-rich foods (especially important for females).
5. Use polyunsaturated fats/spreads instead of saturated varieties.
6. Avoid frying foods; instead grill, boil, steam, poach or bake.
7. Eat five to seven servings of colourful fruits, salads and vegetables daily.
8. Eat foods rich in starch (cereals, potatoes, brown rice and pasta).
9. Eat less saturated fat, sugar and salt, and avoid processed foods.
10. Choose lean meats, poultry and fish; legumes are good alternatives.
11. Drink at least eight glasses of water each day.
12. Keep within the recommended guidelines for alcohol.

LINKS

- The Irish diet (p. 75)
- Meal management and planning (p. 123)

Measuring nutrient intake

Reference Intake is the average daily intake level of a nutrient that is sufficient to meet the nutritional needs of 97–98% of the population based on stage of life (age group) and gender. RI replaces the Recommended Daily Allowances (RDA). RI information is displayed on nutritional food labels (energy format, traffic light format).

Go to health.gov.ie and search for 'The National Guidelines on Physical Activity for Ireland'. Download the pdf to find out more about exercise and healthy living.

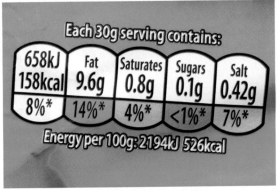

Each 30g serving contains:				
658kJ 158kcal 8%*	Fat 9.6g 14%*	Saturates 0.8g 4%*	Sugars 0.1g <1%*	Salt 0.42g 7%*

Energy per 100g: 2194kJ 526kcal

Traffic light format

Dietary and food requirements

Choosing a balanced diet

A well-balanced diet contains all the nutrients in the correct proportions for each individual, which is achieved by eating a wide variety of foods chosen from the five main food groups on the Food Pyramid.

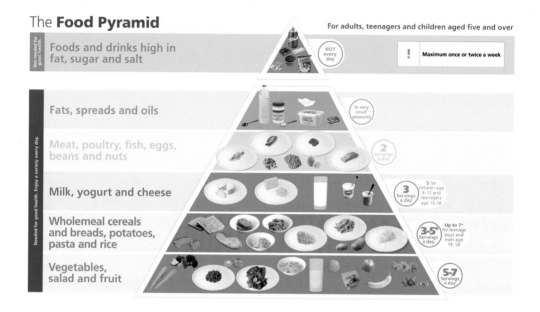

The **Food Pyramid**

The food groups: servings and dietetic value

Food group	Servings per day	Examples of serving sizes	Dietetic value
Vegetables, salad, fruit	5–7	1 medium fruit (apple) 2 small fruits (kiwi) 1 bowl of salad 1 bowl homemade soup 150 ml unsweetened juice	• Carbohydrates • Fibre • Vitamins • Minerals • Water • Almost fat-free
Wholemeal cereals, breads, potatoes, pasta and rice	3–5 (7 for teenage boys and men aged 19–50)	½ cup dry porridge 2 thin slices brown bread 1 pitta bread 2 medium potatoes 1 cup cooked rice, pasta, noodles, couscous 1 cup yam or plantain	• Energy source • Dietary fibre • B-group vitamins • Low in lipids
Milk, yoghurt, cheese	3 (5 for children aged 9–12 and teenagers aged 13–18)	200 ml milk (1 glass) 25 g hard/semi-hard cheese 1 carton yoghurt (125 g) 1 yoghurt drink (200 ml)	• Calcium • Protein • Lipids • Vitamin D

Meat, poultry, fish, eggs, beans, nuts	2 servings per day	50–75 g cooked lean meat/poultry 100 g cooked fish, soya or tofu ½ cup beans or lentils 2 eggs 40 g unsalted nuts or seeds	• Protein • Iron • B-group vitamins • Minerals
Fats, spreads, oils	In **very** small amounts	1 tsp oil per person when cooking 1 portion pack reduced-fat or light spread for 2 slices of bread	• Lipids
Foods and drinks high in fat, sugar and salt	**Not every day** – maximum once a week	Small servings of chocolate, biscuits, cakes, sweets, crisps, ice cream and sugary drinks	

Department of Health, December 2016

key point

Revise the benefits and uses of food composition tables.

Individual dietary requirements

Babies

The early stages of life are a period of rapid growth and development. A baby can be bottle fed with formula feeds or breast fed.

Breast feeding is recommended because breast milk:

- Contains all nutrients in the correct proportions.
- Provides antibodies to protect against infection.
- Is at the right temperature and sterile.
- Reduces risks of respiratory, gastrointestinal and other infections.
- Assists bonding between baby and mother.

If formula milk is used the manufacturer's instructions should be followed strictly. Do not over- or under-dilute.

key point

We should aim to include three of the four main food groups in each meal for all individuals.

LINK

- Nutrients (p. 2)

Dietary guidelines when weaning a baby – introducing solid foods

1. When weaning, introduce single foods at a time: choose soft, sieved/puréed foods, e.g. cereals, fruit, vegetables, potatoes, eggs, meat, chicken, etc.
2. Include a balance of foods from the four main food groups.
3. From six months, the baby needs foods rich in iron and vitamin C.
4. Sieving and puréeing make foods more digestible, and gets the baby used to home-cooked foods.

5. As the baby grows, include more protein and energy foods.

6. Exclude tea, coffee, fatty, fried and spicy foods, sugar and salt. Do not give honey to babies under one year old.

Children

1. 'Faddy' eating should be discouraged.

2. Prepare a variety of nutritious and balanced meals.

3. Regular mealtimes, without rushing, are recommended.

4. Provide healthy nutritious snacks and packed lunches.

5. Serve small, easy-to-manage portions.

6. Choose a balanced diet from the four main food groups.

7. Encourage children to eat breakfast every day.

8. Avoid sweets, sugary foods, salty snacks and fizzy drinks.

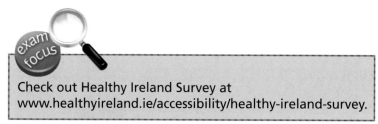

exam focus

Check out Healthy Ireland Survey at
www.healthyireland.ie/accessibility/healthy-ireland-survey.

Specific dietary needs of children

Nutrient	Function	Main sources
Protein	Needed for repair and for rapid growth	Meat, poultry, fish, eggs, cheese
Carbohydrate	Energy production	Cereals, fruit, vegetables
Fibre	Prevents constipation	Cereals, fruit, vegetables
Lipids	Concentrated source of energy, fat-soluble vitamins and essential fatty acids	Milk, cheese, yoghurt, fish
Calcium (aided by vitamin D)	Healthy bones and teeth	Milk, cheese, yoghurt
Vitamin D	Absorption of calcium	Eggs, milk, oily fish, sunlight
Iron (aided by vitamin C)	• Prevents anaemia • General good health	Meat, dark green vegetables
Vitamin C	• Absorption of iron • Healing of wounds	Fruit, vegetables, fortified foods
Water	Prevents dehydration	Beverages, tap water

Adolescents

Adolescence is a time of rapid growth and increased activity. Limit fried foods, junk foods and sugary snacks. Adequate calcium and vitamin D at this stage are essential for life-long bone health.

Specific dietary needs of adolescents

Nutrient	Function	Main sources
Protein	Rapid growth and hormone production	Meat, poultry, fish, eggs, cheese, soya products
Carbohydrate	Energy production	Cereals, fruit, vegetables
Fibre	Prevents bowel disorders and constipation	Whole cereals and products, brown rice, brown bread, fruit, vegetables
Lipids	Concentrated source of energy, fat-soluble vitamins and essential fatty acids	Milk, cheese, yoghurt, fish
Calcium (aided by vitamin D)	● Healthy bones and teeth ● Adequate calcium to prevent osteoporosis	Milk, cheese, yoghurt
Vitamin D	Absorption of calcium	Eggs, milk, oily fish, sunlight
Iron (aided by vitamin C)	Prevents anaemia (especially in females)	Meat, dark green leafy vegetables (cabbage, spinach)
Vitamin C	● Absorption of iron ● Healing of wounds/injuries	Fruit, juices, vegetables, fortified foods
Water	● Healthy skin ● Prevents dehydration	Beverages, tap water, juices

Adults

1. Adults need a well-balanced, varied diet based on their lifestyle, gender and age. Watch portion sizes, read food labels, and limit salt, sugar and high-fat foods.
2. Energy needs are dependent on gender, activity and body size.
3. Reduce intake of salt to prevent high blood pressure.
4. Reduce saturated fats to prevent coronary heart disease (CHD).
5. Give up smoking and reduce/eliminate alcohol consumption.

Specific dietary needs of adults

Nutrient	Function	Main sources
Protein	Growth and repair of body cells	Meat, fish, eggs, soya products
Carbohydrate	Energy production	Cereals, fruit, vegetables, rice, pasta, potatoes
Fibre	● Prevents constipation ● Reduces risk of CHD	Wholegrain cereals, brown rice and pasta, fruits, vegetables
Lipids – unsaturated	● Reduces risk of CHD ● Reduces cholesterol build-up	Chicken, turkey, fish, lean meat
Calcium (aided by vitamin D)	● Healthy bones and teeth ● Maintains bone mass	Milk, cheese, tinned fish
Vitamin D	Absorption of calcium	Oily fish, eggs, sunlight
Iron (aided by vitamin C)	● Prevents anaemia ● Healthy blood	Dark green leafy vegetables, meat
Vitamin C	● Absorption of iron ● Healing of wounds/injuries	Fruits, juices, vegetables, fortified foods
Vitamin B-group	Release of energy from foods/cell metabolism	A wide variety of foods
Water	● For healthy skin ● Prevents dehydration and constipation	Beverages, tap/bottled water, juices

During pregnancy and lactation

1. Choose a well-balanced, varied diet to benefit health of mother and baby.
2. Ensure adequate folic acid prior to and after conception to reduce risks of neural tube defects, e.g. spina bifida.
3. Eliminate risk of listeria and salmonella by avoiding raw eggs, unpasteurised cream cheeses and cook-chill products.
4. Limit salt intake to prevent hypertension and oedema.
5. Avoid fried, spicy or sugary foods and coffee.
6. Give up smoking and alcohol (which cause increased risk of premature birth, foetal alcohol syndrome, etc.).

Specific dietary needs during pregnancy/lactation

Nutrient	Function	Main sources
Folate/folic acid	● Prevents/reduces neural tube defects ● Essential for formation of new cells in foetus	Fortified cereals/bread, spinach, fortified milk, supplementation under doctor's advice
Protein	Foetal growth and development	Meat, fish, eggs, soya products
Carbohydrate	Energy production	Cereals, fruit, vegetables
Fibre	Prevents constipation – common during pregnancy	Wholemeal bread and pasta, brown rice, fruits, vegetables
Lipids – fatty acids	Development of foetus's healthy nervous system	Oily fish, eggs, liver
Calcium (aided by vitamin D)	Healthy bones and teeth	Milk, cheese, tinned fish
Vitamin D	Absorption of calcium	Eggs, sunlight
Iron (aided by vitamin C)	Prevents anaemia in mother and baby	Dark green leafy vegetables, meat
Vitamin C	Absorption of iron	Fruit, vegetables
Water	Prevents dehydration and constipation	Beverages, water, juices

Elderly people

Problems associated with ageing, related dietary issues and some solutions:

Problems	Solutions
Reduced income: limits choice, changes priorities, can result in poverty and inadequate diet, malnutrition	● Use cheaper, nutritious cuts of meat ● Check for meal deals (two/three courses) ● Use own-brand products ● Check special reductions
Poor general health/physical disabilities: dental (false teeth, gum disease), anaemia, arthritis	● Choose foods that are easy to prepare and eat, e.g. eggs, fish, poultry, cheese ● Consider 'Meals-on-wheels' network
Difficulties when shopping: less mobile, too far from the shops, shopping bags too heavy to carry	● Check out local home delivery services ● Keep emergency stores of foods (dried, frozen, canned, bottled)
Difficulties when preparing foods: arthritis in hands	● Specialised kitchen gadgets ● Affordable prepared ingredients
Loss of interest and appetite: buying a limited range of foods	● Follow the Food Pyramid for guidelines ● Avoid too many convenience foods
Loneliness and lack of interest in cooking for one person	● Invite/join others for lunch/dinner/tea ● Consider 'Meals-on-wheels' network ● Join Age Action Ireland – social events

Basal metabolism slows with ageing and for some individuals activity levels may decrease. Energy needs will vary depending on the level of activity.

Specific dietary needs of older people

Nutrient	Function	Main sources
Protein (concentrated and easy to digest)	Replacement or repair of worn cells	Fish, chicken, turkey, eggs
Carbohydrate	Energy production	Cereals, fruit, vegetables
Fibre	Prevents constipation and bowel disease	Wholegrain cereals, fruits, vegetables
Calcium (aided by vitamin D)	• Strong bones • Prevents osteoporosis	Milk, cheese, tinned fish
Vitamin D	Absorption of calcium	Milk, yoghurt, eggs, sunlight
Iron (aided by vitamin C)	Prevents anaemia	Lean meat, offal, dark green vegetables, wholegrains
Vitamin C	• Absorption of iron • Healing of wounds and bruising • Protects against colds and flu • Protects against bed sores	Fruit, vegetables
Vitamin A	Healthy eyes and skin	Carrots, butter, eggs, liver, fish liver oils
Water	Prevents dehydration	Tap/bottled water, juices, milk

Older people should:

1. Choose a varied, well-balanced diet.
2. Serve smaller portions and eat more regular meals.
3. Reduce intake of cholesterol and saturated fats.
4. Reduce salt/salty foods to prevent hypertension.
5. Reduce sugars to prevent diabetes mellitus.
6. Avoid spicy foods to prevent indigestion.

key point

Eat adequate fibre to prevent constipation.

Convalescents

When someone is recovering from illness serve:

1. Concentrated protein foods.
2. Foods that are nutrient-dense and easy to digest.
3. Small portions that are easy to eat.

Meals should be prepared under strict hygienic conditions.

Avoid spicy foods, coffee and fast foods.

Follow the doctor's orders! Prepare meals with fresh ingredients under strict hygiene conditions.

Dietary needs of convalescents

Nutrient	Function	Main sources
Protein	Repairs damaged cells	Fish, chicken, eggs
Carbohydrate	Energy production	Fruits, vegetables, slow-release starches
Fibre	Prevents constipation	Fruits, vegetables
Calcium (aided by vitamin D)	Promotes recovery	Milk
Vitamin D	Absorption of calcium	Milk, yoghurt, eggs
Iron (aided by vitamin C)	Prevents anaemia	Offal, dark green vegetables
Vitamin C	• Absorption of iron • Healing of wounds	Fruit, vegetables
Vitamins/minerals	• Promote healing • Protection from infections	Variety of foods
Water (increase intake)	Prevents dehydration	Water, fruits, juices

Essential for Ordinary and Higher Levels:

Devise a day's menus for each age group, using the correct menu format, meal planning guidelines and healthy eating guidelines. Be able to explain and defend your choices. Check www.healthyireland.ie.

Dietary needs for diet-related health problems

Bowel disorders

Main bowel disorders

Disorder	Symptoms	Dietary deficiency or other reasons
Constipation	• Faeces hard and painful to pass • Irregular bowel movements	Low-fibre diet, pregnancy, medical conditions
Haemorrhoids (piles)	• Enlarged veins in anus and rectum • Severe itching • Passing blood	Low-fibre diet, obesity, straining, pregnancy
Irritable bowel syndrome (IBS)	• Bloating • Abdominal cramps • Constipation • Diarrhoea	Low-fibre diet, stress
Bowel cancer	• Blood loss via the colon • Changes in bowel habits • Weakness, fatigue	Lack of fibre (fruit, vegetables), diet high in saturated fat
Diverticulitis	Formation of pouches in intestinal walls containing food waste; bacteria, acids and gases form, which leads to pain	Low-fibre/high-fat diet low fluid intake, obesity, lack of exercise

Guidelines for preventing bowel disorders – a high-fibre diet

1. Use wholegrain cereals and cereal products.
2. Eat more fruit, vegetables, pulses, seeds and nuts.
3. Use fruits and vegetables with skins where possible.
4. Use fresh/dried fruits, nuts and seeds instead of processed snacks.
5. Drink plenty of water (at least eight glasses a day).
6. Take regular exercise.

Osteoporosis

Osteoporosis occurs when bones become thinner, weaker and brittle. Fractures in hips, spines or wrists can result.

Who is affected?

- Elderly people, especially women. Peak bone mass is reached on average between 25 and 35 years of age. This reduces the risk of osteoporosis later in life.

Benefits of a high-fibre diet:
1. Less saturated fat is consumed.
2. Gives a feeling of fullness.
3. Prevents bowel disorders.

EXAMPLES OF SYMPTOMS:

Brittle bones, unexpected fractures, loss of height, stooped/curved shoulders, neck and back pain.

Main risk factors

1. Age	Risk increases with age, especially for post-menopausal women, due to a lack of the hormone oestrogen which maintains calcium levels
2. Genetic	Heredity or family history of osteoporosis
3. Gender	Females are more at risk than males
4. Hormonal	Menopausal hormonal changes hasten calcium loss
5. Dietary	Inadequate intake of calcium, vitamin D and phosphorus
6. Exercise	Lack of weight-bearing exercise results in weak bones

Specific dietary guidelines

1. Eat a well-balanced diet.
2. Increase intake of vitamin D, calcium-rich and phosphorus-rich foods.
3. Take regular exercise, **daily**.
4. Avoid smoking and reduce alcohol consumption.
5. Reduce salt and caffeine (decreases bone density).
6. Maintain a healthy body weight.

Obesity

When an individual's weight is 20 per cent above the recommended weight for their height, they are considered obese or overweight.

Main causes of obesity

1. Energy intake is greater than energy output.
2. Diet is high in refined, convenience and fast foods.
3. Poor food choices due to inadequate nutritional knowledge.
4. Low-income families buying cheaper foods low in fibre and high in fats, sugars and salt.
5. Increase in consumption of saturated fats and sugar.
6. Hormonal imbalance, e.g. thyroid problems.
7. Lack of exercise, a sedentary lifestyle.
8. Certain medications.
9. Depression, low self-esteem, boredom.

Factors increasing the risk of obesity may be behavioural, environmental or genetic.

Obesity can contribute to social isolation and diminished quality of life.

Health risks associated with obesity

1. CHD, high blood pressure, varicose veins.
2. Respiratory (breathing) difficulties.
3. Diabetes, especially non-insulin-dependent.
4. Gallstones form due to high cholesterol.
5. Infertility or difficulties in childbirth.
6. Psychological problems (depression).
7. Arthritis, joint problems due to excess weight.

Treatments for obesity include: dietary changes to reduce weight, changing eating patterns, exercising regularly, surgical procedures and drug treatments.

Specific dietary requirements/guidelines

1. Consult a doctor before starting a weight-reducing diet.
2. Balance a weight-reducing diet with an exercise programme.
3. Eat balanced regular meals, avoid snacking between meals.
4. Increase intake of high-fibre foods e.g. whole cereals, brown rice, oats, vegetables, nuts and seeds.
5. Avoid convenience foods, fast foods and takeaways (high in fat, sugar and salt).
6. Choose lean meats, poultry, fish, low-fat and low-sugar foods.

> **key point**
>
> Steam, grill or poach instead of frying foods.

Cardiovascular disease

- **Examples:** aneurisms (blood clots), coronary heart disease (CHD), strokes.
- **Main cause:** atherosclerosis.
- **Locations of atherosclerosis in the body:** aorta, cerebral arteries, coronary arteries and femoral arteries.

> **LINKS**
> - Dietary fibre (p. 17)
> - Carbohydrates (p.13)

Coronary heart disease (CHD)

CHD occurs when the coronary arteries become blocked or narrowed due to a build-up of cholesterol. Blood pressure may rise and the restriction of blood flow can lead to heart attack, angina or death.

Fixed risk factors

- **Age:** women over 55 years and men over 45 are most at risk.
- **Gender:** women generally have lower rates of CHD than men, but *after menopause* the rate is the same.
- **Genetics:** family history, high cholesterol, etc.

Dietary and lifestyle risk factors

1. Overweight and obesity.
2. Diets high in saturated fats and salt.
3. High blood cholesterol levels.
4. High blood pressure levels.
5. Diabetes mellitus.
6. High stress levels.
7. Lack of exercise.
8. Smoking and excess alcohol.

exam focus

Check out the government's 'National Physical Activity Plan' at www.getirelandactive.ie.

Dietary and lifestyle measures to reduce CHD

Dietary	1. Reduce intake of saturated fats 2. Choose low-fat alternatives 3. Increase use of polyunsaturated fats 4. Increase fibre (fruit and vegetables) 5. Reduce salt, avoid processed foods and ready meals 6. Use fat-free cooking, e.g. steaming, poaching 7. Avoid refined carbohydrates (sugar), processed foods and takeaways
Lifestyle	1. Exercise regularly to increase levels of HDL and to lower LDL 2. Do not smoke and avoid alcohol 3. Manage stress 4. Reduce weight or maintain correct body weight

exam focus

Be able to elaborate on each dietary and lifestyle measures.

Cholesterol

Functions of cholesterol:

- Involved in the production of hormones.
- Essential component in the production of cell walls.
- Necessary component of bile salts (produced in the liver).

LINKS

- Lipids (p. 23)
- Carbohydrates (dietary fibre) (p. 17)

Types of blood cholesterol:

- Low-density lipoproteins (LDL = 'bad').
- High-density lipoproteins (HDL = 'good').
  1. **LDL** carries cholesterol from the liver to body tissues, delivering triglycerides. High levels of LDL are a risk factor for heart disease.
  2. **HDL** picks up excess cholesterol and transfers it to other lipoproteins, which return it to the liver for recycling or excretion. High levels of HDL reduce the risk of heart disease.

Factors that improve the LDL to HDL ratio are antioxidants, polyunsaturated fats, soluble fibres, weight control and exercise.

Reducing cholesterol levels

Reduce intake of:

- Saturated fats (butter, cheese, red meat).
- High-cholesterol foods (eggs).

Increase intake of polyunsaturated fats (oily fish, olive oil, nuts).

> **key point**
>
> Exercise daily to increase HDL.

Eating disorders

Individuals have a negative view of their body shape and weight, which results in dangerous eating patterns. Inadequate nutrition leads to damaging the digestive system, circulatory system, teeth and bones.

Disorder	Behaviour	Symptoms
Anorexia nervosa	• Refusal to eat a balanced diet • Obsessed with losing weight • Abuse of laxatives • Over-exercising • Self-induced vomiting	• Periods stop (amenorrhoea) • Increased facial and body hair • Hair loss • Extreme thinness • Starvation leading to death
Bulimia nervosa	• Abuse of laxatives • Self-induced vomiting after binge-eating • Regular dieting	• Mottling/decay of teeth • Inflammation of oesophagus • Irritation of throat • Swollen glands • Dehydration

Modified diets

Vegetarianism

Definition: A vegetarian is a person whose diet consists mainly of plant food and who does not eat meat or, in some cases, any animal products.

> **key point**
>
> Eating disorders are most common among females, but males can also develop anorexia and bulimia.

Reasons for vegetarianism

1. **Cultural:** The accepted diet among a family group or community.
2. **Health:** A diet without saturated animal fat and high in fibre is considered healthier.
3. **Moral/ethical:** Killing, harming or intensively rearing animals is believed to be wrong.
4. **Religious:** Some religions do not allow the eating of meat or restrict specific meats.
5. **Aesthetic:** Individuals may not like the look, smell or taste of meat.
6. **Economic:** Meat is too expensive for some families.

Types of vegetarian

Vegan	Lives on plant-based foods; does not eat meat or any animal products
Lacto-vegetarian	Does not eat meat, poultry, fish or eggs but will eat dairy products
Lacto-ovo vegetarian	Eats eggs and dairy products, does not eat animal flesh
Pesco vegetarian (pescatarian)	Eats fish, does not eat meat
Pollo vegetarian	Eats chicken only, no other meat or fish

Benefits of a vegetarian diet

1. Low in saturated fats – reduces risk of obesity and CHD.
2. Low in cholesterol – reduces high blood pressure and CHD.
3. High in fibre – reduces risk of/prevents bowel disorders.
4. Low in salt – lower levels of high blood pressure.
5. Contains less sugar – fewer vegetarians develop diabetes.
6. More fresh foods eaten – contain fewer additives.
7. High intake of fruit/vegetables – reduces risk of obesity.

Main food groups for lacto-vegetarians

Food group	Recommended servings per day
Whole grains and nuts	6–11 (bread, rice, pasta, almonds, etc.)
Vegetables	3–5 (carrots, onions, peppers, broccoli, spinach, etc.)
Fruits	2–4 (oranges, apples, bananas)
Legumes or pulse vegetables	2–3 (peas, beans, lentils)
Milk and dairy products	2–3 (milk, cheese, yoghurt)

Nutrient intake for vegetarians

The **lacto-vegetarian diet** provides sufficient amounts of protein, carbohydrates, dietary fibre, calcium, B-group vitamins, vitamins A, D, E and C, folate, and trace minerals for their dietary needs. Follow the lacto-vegetarian Food Pyramid for planning meals.

The **vegan diet**, because of the absence of all animal products, may lack HBV protein, vitamins B_{12} and D, calcium, iron and zinc. Follow the Vegan Food Pyramid for planning vegan meals.

Nutrients	Sources
HBV protein: plants are usually LBV except for soya	Soya protein, seeds, nuts, legumes, whole grains, Quorn
Fibre	Wholemeal breads, fruits, vegetables, whole cereals

Vitamin B₂ (riboflavin)	Wholegrain cereals, green leafy vegetables, seeds, nuts
Vitamin B₁₂ (cobalamin): not present in plant foods	TVP, fortified cereals, fortified soya milk, supplements
Vitamin D	Fortified cereals, fortified spreads, sunlight
Calcium	Fortified soya milk, tofu, green vegetables, beans, seeds
Iron: not as easily absorbed from plants	Dark green vegetables, whole grains, dried fruit, beans, wheat germ, fortified foods, nuts, seeds
Zinc	Whole grains, beans, lentils, seeds, nuts

Nutrients and sources

Dietary guidelines for vegetarians/vegans

1. Choose a wide variety from the all main food groups.
2. Use vegetables stocks for soups and sauces.
3. Replace animal fats with vegetable oils.
4. Replace meat with alternatives, e.g. legumes, soya, tofu, Quorn.
5. For **vegans**, dairy alternatives include soya milk, yoghurt and tofu.
6. For **lacto-vegetarians**, include milk, yoghurt and cheese.
7. Include wholegrain cereals as sources of vitamin B and fibre.
8. Fortified products are useful in vegans and vegetarian diets.
9. Check food labels for hidden animal fats/animal products.

key point

Make sure that the **nutritional needs** of the individual are met.

Ingredients suitable for vegetarian cookery

Ingredients	Examples
Grains	Wheat, oats, millet, couscous, bulgur wheat, rice, buckwheat, corn (maize), barley, rye
Pulses	*Beans:* butter, adzuki, haricot, kidney, soya, chickpeas *Peas:* green, split green/yellow, chick *Lentils:* brown, green, red
Nuts	Almonds, brazils, cashews, hazelnuts, pecans, peanuts, pistachios, walnuts
Seeds	Linseed, pumpkin, sesame, sunflower
Dried fruit	Apricots, dates, figs, prunes, raisins, sultanas
Sea vegetables	Carrageen moss, dulse (Ireland); laver (Wales)

Vegetarian dishes include: vegetarian lasagne, quiche (modify the ingredients), omelette, mixed vegetable or mixed bean curry and vegetable cobbler.

Vegan dishes include: vegetarian curry, pasta dishes, rice dishes, vegetable stir-fry, vegetarian risotto and stuffed vegetables (tomatoes, aubergines, peppers).

LINK

- Supplementary role of protein (p. 8)

Exam question and sample answer

Higher Level 2013, Section B, Q1 (b)

Identify and give an account of the main factors that are contributing to the prevalence of obesity in Ireland.   (4 points × 4 marks = 16 marks)

1. *Energy intake (food) is greater than energy output (activity).*
2. *Increased intake of processed foods e.g. ready meals, 'fast foods', etc.*
3. *Unhealthy eating patterns e.g. snacking, no breakfast, etc.*
4. *Lack of exercise e.g. sedentary lifestyle, no regular activities, e.g. walking, sports, etc.*

List four points and elaborate on **each** point with examples.

Coeliac disease

Symptoms of coeliac disease:

- **Adults**: anaemia, diarrhoea, reduced body weight, abdominal pain, mouth ulcers, tiredness.
- **Children**: slow growth, weight loss.
- **Other symptoms**: vitamin and mineral deficiency, inflammation in small intestine.

Dietary guidelines

1. Follow the doctor's instructions.
2. Stick to a gluten-free diet.
3. Look for the gluten-free symbol on foods.
4. Read food labels, e.g. on processed foods.
5. Avoid all hidden sources of gluten.

Suitable foods: dairy products, eggs, unprocessed fresh meat, fish (uncoated), poultry, fruit, vegetables, soya products, rice, breakfast cereals made from maize or rice, soups and sauces made with cornflour, gluten-free products.

Diabetes

Diabetes is a disorder of the endocrine system which is caused by:

- a deficiency/lack of insulin; **or**
- not enough insulin being produced.

Insulin, a hormone produced by the pancreas, controls the level of glucose in the blood, which is used to produce energy.

Symptoms: blurred vision, glaucoma, increased thirst, increased urination, tiredness/fatigue, weight loss.

Types of diabetes

TYPE 1: insulin-dependent diabetes (juvenile onset)

- The pancreas produces little or no insulin.
- Found in young children and adolescents.
- Controlled by insulin injections (pen or pump).

Dietary guidelines for **Type 1** diabetes:

1. Co-ordinate times of meals and injections.
2. Eat regular meals: **never** miss meals.
3. Be familiar with carbohydrate sources.
4. Choose low-sugar alternatives or sugar-free dishes.
5. Include fibre in the form of whole grains, wholemeal breads, brown rice and pasta.
6. Choose calcium-rich foods – three portions a day.

TYPE 2: non-insulin-dependent diabetes (maturity onset)

- Occurs in older people.
- Associated with being overweight, lack of regular exercise, family history.
- The pancreas produces insulin, but it is not effective.
- Can be controlled by diet and medication.

Dietary guidelines for **Type 2** diabetes:

1. Eat a balanced diet and regular meals.
2. Reduce intake of saturated fat (risk of CHD).
3. Reduce intake of salt (risk of high blood pressure).
4. Replace sugary snacks with low-sugar fruit.
5. Eat high-fibre starches in fixed amounts at regular times each day.
6. Replace sugar-rich jams with low-sugar varieties/alternatives.
7. Keep alcohol consumption low.
8. **Always** follow the doctor's advice.

key point

Diabetes risk factors include age, genetics, family history and environmental factors.

key point

Always follow the doctor's nutritional guidelines in each case.

exam focus

Revise the following terms: hypoglycaemia, hyperglycaemia, glycemic index.

exam focus

Compiling menus

Learn to devise a day's menus for all modified diets, using the correct menu format and keeping in mind the specific needs for a balanced diet.

LINKS

- Nutrients (p. 2)
- Meal management and planning (p. 123)

Exam questions and sample answers

Higher Level 2014, Section A, Q4 (6 marks) **HL**

What is Basal Metabolic Rate (BMR)?

BMR is the minimum amount of energy needed to keep the body alive, internal organs working and to maintain body temperature when the body is at rest.

Give **two** factors that determine a person's basal metabolic rate.

- *Age: as you get older the BMR slows down.*
- *Body weight.*

Higher Level 2009, Section A, Q3 (6 marks)

Give **three** specific dietary guidelines for a person with diabetes.

- *Eat regular balanced meals to stabilise sugar levels, never miss meals.*
- *Choose slow-release starches for energy, e.g. porridge, pulses.*
- *Replace sugar-rich jams with low-sugar varieties (diabetic jams).*

Ordinary Level 2017, Section A, Q5 (6 marks)

Outline **three** healthy eating guidelines for pregnant women.

- *Include foods rich in protein for the growth and development of foetus.*
- *Increase intake of iron, vitamin C and thiamine.*
- *Avoid raw eggs to reduce risk of salmonella and soft cheese to reduce risk of listeria.*

Ordinary Level 2016, Section A, Q4 (6 marks)

List **three** factors that influence the energy requirements of teenagers.

- *Level and type of activity – more active teenagers require more energy.*
- *Growth spurts due to physical development.*
- *Gender, age and body size.*

Ordinary Level 2015, Section A, Q5 (6 marks)

State **three** lifestyle changes recommended for people at risk of coronary heart disease.

- *Choose a low-fat, low-cholesterol, low-salt and low-sugar diet.*
- *Increase exercise daily to raise HDL and lower LDL levels.*
- *Reduce stress levels (family and work).*

Ordinary Level 2014, Section A, Q4 (6 marks)

Indicate with a tick (✓) whether each of the following statements is true or false.

	True	False
Diabetes can be caused by sedentary lifestyles and unhealthy diets.	✓	
Bowel disease is caused by eating high fibre foods.		✓
A person is considered obese when his/her weight is 20% or more above the recommended weight.	✓	

HL **Higher Level 2017, Section B, Q1**

'Rising levels of overweight and obesity are placing an increasing burden on individuals and society. Currently six in ten adults and one in four children are overweight or obese.' (A Healthy Weight for Ireland: Obesity Policy and Action Plan 2016–25)

Body Mass Index (BMI) is a standardised measure used to estimate whether or not someone is underweight, normal weight, overweight or obese.

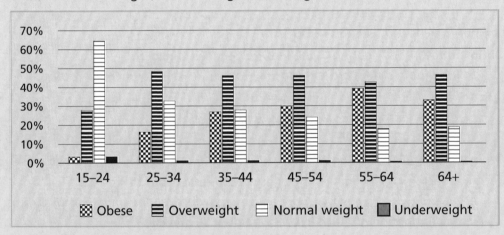

(a) Using the information provided in the chart, comment and elaborate on the variations in Body Mass Index among the different age groups of the Irish population. (4 points × 5 marks = 20 marks)

Underweight: Less than 5% of people are underweight in the 15–24 age groups and it decreases across the other age groups.

- *Reasons for underweight: dieting, eating disorders, increase in physical activities e.g. sports, busy schedules and stress.*

Normal weight: 60–65% of those in the 15–24 age groups have a normal weight, decreasing in the 25–34 age groups (30–35%), decreases again until the 64+ group when there is a slight increase.

- *Reasons for the changes: teenagers are still growing and active and increased awareness of healthy eating has become a priority. For the next age groups work may be sedentary, little exercise, diets may be high in* sugar, saturated fats and low in fibre with poor eating habits. Older people are aware of the importance of a healthy diet and lifestyle which may be a reason for their change in weight.

Overweight: High in 15–24 age group and rising steadily across all the other groups.

- **Reasons for increases:** sedentary lifestyles, decrease in BMR as one ages, reliance on convenience foods high in sugars and saturated fats, increased consumption of foods and larger portion sizes, snacking, no breakfast.

Obese: Obesity rises as one ages up to the 55–64 age groups, after 64+ obesity levels seem to fall.

- **Reasons for rising obesity:** lack of exercise, irregular meal patterns, busy lifestyles and poor food choices.

(b) Carbohydrates: classification, formula, examples and sources   (15 marks)

(c) Sugars: properties and culinary uses   (15 marks)

> **LINKS**
> - Carbohydrates (p. 13)
> - Sugars (p. 15)

(d) Assess the effects of high sugar consumption on the body.   (10 marks)

- **Obesity:** high sugar foods are calorie dense and lacking in other nutrients. Processed foods have added sugar levels and can lead to weight gain.
- **Type 2 diabetes:** high sugar consumption increases risk of diabetes and hypoglycaemia.
- **Dental diseases:** sugary foods/drinks damage the enamel and plaque forms which causes periodontal disease (gums and tissues).

(e) The rate of obesity in Ireland has been increasing despite the fact that it is preventable.

Outline **five** strategies to be considered when purchasing and preparing food in order to reduce sugar consumption. (5 strategies × 4 marks = 20 marks)

Purchasing food:

1. Compare food labels, choose low-sugar varieties. Read the colour coding system (traffic lights) to check if food is high, medium or low in sugar

2. Avoid breakfast cereals coated with sugar, chocolate or honey, eat low sugar fibre-rich varieties

3. Check for added sugars, e.g. cane sugar, corn syrup, fructose, juice concentrates

Preparing food:

1. Reduce sugar in recipes, e.g. cakes, cereals, hot drinks

2. Use fruit juice in desserts instead of syrups, avoid fruits in syrup

3. Plan for low-sugar snacks and meals

exam focus

Give at least one strategy for purchasing, one for preparation, and three other points.

exam focus

Remember to check the current recommended Healthy Eating Guidelines before the exam.

Ordinary Level 2016, Section B, Q2 (a)–(c)

'Going vegetarian is one of the best things you could do for your health. All the nutrients you need are easily provided in a vegetarian diet.' (Vegetarian Society of Ireland, July 2015)

(a) Discuss **four** reasons why some teenagers become vegetarians.

(4 reasons × 5 marks = 20 marks)

- **Moral/ethical:** *some people believe that it is wrong to kill animals for human consumption, or that intensive farming of animals is ethically wrong.*
- **Religious:** *Buddhists practice vegetarianism, Jews do not eat pork, non-vegetarian Hindus abstain from eating meat during special religious practices or holydays.*
- **Health reasons:** *vegetarian diets are considered to be healthier, lower in saturated fats, higher in fibre and reduce risks of CHD, obesity and bowel disorders.*
- **Personal choice:** *Some people do not like the smell, look or taste of meat, poultry or fish and choose from the wide variety of alternatives available, e.g. TVP, Quorn, legumes, seeds, nuts.*

(b) Having regard to current healthy eating guidelines, set out a menu (three meals) for one day for a lacto-vegetarian to ensure their nutritional needs are met. (3 meals × 6 marks = 18 marks)

exam focus

Use the correct menu format when answering this type of question.

LINK
- Current dietary guidelines (p. 53)

Breakfast	Lunch	Dinner
Fresh apple juice *** Porridge with milk and seeds Wholemeal brown bread *** Tea/coffee/water	Lentil soup with wholegrain roll *** Natural yoghurt Apple *** Water/milk/tea	Halloumi and watermelon *** Vegetarian curry with brown rice *** Blueberry and apple crumble *** Water/tea/milk

(c) Explain **three** guidelines that should be followed when preparing and cooking vegetables to retain maximum nutrients.   (3 guidelines × 4 marks = 12 marks)

- *Prepare just before cooking, do not steep (leeching of vitamins into liquid).*
- *Steam, stir-fry or microwave to retain vitamins and minerals.*
- *Cook in a small amount of liquid for the shortest time in a saucepan with a well-fitted lid.*

Past exam questions to check out

Higher Level, Section B: 2013 Q1, 2012 Q3, 2011 Q1, 2009 Q1

Ordinary Level, Section B: 2014 Q1, 2013 Q2, 2011 Q2, 2010 Q2

The Irish diet

Sources of information on Irish eating patterns

- The National Nutrition Surveillance Centre research, e.g. obesity
- SLAN – Survey of Lifestyle, Attitudes and Nutrition 1998, 2002, 2007
- The Irish Health Behaviour in School-aged Children Study 2010
- The National Adult Nutrition Survey 2011
- Irish Universities Nutrition Alliance Survey in 2012
- UK, EU, WHO and international recommendations (2012–15)
- Annual Healthy Ireland Surveys 2015, 2016, 2017

Factors influencing changes in the Irish diet

1. Developments in agricultural practices: new technology, greater yields.
2. Developments in food distribution systems: local, national and global.
3. Improvements in food processing, advertising and retailing.
4. Improved dietary guidelines.
5. World War I and World War II.
6. Influx of people from other countries.
7. Irish people travelling abroad.
8. Consumer demand.

> **LINKS**
> - Food choices (p. 2)
> - Social, economic and technological changes affecting the family (p. 274)

Irish food and eating patterns since 1900

1900–1950

1. Active lifestyle – manual work was common.
2. Rural dwellers used homemade produce.

3. Home-made bread and porridge were staple foods.

4. Good supply of cereals, dairy produce and potatoes.

5. Meat and poultry were served only on special occasions.

6. Few processed foods were available, sugar consumption increased.

7. Increase in food prices during World Wars I and II.

8. Food shortages during World War II led to rationing.

Nutritional significance:

1. High intake of carbohydrates.

2. Low intake of iron – anaemia was common.

3. Low intake of saturated fats.

4. Adequate supply of calcium from milk.

5. Fruit and vegetable intake increased after the 1940s.

- Little knowledge of nutrition.
- High levels of anaemia in women.
- Food choices were based on economic status of family.

Effects of World Wars I and II:

1. Rise in unemployment.

2. Higher food prices.

3. Insufficient supplies of basic foods.

4. Diets limited; deficiency diseases became common.

5. Diets were low in iron, vitamins and minerals.

Post-World War II (1950–1990)

1. Increased availability of white bread, tea and processed foods.

2. Meat and dairy produce consumption increased.

3. Diets higher in fat and lower in unrefined carbohydrates.

4. Anaemia common among females.

5. Decreased intake of fruit, vegetables, porridge, potatoes and homemade foods.

6. Food imports increased, greater variety available.

7. Improvement in food storage, e.g. refrigeration, freezing.

8. Consumer demands for processed foods, new foods.

Rural electrification and water schemes became available.

Nutritional significance:

1. Decreased intake of fibre, vitamins and minerals.

2. Increase in saturated fats.

3. Increase in sugar and salt.

4. Dramatic increase in the use of additives.

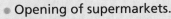

- Opening of supermarkets.
- New foods for consumer markets.

1990–present day

1. Increase in convenience, processed, take-away, ready meals.
2. Wide variety of foods, meats, fish, breads, pasta, fruits, vegetables.
3. Increased variety of pastries, sweets, fizzy drinks.
4. Low-fat varieties and fortified foods available.
5. Increase in pre-prepared family meals.
6. Increase in families snacking, 'eating on-the-go'.
7. More nutritional information available to the public.
8. Individuals becoming more health conscious.
9. Sedentary lifestyles, irregular eating patterns, snacking.

There has been an increase in snack foods, take-aways, sweets and fizzy drinks.

Nutritional significance:

1. Increase in saturated fats, salt and sugar.
2. Increase in HBV protein and iron.
3. Diet low in fibre, calcium and vitamin D.
4. Further increase in additives and preservatives.
5. Consuming more energy than is needed, increase in obesity.
6. Increase in alcohol consumption.
7. Increase in range of nutritional supplements available.

LINKS
- Nutrients (p. 2)
- Food processing (p. 147)
- Food labelling (p. 157)

Trends – 21st century

- Establishment of farmers' markets.
- Availability of organic produce.
- Consumer demands for organic/free range produce.
- Traceability of meat, poultry, eggs, etc.

1. Improvements in knowledge of nutrition.
2. Development of low-fat foods, gluten-free foods.
3. By 1990, vegetable intake reduced to half that of 1948.

Comparing the Irish diet with current dietary guidelines

	Current findings – recent trends	Current recommended guidelines
Energy	Intake is higher than recommended	Balance energy intake with energy output
Protein	Intake is greater than needed	Replace with alternatives, e.g. pulses, soya

Lipids	Consumption of saturated fat and trans fat continues to be too high; 58–63% of people eat more than the Recommended Intake	• Limit food from top of food pyramid (HFSS) to once or twice a week – do not eat daily • Avoid takeaways, processed, convenience foods • Choose low-fat food products • Replace saturated fats with polyunsaturated oils
Carbohydrates	Recommended daily servings have been falling since 1998	Choose slow-release starches rather than sugars
Sugars	Highest consumption of sugar in EU; only 14–18% eat recommended intake	Reduce and limit sugar intake
Fibre	26% meeting RI target, majority of people are not meeting the RI target	• Increase intake to 25–35 g per day • Increase fruit and vegetables in diet • Eat more whole grains, brown rice, cereals
Fruits and vegetables	Increase intake, most not meeting the recommended target	• Increase fruits, vegetables, salad (5–7 servings) • Choose as snack foods
Calcium	Lower intake than recommended, women's intake less than men	• Use low-fat milk, cheese and low-sugar yoghurts • Choose fortified foods
Iron	Females have a lower intake than recommended, anaemia is common	• Eat more dark green vegetables and red meat. • Supplements may be necessary
Salt	Majority of population (93%) consume more than the recommended intake	• Less than 5 g a day of salt (6 g recommendation FSAI 2016) • Limit salt from the top of the Food Pyramid
Alcohol	Consumption levels have risen outside recommended units, binge-drinking is a problem	• Reduce/limit alcohol intake • Drink within the guidelines or not at all

Major concerns about the current Irish diet

1. High in saturated fats, salt and sugars.
2. Low in dietary fibre, calcium, vitamin D and iron.

LINK
• Dietary needs for diet-related health problems (p. 62)

Aspects of malnutrition

Low dietary fibre intake

Causes	Effects on body	Corrective measures
● Insufficient fibre-rich foods ● Over-use of processed foods	● Bowel disorders, constipation, IBS ● Gallstones ● Piles	● Eat more fibre ● Avoid processed foods ● Eat more fruit and vegetables ● Drink more water

LINKS
- Carbohydrates (p. 13)
- Fruit and vegetables (p. 109)

LINKS
- Lipids (p. 23)
- Obesity (p. 63)
- CHD (p. 64)
- Methods of cooking (Chapter 3, Extension 1, see www.moresuccess.ie)

High saturated fat intake

Causes	Effects on body	Corrective measures
● Increased intake of foods high in saturated fats ● Eating too many processed foods, takeaways and fast foods	● Diabetes ● CHD ● Obesity ● High cholesterol	● Reduce saturated fat ● Increase intake of polyunsaturated fats ● Remove visible fats on meat, select lean cuts ● Grill, poach or steam; do not fry ● Use low-fat foods ● Avoid convenience foods

Low iron intake

Causes	Effects on body	Corrective measures
● Lack of iron-rich foods ● Inadequate vitamin C ● Lack of variety in type of iron (haem, non-haem) ● Inhibiting factors (phytic acid, fibre) ● Menstruation	● Anaemia ● Tiredness ● Fatigue ● Feeling 'run down' ● Breathlessness	● Eat iron-rich foods ● Include adequate vitamin C for iron absorption ● Reduce intake of inhibiting factors

LINKS
- Iron (p. 43)
- Vitamin C (p. 35)

LINKS
- Calcium (p. 42)
- Vitamin D (p. 33)
- Functional foods (p. 151)

Low calcium intake

Causes	Effects on body	Corrective measures
● Insufficient vitamin D ● Insufficient calcium-rich foods ● Inhibiting factors (phytates, oxalates and dietary fibre)	● Rickets ● Osteomalacia ● Osteoporosis ● Dental decay	● Increase intake of calcium-rich foods ● Increase intake of vitamin D ● Increase intake of protein-rich foods ● Use fortified foods

Exam questions and sample answers

Ordinary Level 2009, Section A, Q3

Outline **three** changes that have taken place in Irish eating habits from the beginning of the 20th century. (6 marks)

- *Increased consumption of prepared convenience, processed, takeaway foods and meals.*
- *Increased knowledge of healthy eating guidelines, nutritional needs and special diets.*
- *Decrease in consumption of potatoes and bread, increase in use of rice and pasta.*

> **LINK**
> - The Irish diet (pp. 75)

Ordinary Level 2015, Section B, Q2 (c) (linked to CHD)

Write an information account of the changes in the Irish diet in the 21st century.

(3 points × 4 marks = 12 marks)

- *Nutritional food labelling encourages people to increase intake of fibre, and reduce intake of salt, sugar and saturated fats.*
- *Meal times have become irregular with family members eating at different times due to busy school, work and leisure schedules.*
- *Traditional cooking methods are being replaced by new methods as people travel more, new foods become available and Ireland is becoming a multi-cultural society.*

> **exam focus**
> Elaborate on **each** point and give examples.

Ordinary Level 2014, Section A, Q7 (6 marks)

Identify **three** changes in the eating habits of Irish people in recent years.

- *Staples from other countries have become popular, e.g. rice, pasta, couscous.*
- *Increase in the use of convenience meals, pre-prepared meals, 'take-away' and snack foods.*
- *Eating habits are being influenced by media, e.g. TV cookery, marketing.*

3 Food Studies: Part One

 aims

To learn and revise:

- Food commodities
- Meal management and planning
- Food preparation and cooking processes
- Recipe balance
- Aesthetic awareness
- Sensory analysis
- The Irish food industry

 exam focus

This section is examined in **Section A** and in **Section B**. For each food commodity, revise classification, structure, nutritive significance, contribution to the diet, processing, effects of heat, buying, storing and cooking methods.

Food commodities

 exam focus

Check Food Composition Tables in a Home Economics textbook for the composition of foods.

LINKS

- Properties of nutrients (Chapter 1)
- Food preparation and cooking processes (p. 123)
- Food processing (p. 147)
- Consumer choice (p. 254)

 exam focus

Remember:

- **Nutritive value** = the nutrients in the food.
- **Dietetic value** = the contribution each of those nutrients makes to the diet.

Meat and poultry

Classification of meat

Carcass meat: beef, veal, sheep, pig.

Poultry: poultry, turkey, duck, goose.

Offal: kidney, liver, heart, tripe, tongue.

Game: rabbit, hare, venison, pheasant.

Examples of meat products: sausages, burgers, cooked meats (e.g. salami, ham), paté, gelatine.

Nutritive value/nutritional significance

Nutrient	Value in the diet
Protein	• HBV protein • Actin, myosin and globulin in meat fibres • Collagen and elastin in connective tissue
Fat/lipid	• Saturated fats (visible and invisible) • Amount depends on the type, cut and age
Carbohydrate	• None present
Vitamins	• B-group vitamins (B_1, B_2, B_6, B_{12}, niacin, folic acid) • Traces of vitamins A and D in offal
Minerals	• Good source of haem iron • Zinc, phosphorus, potassium, sulphur
Water	• Leaner meat has higher water content • Fat meat has lower water content

Dietetic value/contribution to the diet

Protein	Needed for cell growth and repair (children, adolescents, pregnant women)
Fat	Provides heat and energy. People at risk of CHD and high cholesterol should avoid/reduce intake of saturated fat
Iron	Haem iron is easily absorbed and prevents anaemia (females, children, teenagers, adults)
Nutrients lacking	Carbohydrates, calcium, vitamin C. Serve with foods rich in these nutrients

Structure of meat

LINKS
- Protein (p. 3)
- Lipids (p. 23)
- Vitamins (p. 32)
- Minerals (p. 42)

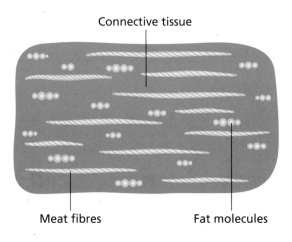

Connective tissue

Meat fibres   Fat molecules

Rules for buying meat

Buy meat from a reputable shop where:

1. Surfaces and equipment are clean and hygienic.
2. Staff wear protective clothing and follow hygienic procedures.
3. Raw and cooked meats are stored and handled separately.
4. The meat supplied is produced under the Bord Bia Quality Assured Programme (traceability, quality and safety standards).

Staff should not handle both meat and money.

Rules for choosing meat

When choosing meat:

1. Buy fresh meat in small quantities.
2. Choose meat which has a good bright colour, is firm, moist and free of odours.
3. Avoid meats with gristle or a lot of fat.
4. Match the cut of meat to the cooking method.
5. Cheaper cuts are as nutritious as expensive cuts.

Frozen meat must be frozen solid when you buy it.

Rules for storing meat

1. Store fresh meat quickly after purchase, below 5°C.
2. Unwrap, put on a clean plate, cover, store in a refrigerator below cooked foods.
3. Store raw and cooked meats separately, never on the same plate or shelf. Use within 2–3 days. Use offal the day you buy it.
4. Leave vacuum-packed meat in wrapping until needed.

Causes of toughness in meat

1. Age	Older animals have longer fibres and produce tougher meat; meat from younger animals is tender
2. Activity	Less active parts of animals are tender, active parts are tougher
3. Conditioning of animals	• Resting before slaughter allows glycogen to build up in muscles • Hanging after slaughter changes glycogen to lactic acid – tenderises meat
4. Cooking method	• Slow, moist methods tenderise tougher cuts of meat, e.g. stewing • Fast methods are better suited to tender cuts of meat

Methods of tenderising meat

1. Injecting animals with proteolytic enzymes.
2. Sprinkling tenderising enzymes on raw meat, e.g. papain.
3. Mechanical methods (pounding, mincing, piercing).
4. Slow, moist methods of cooking, e.g. stewing, braising, casseroling.
5. Marinating in acids, oils, spices and herbs.

Effects of heat/cooking on meat

Protein	Coagulates, meat shrinks, becomes firmer, collagen changes to gelatine, fibres become tender and digestible
Fat/lipid	Melts and improves flavour
Vitamins	Some B-group vitamins are destroyed
Minerals	Some lost during cooking
Extractives	Are released, flavours improve
Bacteria	Are destroyed
Colour	Changes from red to brown (denaturation of myoglobin)

Methods of preserving and processing meat

Process	Method	Effects
1. Canning	Ingredients heated to high temperatures, canned and sealed *Examples*: meat stews, corned beef	• Loss of B-group vitamins • Colour, flavour and texture changes • Increase in fat content
2. Curing/salting	Brine solution injected into meat; meat soaked for 4 days, hung for 5 days more to develop colour; may be smoked after curing *Examples*: bacon, ham	• Changes in colour and flavour • Increase in salt content • Prevents growth of bacteria **LINK** • Food preservation (p. 182)
3. Drying	Removal of water from small pieces of meat: accelerated freeze drying (AFD) *Examples*: packet soups, sauces	• Loss of moisture • Loss of B-group vitamins • Colour, flavour and texture changes
4. Freezing	Commercial blast freezing at −30°C *Examples*: most meats	Loss of B-group vitamins
5. Vacuuming	Meat is placed in polythene, air is removed and edges are heat-sealed *Examples*: rashers, gammon	• Little change in food value • No change in colour, flavour and texture

Offal

Offal is the edible internal organs of animals, e.g. heart, kidney, liver, sweetbreads and tongue. It is cheap and nutritious.

Nutritional value/nutritional significance

Protein	HBV (high biological value) protein
Fat/lipid	Most offal is low in fat
Carbohydrates	Traces of glycogen in liver
Vitamins	• B-group vitamins • Vitamin C • Vitamins A and D (liver, kidney)
Minerals	Good source of iron (liver, kidney)

Exam questions and sample answers

Higher Level 2014, Section B, Q2 (a), (b)

(a) Discuss the nutritional significance of meat in the diet.

(5 points × 4 marks = 20 marks)

- *Protein: HBV protein for growth of cells and tissues, myosin, actin and globulin in meat fibres, collagen and elastin in connective tissue.*

  LINK
  - Meat (p. 81)

- *Fats: Saturated fats (visible and invisible) for heat and energy, amount depends on type and cut of meat, some meats are lower in fat, e.g. poultry.*

- *Carbohydrate: Serve with carbohydrate-rich foods, trace of glycogen in liver.*

- *Vitamins: Source of B-group vitamins (niacin, thiamine, riboflavin, pyridoxine) required for release of energy, small amounts of fat-soluble vitamins A and D in liver.*

  List each nutrient and then note its significance.

- *Minerals: Haem-iron in red meat and offal is easily absorbed and prevents anaemia; source of phosphorus, zinc and potassium.*

(b) Describe **each** of the following: (15 marks)

(i) Factors that cause **toughness** in meat. (3 factors × 3 marks = 9 marks)

- *Age: Meat from older animals is tougher due to longer fibres; meat from younger animals is tender.*

- *Activity: Active parts of animals are tougher, e.g. legs. Less active parts are tender.*

- *Treatment before slaughter (conditioning): Not allowing animals to rest before slaughter prevents glycogen building up in muscles which after slaughter and hanging results in a lack of lactic acid necessary to tenderise meat.*

(ii) **Two** methods of tenderising meat. (2 methods × 3 marks = 6 marks)

- *Cooking: Long, slow, moist methods tenderise tougher cuts, collagen softens and muscle fibres separate, e.g. stewing, braising, casseroles.*

- *Mechanical breakdown: Marinating with oils, vinegar and herbs, mincing, pounding, piercing.*

Ordinary Level 2017, Section B, Q3 (a)–(c) (20 marks)

(a) Give an account of (i) nutritive value and (ii) the dietetic value of meat.
(4 points × 5 marks = 20 marks)

(i) Nutritive value

Protein: HBV protein, myosin, actin and globulin, connective tissue (elastin and collagen).

Vitamins: B-group vitamins in meat, vitamin A in offal, lacking in vitamin C.

(ii) Dietetic value

Protein: Excellent source of HBV protein needed for growth and repair of body cells, especially important in the diet of children, teenagers, pregnant women.

Fat: Saturated fat provides heat and energy, should be reduced in the diet of those at risk of CHD or with high cholesterol.

> **exam focus**
> It is necessary to give **two** points for both (i) and (ii).

(b) Outline the following: (16 marks)

(i) Effects of cooking on meat (2 effects × 4 marks = 8 marks)
  ● Protein coagulates, becomes firm and meat shrinks due to loss of juices
  ● Fat melts and adds flavour to foods

(ii) Guidelines for storing meat (2 guidelines × 4 marks = 8 marks)
  ● Remove from wrapping, place on plate, cover and place in fridge.
  ● Place raw meat below cooked meats or meat products to prevent cross-contamination.

(c) Explain **two** causes of toughness in meat and name two different methods of tenderising meat. (14 marks)

Causes of toughness: (2 causes × 4 marks = 8 marks)
  ● *Age: Older animals have longer, thicker and tougher muscle fibres; younger animals have shorter and smaller muscle fibres which produce more tender meat.*
  ● *Activity: the more active sections of the animal the longer the muscle fibre which results in toughness in meat, e.g. neck, legs; less active parts have shorter fibres which provide more tender meat.*

Methods of tenderising: (2 methods × 3 marks = 6 marks)
  ● *Injecting with proteolytic enzymes before slaughter.*
  ● *Long slow methods of cooking, e.g. stewing, braising.*

Ordinary Level 2014, Section A, Q6 (6 marks)

Using the words listed complete the statements in relation to the preparation and cooking of meat.

denaturation   **mincing**   **collagen**

Mincing helps break up the fibres of tougher cuts of meat.

During cooking *collagen* is converted to gelatine and meat becomes tender.

Colour changes from red to brown due to the *denaturation* of myoglobin.

Poultry

Classification

Domestic (chicken, duck, goose, turkey), game (duck, pheasant).

Nutritive value/nutritional significance

Nutrient	Value in the diet
Protein	HBV proteins – high biological
Fat/lipid	• Small amount of saturated fat • Amount depends on the type of bird
Carbohydrate	None present
Vitamins	B-group vitamins (B_1, B_2, B_6, B_{12}, niacin)
Minerals	• Iron (less than in meat) • Traces of calcium, phosphorus, zinc
Water	Significant amount: 50–70%

Dietetic value/contribution to the diet

Protein	HBV protein for growth and repair (children, convalescents)
Fat/lipid	Lower fat content, good alternative for low-cholesterol and low-calorie diets
Carbohydrate	Serve with carbohydrate-rich foods
Digestibility	Easy to digest, suitable for invalids and the elderly
Economic value	Inexpensive and versatile

Rules for buying poultry

1. Buy from a reliable source that is clean and hygienic.
2. Check origin and 'use by' or 'best before' label.
3. Check for signs of freshness – firm, plump flesh.
4. Avoid poultry with a bad smell and poor colour.
5. Frozen poultry should be **frozen solid**.

Rules for storing poultry

- **Frozen poultry:** place in a freezer as soon as possible after purchase.
- **Fresh poultry:** store as for fresh meat.

key point

Poultry can be free range, organic or factory reared. Bord Bia operates the **Poultry Products Quality Assurance Scheme.**

Fish

Classification of fish

Fish may be classified according to:

- Habitat (saltwater, freshwater).
- Shape: flat (e.g. plaice, sole) or round (e.g. salmon, trout).
- Nutritive value.

> **LINK**
>
> - Methods of cooking (Chapter 3, Extension 1, see www.moresuccess.ie)

Habitat

Freshwater	Saltwater	Farmed
Rivers, lakes *Examples:* salmon, trout, pike, eel	**Demersal:** on the seabed *Examples:* cod, plaice, sole **Pelagic:** in shoals near the surface *Examples:* herring, mackerel	Aquaculture *Examples:* oysters, mussels, salmon, trout

Nutritive value (based on fat content)

White fish	Oily fish	Shellfish
Low in fat, fat stored in liver *Examples:* cod, haddock, plaice	High in unsaturated fatty acids in flesh *Examples:* herring, mackerel, salmon, tuna	Lower in fat, higher in cholesterol **(a) Molluscs:** shells *Examples:* mussels, oysters **(b) Crustaceans:** claws *Examples:* prawns, crabs, lobsters

Nutritive value/nutritional significance

Nutrients	Nutritive value
Protein	- HBV protein, easy to digest - Actin, myosin and collagen
Fat/lipid	- Oily fish – polyunsaturated fatty acids (PUFA), omega-3 - Traces in liver of white fish
Carbohydrates	None present
Vitamins	- B-group in all fish - Vitamins A and D in oily fish
Minerals	- Phosphorus, potassium, zinc, iodine in salt water fish, iron in shellfish - Calcium in canned fish, e.g. sardines, salmon
Water	- 65–80% water - Highest in white fish, lowest in oily fish due to fat content

Dietetic value/contribution to the diet

Protein	HBV protein for growth (children, teenagers, pregnant women)
Fat/lipid	Omega-3 fatty acids useful in low-cholesterol diets and low-calorie diets: reduce risks of CHD, good for brain health
Carbohydrates	Serve with carbohydrate-rich foods, e.g. potatoes, rice, pasta
Digestibility	Easy to digest, ideal for invalids and the elderly
Economic value	Most are cheaper when in season; some are expensive
Availability	Widely available in a variety of forms: fresh, frozen, canned, etc.
Cooking	Easy and quick to prepare and cook; versatile; short cooking time

Structure of fish

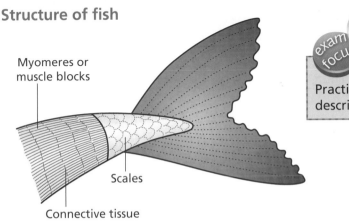

Myomeres or muscle blocks

Scales

Connective tissue

exam focus

Practise drawing, labelling and describing the structure of fish.

LINKS
- Protein (p. 3)
- Lipids (p. 23)
- Vitamins (p. 32)
- Minerals (p. 42)

Spoilage (staling)

Fish is perishable and spoils because of:

1. **Oxidative rancidity:** fish oils reacts with oxygen in the air.
2. **Enzymes:** spoil fish even at low temperatures.
3. **Bacteria:** when caught, fish struggle and use up glycogen stored in muscles and liver. Lactic acid is not formed, fish stales quickly, bacteria multiply rapidly and fish begins to 'go off', producing tri-methylamine.

Rules for buying fish

Fresh fish:

key point

Polluted waters may contaminate shellfish.

1. Choose fish in season.
2. Eyes should be fresh, bright and bulging.
3. Flesh should be firm, shiny and moist, gills bright red or pink in colour.
4. Colour should be characteristic of species.
5. Smoked fish should have a glossy skin and smoky smell.
6. Shellfish should be clean: *molluscs* should not be open; *crustaceans* should be active and alive.
7. When buying canned or tinned fish, ensure there are no dents, bulges, leaks or rust on the packaging.

Frozen and pre-packed fish:

1. Check the sell-by date.
2. Ensure the fish is frozen solid.
3. Packaging must not be damaged.
4. Place in the freezer soon after purchase.

> **key point**
>
> Cooking methods for fish include poaching, frying, grilling, baking and steaming.

Rules for storing fish

Place in the fridge or freezer immediately.

Fresh fish:

1. Remove wrapping, rinse and cover.
2. Place on a bed of ice in the fridge.
3. Store away from other foods.

> **key point**
>
> Overcooking causes fish to become tough and dry.

Tinned fish: use immediately after opening.

Store **hot smoked** and **cold smoked** fish separately.

Wash **shellfish**, cover with a damp cloth and store at the bottom of fridge (never steep them in water).

Use **frozen** white fish within six months, and frozen oily fish within three months.

Effects of cooking on fish

1. Bacteria and parasites are destroyed.
2. Protein coagulates and sets between 60° and 70°C.
3. Collagen changes to gelatine, fish flakes easily.
4. Fish shrinks, flesh becomes opaque.
5. Loss of B-group vitamins and minerals.

Commercial fish processing

Method	Process	Effects	Examples
Canning	Fish is heated to high temperatures, put in sterile cans with brine, oil, water or sauce, and then sealed	• Softens bones • Increase in calcium • Loss of B vitamins • Bacteria are destroyed	Sardines, tuna, salmon, herring, crab, anchovies
Freezing	Commercial freezing is at −30°C; home freezing is at −25°C	• Inactivates micro-organisms • No change in colour, flavour and texture unless breaded, etc.	Whole, steaks, fish fingers, pies
Smoking	Fish is covered in brine or salt, and 'cold' smoked at 27°C or 'hot' smoked at 80°C	• Change in colour and flavour • Increase in salt content • Bacteria are destroyed	Mackerel, salmon, eel

Fish products: Crab sticks, shredded crab meat, fish goujons, fish fingers, fish cakes, fish stock/cubes.

Exam questions and sample answers

Higher Level 2016, Section B, Q2 (a)–(c)

'Fish has been recognised as one of nature's best foods and with its rich supply of nutrients it is one of the few foods that can truly be called a super food.'

(a) Discuss the nutritive value and contribution of fresh fish/fish products to the diet. (5 points × 4 marks = 20 marks)

Nutritive value:

- *Fish is an excellent source of high biological protein (HBV).*
- *Oily fish are high in PUFTA (omega-3, EPA and DHA). White fish has no fat.*
- *Fish is an excellent source of iodine, good source of potassium, phosphorus; calcium in canned fish.*

Always read statements carefully. They are helpful when analysing information and tables.

Contribution to diet:

- *Excellent source of omega-3, reduces risk of coronary heart disease.*
- *Low in saturated fats, fish is suitable for low-cholesterol and low-calorie diets.*
- *Fish is a good alternative to meat.*
- *Easy to digest, useful for children and the elderly.*

Give **two** points on nutritive value and two points on contribution to diet, plus one additional point. Elaborate on each point.

(b) Outline the main causes of fish spoilage. (3 points × 5 marks = 15 marks)

- *Oxidative rancidity: fish oils react with oxygen in the air, resulting in an unpleasant smell and taste.*
- *Enzymes: action of enzymes causes fish to deteriorate even at low temperatures.*
- *Bacteria: fish struggle when caught and use up glycogen stores. If lactic acid does not form fish stales quickly, bacteria multiply producing trimethylamine and a strong unpleasant smell.*

(c) 'Oily fish and fish liver oils make a significant contribution to a person's intake of vitamin D.'

Give an account of vitamin D and refer to:

LINK

- Type/form of vitamin D (p. 33)

(i) Type/form (1 point × 3 marks = 3 marks)

(ii) Properties (3 points × 2 marks = 6 marks)

- *Fat-soluble vitamin*
- *In-soluble in water*
- *Stable to heat, acids, alkalis and oxygen*

(iii) Effects of deficiency (2 points × 3 marks = 6 marks)

- *Rickets in children*   • *Osteomalacia*
- *Osteoporosis*

Name = 1 mark, details = 2 marks.

Ordinary Level 2015, Section B, Q3 (a)–(c)

'Low in calories and packed with goodness, fish is the perfect food.'

(a) Give an account of the (i) nutritional value and (ii) the dietetic value of fish.

   (i) Nutritional value   (4 points × 6 marks = 24 marks)

- *Minerals: iodine, phosphorus, fluoride and zinc, calcium in tinned fish, iron in sardines.*
- *No carbohydrates, serve with carbohydrate-rich foods.*
- *Lipids: polyunsaturated fatty acids (PUFAs), omega 3.*

Give one point on nutritional value, one on dietetic value, plus two other points.

   (ii) Dietetic value

- *Easy to digest food, suitable in the diets of children, invalids and the elderly.*
- *Good source of HBV for growth and development in children and teenagers.*
- *Excellent source of omega-3, reduces CHD, ideal for those on low-cholesterol diets.*

(b) Name **three** different methods of cooking fish and explain how **one** cooking method is carried out.

Methods: (3 methods × 4 = 12 marks)

- *Grilling*
- *Frying*
- *Poaching*

Other methods of cooking fish are steaming, frying, deep-frying, grilling, baking and roasting.

Cooking method: *Poaching*   (2 points × 4 marks = 8 marks)

- *Cooking food gently in below simmering liquid (85°C).*
- *Cook in a saucepan on the hob or in a casserole in the oven.*

(c) State the benefits of omega-3 fatty acids in the diet.

                      (6 marks)

LINK
- Lipids (p. 23)

Higher Level 2010, Section B, Q2 (a)–(c)

'Few Irish people consume the two portions of fish recommended each week. Despite being surrounded by some to the best fishing and fish in the world we are often reluctant to try this incredibly healthy food.'

(a) Evaluate the nutritional and dietetic contribution that fish makes in the diet   (20 marks)

LINK
- Fish (p. 88)

(b) Recommend **one** dry method of cooking and **one** moist method of cooking suitable for fish. In relation to each method recommended:

- State the underlying cooking principle involved.
- Comment on the palatability of the cooked fish.

Method = 2 marks; principle: 2 points × 3 marks = 6 marks; palatability = 2 marks

Dry method: *Grilling*   (10 marks)
Fish cooks by radiant heat, heat from the grill seals the surface of the food, sealing in moisture, nutrients and flavour.

Moist method: *Stewing*   (10 marks)
Fish is cooked by conduction and convection in a small amount of simmering liquid (80°C–90°C), fish becomes digestible and flavour is retained. Overcooking can cause the fish to fall apart.

(c) Identify and discuss **two** contemporary trends in Irish eating patterns.   (10 marks)
  ● *Availability of pre-prepared cooked and uncooked foods and complete meals.*
  ● *Increased awareness of nutrition and food labelling.*

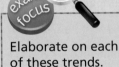

exam focus

Elaborate on each of these trends.

Ordinary Level 2005, Section A, Q7   (6 marks)
Classify fresh fish and give **one** example of each class.

Classification	Example (1 per class)
Oily fish	Mackerel
White fish	Haddock
Shellfish	Prawns

Eggs

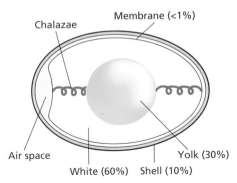

Chalazae

Membrane (<1%)

Air space

White (60%)   Shell (10%)

Yolk (30%)

Nutritive value/nutritional significance

Protein	● Rich source of 100% HBV protein
	● *White:* ovalbumin and globulin
	● *Yolk:* vitelin and livetin
Fat/lipid	● Saturated fat in yolk, held in a fine emulsion by lecithin, trace in egg white
	● Cholesterol present in yolk
Carbohydrates	None
Vitamins	● B_1, B_2, B_{12}, niacin (water-soluble)
	● A, D and E (fat-soluble)
Minerals	Calcium, iron, phosphorus, zinc, sulphur, selenium
Water	High content: 74% in whole egg

Dietetic value

Protein	• Contains all the essential amino acids • Ideal for children, adolescents, lacto-ovo vegetarians • Good alternative to meat
Fat/lipid	• Restrict in low-cholesterol diet • Easy to digest, ideal for elderly people
Carbohydrate	Serve with carbohydrate-rich foods
Vitamins and minerals	Useful source of vitamins B_1, B_{12}, iron, phosphorus and zinc
Digestibility	Easy to digest, ideal for elderly people, children, convalescents
Water	High water content (74%)
Versatility	Used in a variety of dishes, economical, cooks quickly

Rules for buying eggs

1. Buy from a clean shop with a good turnover.
2. Check for the Quality Assurance logo (Bord Bia).
3. Check shells are not broken/cracked.
4. Check egg size, class and use-by date.
5. Check that eggs are heavy for their size.

LINKS
• Protein (p. 3)
• Lipids (p. 23)
• Vitamins (p. 32)
• Minerals (p. 42)

Sustainable Egg Assurance Scheme (SEAS)

- Monitoring and testing carried out by Bord Bia and the Department of Agriculture and the Marine.
- Strict regulations cover hygiene, disease control, flock welfare and environmental protection of poultry.
- Hens are tested and certified salmonella-free.
- All feed used is heat-treated.
- Farms are inspected and monitored.

LINK
• Bord Bia (p. 138)

Grading and labelling of eggs

Weight/size	Quality/class/uses

XL (very large) = 73 g
L (large)   = 63–73 g
M (medium)   = 53–63 g
S (small)   = under 53 g
	A = top quality, small air space,
	     suitable for boiling, poaching
	B = large air space, suitable for
	     baking, sauces, scrambling
	C = sold to industry only

Egg boxes must carry the following information:

- Country of origin
- Name, address and registration of producer/packer
- Class/quality of eggs (Class A, etc.)
- Quantity (number of eggs)
- Week number (1–52)
- Best before date on Class A
- Size of eggs (XL, L, M, S)
- Storage instructions
- Farming method (0, 1, 2, 3)

Eggs must carry the following codes:

- Farming method code: 0 = organic;
  1 = free range; 2 = barn; 3 = cage.
- Country of origin (e.g. IR = Ireland).
- County and farm code/ID.
- Best before date.

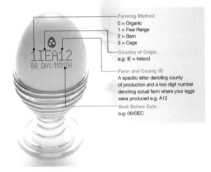

Rules for storing eggs

1. Store in a fridge with the pointed end down.
2. Do not store near strong-smelling foods.
3. Use eggs in rotation.
4. Egg whites and yolks can be frozen separately.
5. Remove eggs from the fridge one hour before use.

Effects of heat and cooking on eggs

1. Bacteria are destroyed.
2. Proteins are denatured and coagulate.
3. Albumin becomes insoluble, changes colour and becomes opaque.
4. Overcooking causes curdling, eggs become indigestible.
5. Sulphide ring forms if overcooked.
6. Some loss of vitamin B.

key point

Store leftover egg whites in the fridge in an air-tight container; cover leftover egg yolks with a little water to keep them from drying out, and store in the fridge.

key point

'Free range' status may vary due to incidents of avian flu.

LINK

- Properties of protein (p. 8)

Properties of eggs

Method	Effects	Application
Aeration	1. Whisking unfolds the structure of protein 2. Whisking traps and holds air, creates foam 3. Beating creates heat, which coagulates the foam 4. Cooking sets the foam	Sponge cakes, meringues, soufflés
Coagulation	1. Eggs coagulate or set when heated (white at 60°C and yolk at 68°C) 2. Overheating causes curdling/ denaturation – protein tightens, shrinks, water escapes	• Boiling, poaching • Coating food • Glazing food • Thickening sauces • Binding ingredients
Emulsifying	Lecithin is an emulsifier in egg yolk: 1. Enables two immiscible liquids to mix together and form an emulsion 2. Mixture becomes stable and does not separate	• Mayonnaise (oil/vinegar) • Cakes (fat/sugar) • Hollandaise sauce (yolks only, butter/vinegar)

Culinary uses of eggs	Examples
Binding	Burgers, omelettes, potato cakes, rissoles
Coating	Batters, coating sweet or savoury fried foods
Garnishing	Halved, sieved or sliced for savoury dishes (hard-boiled)
Glazing	Pastry flans, pies, scones, tarts
Thickening	Custards, quiches, sauces, soups
Other uses	As a food on its own or as a main ingredient, aerating, enriching, clarifying

key point

Pasteurised eggs are sold as liquid egg products in the supermarkets.

exam Q

Exam questions and sample answers

Higher Level 2015, Section B, Q2 (a), (b)

'Over 85% of adults in Ireland enjoy eggs at least once a week, with 56% of men and over 47% of women eating eggs two to three times per week.' (Bord Bia, 2014)

LINK
● Eggs (p. 93)

(a) Set out the result of a study you have carried out on eggs. Refer to nutritional significance, contribution to the diet and properties and culinary uses.   (6 points × 4 marks = 24 marks)

Nutritional significance:
- *Fat: saturated fat (12%) in the yolk in a fine emulsion due to the presence of lecithin, makes it easy to digest, cholesterol is also present.*
- *Protein: HBV (13%) for cell growth and repair. Albumin, globulin in white; livetin, vitellin in the yolk.*
- *Carbohydrates: none present, serve with carbohydrate-rich foods.*

exam focus

Give **one** point on nutritional significance, **one** point on contribution to the diet and **four** other points.

Contribution to the diet:
- *Cheap, nutritious food, ideal for those on low-incomes/low-budgets.*
- *Easily digested food, ideal for children, invalids and the elderly.*
- *Versatile food, can be used on its own or as part of a dish.*

Properties and related culinary uses: (2 points × 8 marks = 16 marks)
1. **Coagulation**
   Protein coagulates and sets when heated, white at 60–65°C, yolk at 65–70°C, protein chains untwist and denature, overheating causes proteins to curdle and water to squeeze out.

Culinary use: eggs on their own, e.g. poached, scrambled, fried, boiled; as a main ingredient, e.g. omelette; binding, e.g. burgers, potato/fish cakes; thickening quiches and custards; coating, e.g. chicken goujons, fish; clarifying, e.g. consommé (soup); glazing scones, pastries and breads.

Properties include coagulation, emulsification, aeration.

2. Emulsification

Lecithin, an emulsifier in egg yolk, enables two immiscible liquids to join together (vinegar and oil).

Culinary use: mayonnaise, Hollandaise sauce.

(b) Explain how quality is assured in egg production in order to minimise food safety risks. **(2 points × 5 marks = 10 marks)**

- *The EU-approved Salmonella Plan maintains the health of Ireland's laying stock. Laying hens are checked for salmonella on a monthly basis, and incoming hens are certified as salmonella free.*
- *Management systems guarantee full traceability of eggs.*

LINK
- SEAS (p. 94)

Ordinary Level 2016, Section B, Q3 (b), (c)

(b) Outline the following:

(i) Factors to be considered when storing eggs.

(2 points × 5 marks = 10 marks)

- *Store in the fridge in the egg compartment (on door) at 4°C with the pointed end downwards.*
- *Never wash the egg shell to avoid staling and contamination.*

(ii) Effects of heat on eggs. **(2 points × 5 marks = 10 marks)**

- *Protein coagulates and sets, egg white changes colour and yolk hardens.*
- *Overcooking eggs causes them to curdle and eggs become rubbery.*

(c) Describe **two** items of consumer information found on an egg carton (box).

(2 points × 5 marks = 10 marks)

Give one point on storing, one on effects of heat, plus two more.

- *Quality assurance mark.*
- *Name and address of producer.*

LINK
- Eggs (p. 93)

Other examples of consumer information include country of origin, registration number of producer/packer, class, week number, size, use by/best before date, storage, organic or free range, etc.

Alternative protein foods – novel proteins

Novel proteins are derived from two non-animal sources:

- **Processed plant foods:** soya beans, wheat, ground nuts, cotton seeds.
- **Micro-organisms:** fungi, yeast, bacteria, algae.

Soya foods

Examples of soya foods:

- Textured vegetable protein (TVP).
- Tofu (soya bean curd).
- Tempeh (fermented soya bean plant).
- Miso (soya bean paste).
- Soy sauce, soya oil, soya flour.
- Soya margarine, milk and yoghurt.

Nutritive value/nutritional significance

Protein	HBV protein (74%), low in methionine
Fat/lipid	Unsaturated fat, polyunsaturated fatty acid (linoleic acid)
Carbohydrates	Starch and fibre
Vitamins	B-group vitamins (soya beans)
Minerals	Calcium, non-haem iron
Water	Low amount (14%)

Dietetic value

Protein	HBV protein, useful for all groups including vegetarians
Fat/lipid	• Polyunsaturated fat, which helps to reduce cholesterol • Suitable for low-cholesterol and low-calorie diets
Carbohydrate	Fibre helps prevent bowel disorders
Versatility	• Versatile, available in a variety of forms, easy to use • Good alternative to meat in the diet

Textured vegetable protein (TVP)

Manufacture:

1. Oil is extracted from soya beans.
2. Beans are ground into flour.
3. Carbohydrates are removed, leaving only protein.
4. Oil, additives and flavouring are added.
5. Mixture is heated and extruded to create specific textures.
6. It is dried, fortified, weighed and packed.

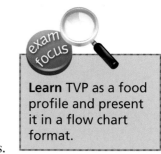

exam focus

Learn TVP as a food profile and present it in a flow chart format.

Advantages and disadvantages of TVP:

Advantages	Disadvantages
• Nutritious and cheap substitute for meat	• Inferior flavour to meat, tends to be bland
• Low in saturated fat	• Extra flavouring is usually required
• Source of dietary fibre	• Inferior texture
• Little waste, very versatile, long shelf-life	• Limited range of forms/shapes

Culinary uses of TVP: burgers, casseroles, curry, lasagne, stews.

Rules for storing TVP:

1. Store in a dry, well-ventilated press.
2. Once rehydrated, use as for raw meat.

exam focus

Revise the guidelines for cooking/using TVP.

Mycoprotein

Nutritive value/nutritional significance

Protein	HBV protein, low in methionine
Fat/lipid	Low in saturated fat, cholesterol free
Carbohydrate	Source of dietary fibre
Vitamins	B-group vitamins
Minerals	Zinc, low in non-haem iron
Water	Low water content

Manufacture of mycoprotein (Quorn)

1. Produced from a fungus, *Fusarium graminearum*.
2. Fungus cells are grown in a fermenter at 65°C – pH balance, temperature, oxygen and nutrients are monitored and adjusted.
3. Oxygen, glucose, nitrogen and minerals are added. Mycoprotein solids form.
4. Mixture is harvested and filtered. A binder is added to the mixture.
5. Flavourings and colourings are added.
6. Mixture is textured to resemble meat.
7. It is shredded, diced or sliced.

Main uses of Quorn

Pies, curries, casseroles, stews.

Exam questions and sample answers

Higher Level 2016, Section A, Q5 (6 marks)

State **two** advantages of including tofu in the diet.

- *Good source of HBV protein, low in saturated fat.*
- *Easy to prepare, little cooking involved, suited to sweet or savoury dishes.*

Other than tofu, name **two** protein alternatives that can be used in a vegan diet.

- *Textured Vegetable Protein (TVP)*
- *Soya cheese*

> **LINK**
> - Novel proteins (p. 98)

Higher Level 2009, Section B, Q1 (a) (24 marks)

	Energy	Protein	Fat	CHO	Fibre	Vitamins	Minerals
Minced beef (raw)	225 kcal	19.7 g	16.2 g	0	0	B-group	Iron 1.4 mg Sodium 80 mg
Quorn mince	94 kcal	14.5 g	2.0 g	4.5 g	5.5 g	0	Sodium 100 mg

(a) Using the information provided in the table, evaluate the contribution of Quorn mince to the diet of vegetarians.   (6 points × 4 marks = 24 marks)

- *Contains protein, mycoprotein, which is a good alternative to meat.*
- *Contains carbohydrate, which provides heat and energy.*
- *Lacks saturated fats, ideal for those with CHD and high cholesterol.*
- *Low in haem-iron and vitamins, vegetarians may need to supplement.*
- *Source of fibre; help to maintain a healthy digestive system.*
- *Its low sodium content makes it ideal for those with high blood pressure.*

Milk

Nutritive value/nutritional significance

Protein	• HBV protein • Caseinogen, Lacto-albumin, Lacto-globulin
Fat/lipid	• Mainly saturated fat • An emulsion stabilised by lecithin
Carbohydrate	• Milk sugar, lactose, a disaccharide

Vitamins	• Fat-soluble vitamins A and D in milk fat
	• Water-soluble B_1, B_2 and niacin
	• Lacks vitamin C (due to processing)
Minerals	• Rich source of calcium
	• Phosphorus, potassium, iodine
	• Lacks iron
Water	• High water content (87%)

Check the composition of the different forms of milk. Be able to evaluate and compare them.

Dietetic value/contribution to the diet

Protein	• HBV protein for growth (babies, children, adolescents, pregnant/nursing mothers)
	• For repair of cells (sportspeople, invalids, elderly)
Fat/lipid	• Easily digested form of fat
	• Low-fat milk is suitable for low-cholesterol or low-kilocalorie diets.
	• Omega-3 fatty acids added to milk reduces risk of CHD, suits those with high cholesterol
Carbohydrates, vitamins and minerals	Serve with foods rich in fibre, starch, vitamin C and iron. Choose milk fortified with vitamins and minerals
Digestibility	Easy to digest, ideal for all groups
Versatility	Many uses (savoury and sweet dishes)
Economic value	An economical, balanced food, widely available. Some milks are fortified

Culinary uses of milk

1. As a beverage on its own, in milk shakes, smoothies.
2. As a main ingredient, e.g. batters, puddings, desserts.
3. In sauces, e.g. parsley sauce, custard sauce.
4. In soups, e.g. cream of vegetable soup.
5. Enriching dishes/increasing nutritive value, e.g. creamed potatoes.
6. Glazing scones, tarts, breads.

LINKS
• Protein (p. 3)
• Lipids (p. 23)
• Vitamins (p. 32)
• Minerals (p. 42)

Types of milk

Whole milk (full fat milk)	Minimum of 3.5% fat
Semi-skimmed milk	2% fat (low fat or light milk)
Skimmed milk	0.2% fat, fewer fat-soluble vitamins
Fortified milk	Fortified with vitamins and minerals (calcium, folic acid, vitamin A + D, etc.), made from whole or low-fat milk
Organic milk	From cows grazed on pasture on which no chemical fertilisers or pesticides have been used
Buttermilk	Soured milk used in bread making
Flavoured milk	Chocolate, strawberry, banana
Dried milk	Water is removed from milk
Evaporated milk	Canned milk with 60% water removed
Condensed milk	Evaporated milk with added sugar
Soya milk	Milk substitute from soya beans

Reasons for processing milk:

- To destroy micro-organisms.
- To increase shelf life.
- To improve flavour.

Methods and effects of processing on milk:

Method	Effects
Homogenisation: heated to 65°C, forced under pressure through tiny valves, fat globules are decreased in size and dispersed	• Uniform consistency • No nutrients lost • Easy to digest
Pasteurisation: heated to 72°C for 25 seconds, cooled rapidly to 10°C, packed into sterilised containers and sealed	• Destroys pathogens • Some loss of vitamins B_1 and C • Extends shelf life • Little change in flavour/texture
Sterilisation: homogenised, packed and sealed, then heated to 110°C for 30 seconds and cooled	• Destroys bacteria • Loss of vitamin B_1, folic acid and vitamin C • Changes in flavour and colour • Longer shelf life (unopened)
Ultra-heat treated (UHT) : homogenised, heated to 132°C for 1–3 seconds, cooled quickly to 102°C and packed in sterile containers	• Destroys pathogens • Longer shelf life (unopened) • Little change in colour and flavour

Evaporated milk: pasteurised, evaporated to 50%, homogenised, sealed in tins and heated to 115°C for 20 minutes	<ul><li>Destroys bacteria</li><li>Shelf life of one year or more</li><li>Has a cooked flavour</li><li>Colour changes</li><li>Loss of vitamins B_1 and C</li></ul>
Condensed milk: homogenised, pasteurised, evaporated by two-thirds, sugar is added, sealed in tins	<ul><li>Destroys bacteria</li><li>Change in colour and flavour</li><li>Increase in sugar (higher in calories)</li><li>Loss of vitamins B_1 and C</li><li>Long shelf life</li></ul>
Dehydrated milk Spray dried Roller dried	<ul><li>Destroys bacteria</li><li>Loss of vitamins – B-group, C</li><li>Reduced fat content</li><li>*Spray dried:* reconstitutes easily, uniform in shape</li><li>*Roller dried:* has cooked flavour, tends to form lumps when mixed with water</li></ul>

LINK

- Food profile – milk (p. 150)

Effects of heat/cooking on milk

Revise the above table on milk processing.

Buying and storing milk

1. Check 'best before' date.
2. Store fresh milk in its own container in a fridge.
3. Never mix new and old milk; use in rotation.
4. Store away from strong-smelling foods.

key point

Milk substitutes are available for people who are lactose intolerant, allergic to cow's milk, or vegan.

exam Q

Exam questions and sample answers

Higher Level 2017, Section A, Q8 (6 marks)

Complete the table below in relation to the processing of milk.

Process	Temperature	Time	Effect
Ultra-heat treatment	*132°C*	*1–3 seconds*	Destroys all bacteria, longer shelf-life, change in flavour, loss of vitamins B_1 and C

Ordinary Level 2013, Section A, Q5 (6 marks)

Name **two** of the main nutrients found in skimmed milk.

- *Protein*
- *Carbohydrate*

Name **two** heat treatments applied to milk to extend its shelf-life.

- *Pasteurisation e.g. whole milk, skimmed milk, etc.*
- *Dehydration e.g. dried skimmed milk, milk powder.*

Ordinary Level 2014, Section B, Q2 (b)

(b) Explain the difference between whole milk, skimmed milk and fortified milk.

(3 points × 4 marks = 12 marks; one reference to each type)

Whole milk: *Full fat milk, 3.5% to 4% fat.*

Skimmed milk: *0.1% to 0.4% fat as the remainder has been removed during processing.*

Fortified milk: *Available as full fat, low fat or skimmed. Has added vitamins.*

Check out Section B in Higher Level 2011, and Section B in Ordinary Level 2010.

Dairy products

Yoghurt

Classification of yoghurt:

- Full-fat
- Low-fat/fat-free
- Set
- Live/bio-yoghurt
- Drinking
- Frozen
- Greek
- Natural
- Flavoured
- Fromage frais (cheese culture)

Production of yoghurt:

1. Milk is homogenised and pasteurised for 15–30 minutes at 85–95°C.

2. Milk is cooled and inoculated with a starter culture.

3. Mixture is incubated at 37°C for 6–8 hours.

4. Lactose changes to lactic acid, protein coagulates, mixture thickens and flavour develops.

5. Yoghurt is cooled to 4.5°C.

6. Fruits, nuts, cereals, colourings, sweeteners or flavourings are added.

7. Yoghurt is packaged, labelled and refrigerated.

Nutritive value/nutritional significance

Protein	HBV protein, similar value to milk
Fat/lipid	Saturated animal fat: amount depends on type of milk
Carbohydrates	Milk sugar, lactose Sugar increased with fruit and sweeteners, contains fibre
Vitamins	Fat-soluble A and D Water-soluble B_1, B_2, niacin
Minerals	Calcium Potassium and phosphorus (trace)
Water	Varies depending on fat content (type)

Dietetic value

1. A nutritious, inexpensive food.
2. Provides HBV protein for growth and development in children, adolescents, pregnant and nursing mothers.
3. Excellent source of calcium for healthy bones and teeth.
4. Easy to digest, ideal for babies, elderly people and invalids.
5. Ideal snack food, for packed lunches and desserts.
6. Low-fat varieties are useful in low-kilocalorie diets.

Culinary uses

- On its own, as a dessert or snack.
- On breakfast cereals.
- Dips, salad dressings, marinades, smoothies.
- In sauces and savoury dishes.

Exam question and sample answer

Ordinary Level 2008, Section A, Q5(b) (3 marks)

State the benefit to the consumer of adding bacterial cultures, such as acidophilus, to bio yoghurt.

Acidophilus aids digestion.

Cheese

Classification of cheese

Hard	Semi-hard	Soft	Others
Cheddar	Edam	Brie	Cottage
Emmenthal	Port Salut	Camembert	Processed
Parmesan	Stilton	Mozzarella	Farmhouse

Nutritive value/nutritional significance

Protein	HBV protein, casein is present
Fat/lipid	Saturated animal fat, higher in hard cheese
Carbohydrates	None – lactose is drained away in the whey
Vitamins	B_2, A and D, lacks vitamin C
Minerals	Excellent source of calcium, low in iron, sodium present from processing
Water	Varies with the type of cheese: hard cheese has less water than soft cheese

Dietetic value

1. A concentrated source of HBV protein and calcium, which are essential for growth.
2. Its saturated fat content makes it a high-energy food.
3. Serve with foods rich in carbohydrates.
4. A good alternative to meat, fish and poultry.
5. Suitable for snacks and packed lunches.
6. Quick, convenient, economical and versatile.

key point

Pregnant women should avoid soft cheese due to the danger of listeria.

LINKS
- Nutrients (p. 2)
- Food pyramid (p. 54)

exam Q

Exam questions and sample answers

Ordinary Level 2016, Section A, Q6   (6 marks)

Using the words listed below, complete the statements in relation to cheese.

curds   **lactic acid**   **rennin**

In the production of cheese a culture is added to milk to convert the lactose to *lactic acid*, the enzyme *rennin* changes caseinogen to casein. The mixture is allowed to rest for 30 minutes and separates into *curds* and whey.

Higher Level 2017, Section B, Q2 (a)–(c)

'Ireland produces more farmhouse cheese per capita than any other country in the world. Our reputation for quality extends overseas, with Ireland exporting 90% of the cheese it produces.' (Irish National Dairy Council)

This question integrates cheese with the Irish food industry.

(a) Evaluate the nutritional value **and** the dietetic contribution of cheese to the diet. **(5 points × 4 marks = 20 marks)**

Nutritional value:

1. *Protein: 10–27%, good source of HBV protein (casein) for growth. Cheddar cheese has the highest content at 27% with soft cheeses lower at 10–14%.*
2. *Fat/lipid: 4–35%, high in saturated fats but lower if made from skimmed milk. Hard cheese has more fat than soft cheese.*
3. *Minerals: 1.5–4% depending on cheese type. Cheese is a rich supply of calcium for bones and teeth, but sodium is present due to salt added during production, and it lacks iron.*

Dietetic contribution:

1. *A versatile, inexpensive food with no waste, suited to those on low incomes.*
2. *A rich source of protein and calcium essential for growth in babies, children, teenagers and pregnant women. Pregnant women should avoid soft cheese due to risk of listeria.*
3. *Restrict in low-cholesterol diets or low-calorie diets due to high levels of saturated fats. You can use low-fat cottage cheese (4% fat) as an alternative.*

Give **two** points for nutritional value, **two** for dietetic contribution, and **one** other point.

(b) Describe the production of cheese. **(18 marks)**

Production: **(7 stages × 2 marks = 14 marks)**

- *A culture of lactic acid bacteria is added to pasteurised milk to convert lactose to lactic acid which acts as a preservative and adds flavour.*
- *Milk is heated to 30°C, rennet is added and the enzyme rennin coagulates milk protein converting caseinogen to casein. The mixture separates into curds and whey.*
- *Curds are cut and the whey is drained off.*
- *Curds are scaled by heating to 40°C to achieve the correct consistency. More whey is released.*
- *Curds are cut again into blocks and 2% salt is added.*
- *Salted curds are pressed into moulds which may be sprayed with hot water to produce a protective rind.*

Refer to stages of production, packaging and labelling.

- *Cheese is removed from moulds, stored for 3–12 months at 5–10°C to ripen and then graded.*

  Packaging: *Wrapped in waxed paper or in plastic tubs or vacuum packed with a use-by date.* (2 marks)

  Labelling: *Provides information on type, quantity, nutritional information, date stamp.* (2 marks)

  LINK
  - Irish food industry (p. 138)

(c) Discuss the role of artisan producers/small businesses in the Irish food industry. (4 points × 3 marks = 12 marks)

- *Speciality foods are produced using traditional skills, e.g. cheese-making, preserving.*
- *Produce quality foods using local ingredients, implementing high standards of hygiene.*
- *Businesses are small and frequently family-run in rural areas.*
- *Provide local employment and develop a small skilled workforce.*

exam focus

Revise the Irish food industry and link it with food commodities.

Buying and storing cheese

1. Buy in small amounts from a clean shop where it is stored in a chilled cabinet.
2. Check use-by date on pre-packed cheese.
3. Ensure seals are not damaged on pre-packed cheese.
4. Store freshly cut cheese wrapped in greaseproof paper in the fridge.
5. Store soft cheese in a covered container in the fridge.

Using cheese

- Use fresh cheese within 2–3 days.
- Remove from fridge 30 minutes before use.
- Serve cheese at room temperature.
- Grate leftover hard cheese and use as a garnish.

Culinary uses of cheese:

Snacks	Cheese sandwich
Main dish	Quiche Lorraine, cheese fondue
End of meal	Cheese board
Sauces	Lasagne, cauliflower cheese

Fillings	Omelettes, baked potato, toasted sandwiches
Toppings	Lasagne, macaroni cheese, pizza
Accompaniment	Dips, spreads, salads, grated on salads
Dessert	Cheesecakes, tiramisu
Baking	Scones, pastry and biscuits

Effects of heat/cooking on cheese:

1. Protein coagulates, shrinks and denatures.
2. Fat melts at high temperatures.
3. Overcooking causes fat to separate and become stringy.
4. Dry heat causes cheese to brown.
5. Overheating causes cheese to become indigestible.

Improve the digestibility of cheese by cooking it for the shortest possible time, grating or slicing it, adding mustard when cooking, or using low-fat varieties.

Exam question and sample answer

Ordinary Level 2014, Section A, Q5 (6 marks)

Tick (✓) which of the following nutrients is not found in cheese.

Protein	Vitamin C	Calcium
	✓	

List **two** effects of cooking on cheese.
- Protein coagulates and shrinks.
- Overcooking causes cheese to become tough and indigestible.

Fruit

Classification of fruit

Berries	Blackcurrants, blueberries, cranberries, gooseberries, raspberries, strawberries
Citrus	Grapefruit, lemons, limes, oranges
Dried	Apricots, dates, raisins, prunes, sultanas
Hard	Apples, pears
Stone	Cherries, nectarines, peaches, plums
Tropical	Bananas, kiwis, passion fruit, pineapples, mangoes
Other	Rhubarb

Nutritive value/nutritional significance

Protein	Traces of LBV protein
Fat/lipid	None except avocadoes (polyunsaturated fat)
Carbohydrates	• Starch in unripe fruit • Glucose and fructose in ripe fruit • Dried fruit high in sugar • Source of dietary fibre (NSP) and pectin
Vitamins	• Rich supply of vitamin C • Beta-carotene in yellow, orange and red fruits
Minerals	• Calcium in some fruits • Traces of iron (non-haem)
Water	High in fresh fruit, low in dried fruit

Dietetic value

1. Rich in vitamin C, which aids absorption of iron.
2. Vitamins and minerals protect against disease.
3. Excellent source of dietary fibre (NSP).
4. Ideal in low-kilocalorie and high-fibre diets.
5. Economical and versatile; can be eaten raw or cooked.
6. Provides colour, flavour and texture.

LINKS
- Nutrients (p. 2)
- Food pyramid (p. 54)

Rules for buying, storing and using fruit/vegetables

Buying	1. Buy in season when cheapest 2. Choose young fresh produce free from blemishes 3. Buy loose or netted 4. Check the use-by date 5. Buy in useable quantities
Storing	1. Remove from wrapping 2. Store in a cool area with good air circulation to slow down the action of enzymes and moulds
Using	1. Wash to remove residues of sprays 2. Use quickly, eat raw if possible, remove peels or skins where necessary

Effects of cooking on fruit/vegetables

1. Enzymes and micro-organisms are destroyed.
2. Texture softens, fruits become digestible.
3. Colours and flavours change.
4. Vitamin C is destroyed (greatest nutrient loss).
5. Loss of water-soluble vitamins and minerals.

LINK
- Food preparation and cooking processes (p. 123)

Culinary uses of fruits

- Decoration on flans, pies, tarts.
- Garnishes, e.g. lemon wedges with fish.
- Starters, e.g. grapefruit and snacks (whole fruit).
- Beverages, e.g. milk shakes, smoothies.
- Main courses, e.g. pineapple on pizza.
- Desserts, e.g. Pavlova, fruit salad.
- Cheeseboard (cheese, crackers, fruit).
- Preserves: jams, jellies, chutneys, pickles.

exam focus

Revise the ripening of fruit (Chapter 3, Food Studies: Part Two).

Effects of processing on fruit/vegetables

Method	Examples	Effects
Canning	Pears, strawberries Beans, peas, sweetcorn	• Loss of B-group and C vitamins • Changes in colour, flavour and texture • Bacteria and enzymes are destroyed • Increased sugar content
Drying	Apricots, raisins, sultanas Peas, beans, lentils	• Reduced water content • Loss of B-group and C vitamins • Enzymes and bacteria are inactivated • Changes in colour, flavour and texture • Increased sugar content • Iron is concentrated
Freezing	Apples, berries, rhubarb Carrots, peas, broccoli	• Little loss of nutrients • Change in texture • Enzymes and bacteria are inactivated
Irradiation	Strawberries, berries Onions, potatoes	• Destroys enzymes and micro-organisms • Extends shelf life • Prevents sprouting • Some vitamin loss • No change in appearance

Irradiation

Irradiation involves exposing food to ionising radiation. The purpose of irradiation is to:

- Control damage by insects.
- Reduce pathogenic micro-organisms.
- Delay ripening, germination or sprouting.

In many countries irradiated foods carry the word 'irradiated' and they may also carry the Radura symbol.

LINK
- Food preservation (p. 182)

Radura symbol

LINK
- Food labelling (p. 157)

Exam question and sample answer

Ordinary Level 2012, Section A, Q6 (6 marks)

Name **three** classes of fruit and give one example of each class.

Class of fruit	Examples
Citrus fruit	Oranges
Stone fruit	Peaches
Hard fruit	Apples

Vegetables

Classification of vegetables

Class/type	Examples
Leafy greens	Cabbage, kale, spinach
Flowers	Broccoli, cauliflower
Pulses (legumes)	Peas, beans, lentils
Stems	Asparagus, celery
Fruit	Aubergines, courgettes, cucumbers
Bulbs	Garlic, leeks, onions, shallots
Roots	Beetroot, carrots, parsnips
Tubers	Potatoes, sweet potatoes

key point

Fungi such as mushrooms and truffles are used in savoury dishes with vegetables.

Nutritive value/nutritional significance

Protein	Low in LBV protein *except* soya beans
Fat/lipid	Low, except soya beans, avocados, olives
Carbohydrates	<ul><li>High in starch (potatoes)</li><li>Sugar in carrots, onions, tomatoes</li><li>Fibre in outer skins, flesh and husks</li></ul>
Vitamins	<ul><li>Excellent supply of beta-carotene (vitamin A) in brightly coloured vegetables</li><li>Water-soluble B-group and C</li></ul>
Minerals	<ul><li>Non-haem iron in green leafy vegetables</li><li>Calcium and traces of potassium, iodine and zinc</li></ul>
Water	High % of water unless dried

exam focus

Review the average composition chart of vegetables. Be able to evaluate and compare the information in the table.

exam focus

Revise carbohydrates (p. 11); vegetarian/vegan diets (p. 66–68).

Dietetic value

1. Provide a rich supply of nutrients for all age groups.
2. Important sources of dietary fibre.
3. Contain anti-oxidant vitamins A, C and E.
4. Useful in low-calorie and low-cholesterol diets.
5. Pulses are important for vegans (substitute for meat).
6. Versatile, used in a variety of dishes, raw/cooked.

LINKS

- Nutrients (p. 2)
- Vegetarianism (p. 66)

Rules for buying vegetables

1. Buy in season in useable quantities.
2. Choose fresh, medium-sized vegetables that are even in colour.
3. Select crisp fresh greens, avoid wilted greens.
4. Choose roots and tubers heavy for their size.
5. Check grade/quality and best before dates.
6. Check pre-packed vegetables for bruising and wilting.

key point

- Green vegetables are a good source of calcium and iron.
- Economical, cheap when in season.
- Serve with foods rich in vitamins D and B$_{12}$.

Rules for storing vegetables

1. Store potatoes in a dark place to prevent greening and sprouting.
2. Store salad vegetables/greens in sealed bags in the fridge.
3. Place frozen vegetables in freezer.
4. Store dried pulses in airtight jars.

key point

Choose loose or netted vegetables rather than those washed or packed in plastic.

Rules for preparing vegetables

1. Use raw or prepare just before cooking.
2. Avoid early preparation and steeping.
3. Wash, scrub and peel, trim sparingly.
4. Use a sharp knife to prevent nutrient loss, tear leafy green vegetables.
5. Wash under cold running water to remove dirt, prepare according to kind.

key point

Use vegetables up quickly and in rotation. Store unwashed vegetables in a dark, dry, cool place.

Rules for cooking vegetables

1. Cook in a small amount of boiling water, for the shortest possible time.
2. Keep a lid on the saucepan; never use copper pans.
3. Cook vegetables *al dente*.
4. Using bread soda and overcooking destroys vitamin C.
5. Use leftover cooking liquid for stocks, sauces, soups.

Effects of cooking on vegetables

See under Fruit, page 111.

exam focus

Revise guidelines for cooking fruits and vegetables to maintain the maximum nutrients.

Spoilage

1. Browning/bruising due to oxidation.
2. Leafy vegetables go limp and yellow.
3. Root vegetables go woody and limp and develop soft patches.
4. Vegetables shrivel and reduce in size.

LINK

- Food preparation and cooking processes (p. 123)

Methods of processing vegetables

- **Home:** dehydration (herbs), freezing, pickling.
- **Commercial:** bottling, canning, dehydration, freezing, pickling, irradiation.

exam focus

Revise effects of processing on fruits and vegetables, and culinary uses of vegetables, legumes, nuts and organic produce.

Organic symbols

Grading of fruit/vegetables

Class	Explanation
Extra Class	Top quality, no defects in colour, shape, size
Class 1	Good quality, free from bruising, cracking, uniform in shape
Class 2	Marketable, some blemishes, defects in colour and shape
Class 3	Inferior quality but marketable, slight blemishes

Exam questions and sample answers

Higher Level 2006, Section A, Q5 (6 marks)

(a) Identify and explain **two** EU grading classes used for fruit and vegetables.

(4 marks)

- *Extra class: superior quality, free from defects in shape, size and colour.*
- *Class 1: good quality, no bruising or defects.*

(b) What does this symbol convey to the consumer? (2 marks)

The **Radura symbol** *indicates that the food has undergone irradiation.*

Ordinary Level 2016, Section A, Q8 (6 marks)

Give **two** examples of vegetables in each of the following classes.

Classes	Example 1	Example 2
Pulse vegetables	Peas	Kidney beans
Root vegetables	Potatoes	Beetroot
Green vegetables	Cabbage	Kale

Higher Level 2012, Section B, Q2 (a) (b)

(a) Discuss the options available to consumers when selecting and purchasing fruit and vegetables. (4 points × 3 marks = 12 marks)

- *A wide variety of forms are available, e.g. fresh, frozen, canned, dried, or in other products.*
- *They can be bought loose or pre-packed in nets or plastic bags/containers.*
- *They are available all year round, e.g. fruits/vegetables in season and out of season, tropical varieties.*
- *Pre-prepared fruits/vegetables are useful for salads, stir-fries, snacks, smoothies.*

(b) Give details of the nutritional significance **and** contribution to the diet of either fruit or vegetables. (5 points × 4 marks = 20 marks)

FRUIT

Nutritional significance	Contribution to the diet
• **Protein**: none in fruit. • **Fat**: none in fruit except avocados (polyunsaturated). • **Carbohydrates**: Starch in unripe fruit, fibre in the cell walls of fruit; fruit contains sugar (glucose, fructose), pectin. • **Vitamins**: valuable source of vitamin C, e.g. blackcurrants, brightly coloured fruits are excellent sources of pro-vitamin A.	• Versatile and economical food, e.g. on their own, in snacks, in main courses or as accompaniments. • Rich in vitamin C, which aids absorption of iron. • Antioxidant property protects against disease. • Ideal for low-calorie, low-cholesterol and high-fibre diets. • Excellent source of fibre.

Choose a mix of 5 points from each column.

(c) Give an account of vitamin A. (18 marks)

LINK
• Vitamin A (p. 32)

Ordinary Level 2014, Section B, Q1 (d)
(d) Discuss how **each** of the following could influence the consumer when buying fresh fruit and vegetables.

(4 points × 5 marks = 20)

Cost:
In season produce is the cheapest, freshest, often best quality and most plentiful.

Skills:
Knowledge of preparation and cooking minimises vitamin and mineral loss, e.g. not steeping, peeling thinly with a sharp knife.

Time available for preparation:
Preparation time depends on the type, e.g. root vegetables need to be washed before peeling, chopping or slicing, fruits need washing to remove traces of chemicals. Using prepared fruits/vegetables saves time.

Storage space:
Incorrectly stored fruit/vegetables deteriorate quickly, so they must be stored in a cool, dry, dark, well-ventilated place. Some can be packed loosely and placed in the vegetable drawer of a fridge.

Cereals

The **main sources** of cereals are the grains of cultivated grasses, e.g. barley, oats, maize, millet, rice, rye and wheat.

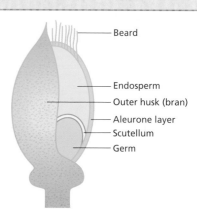

Beard

Endosperm

Outer husk (bran)

Aleurone layer

Scutellum

Germ

Structure of wheat grain

Bran layer or outer husk: tough layer of indigestible fibre	13%	Contains cellulose, rich in fibre, B-group vitamins (especially niacin), calcium, iron, phosphate
Endosperm: energy store of the grain, largest part of grain	85%	Contains the energy store of the grain (mainly starch), protein and B-group vitamins *Aleurone* is the outer layer of the endosperm; contains protein
Germ or embryo: contains all nutrients for germination and growth	2%	Rich in protein, fat, vitamins (B-group, E), iron and the nutrients for the germination of a new plant, mainly essential fatty acids
Scutellum		A thin layer between germ and endosperm

Nutritive value/nutritional significance of wheat

Protein	● LBV proteins, higher in wholemeal flour than in white flour ● Gluten, lysine, threonine, tryptophan ● Lacks some amino acids
Fat/lipid	Polyunsaturated fats in the germ
Carbohydrates	● High in starch ● Rich in cellulose (outer husk/bran)
Vitamins	● Rich in B-group vitamins (niacin and thiamine) ● Vitamin E in germ
Minerals	Useful amounts of calcium, non-haem iron, traces of phosphorus
Water	Low water content, about 13%

Dietetic value of cereals

1. A cheap, nutritious and versatile food.
2. Ideal energy food.
3. Suited to low-calorie, high-fibre diets.
4. Whole grains provide B-group vitamins, non-haem iron and calcium.
5. Coeliacs should avoid cereals with high gluten content.

LINKS
- Carbohydrates (p. 13)
- Vitamins (p. 32)
- Minerals (p. 42)

Flour

Classes of flour

- Strong flour – high in gluten.
- Weak flour – lower gluten content.
- Plain flour – mixture of weak and strong flour.

LINK
- Coeliac disease – dietary guidelines (p. 69)

LINK
- Food profile – flour (p. 149)

Types of flour

Types of flour	Extraction rates	Key points, description and uses
Wholemeal/ wholegrain	100%	All of the grain remains, none removed Uses: breads, scones
Wheatmeal/ brown	85%	Some bran removed Uses: breads, scones
White (cream/ plain)	70–75%	Bran and germ removed, endosperm remains Uses: cakes
Self-raising	less than 75%	Raising agents added, sodium bicarbonate, cream of tartar Uses: buns, cakes
Strong		High-gluten flour, suits yeast baking
High-ratio	less than 50%	A 'soft' finely milled high quality flour, low in gluten Use: commercial
Gluten-free		Gluten is removed, flour lacks elasticity Uses: breads, cakes, sauces, etc.

Effects of heat/cooking on cereals and cereal products

1. Protein coagulates, dry heat sets bread/cakes.
2. Moist heat causes gelatinisation and liquids to thicken.
3. Dry heat causes starch grains to swell, burst and absorb oils/fats, e.g. popcorn.
4. Dextrinisation and caramelisation occur.
5. Starch becomes digestible.
6. B-group vitamins are destroyed.

Revise rice and pasta.

Exam questions and sample answers

Higher Level 2015, Section A, Q5 (6 marks)

State the nutritional significance of **each** of the following parts of the wheat grain.

Part of grain	Nutritional significance
Bran	*Source of fibre which aids digestion by peristalsis, calcium for bones*
Endosperm	*Mainly starch as energy source, B-group vitamins for metabolism*
Germ	*Rich in protein for growth and repair, iron to prevent anaemia*

Higher Level 2008, Section A, Q5   (6 marks)

Name **three** cereals grown for food production and give **one** example of a
different product manufactured from each cereal.   (6 points × 1 mark = 6 marks)

Cereal	Products
Wheat	Flour
Rice	Rice cakes or rice noodles
Maize	Cornflakes

Ordinary Level 2017, Section A, Q7   (6 marks)

Using the words listed below complete the following statements in relation to
cereals.

bran   **endosperm**   **staple**

The largest part of the grain is the *endosperm* which contains starch.

Cereals are *staple* foods in many countries.

The *bran* layer is composed mainly of cellulose.

> **LINK**
> • Cereals (p. 116)

Ordinary Level 2012, Section B Q2 (a)–(c)

(a) Identify the main sources of cereals in the Irish diet and state why some people
    avoid/limit their intake of cereals.   (20 marks)

Main sources (3 sources × 4 marks = 12 marks)	Why people avoid/limit their intake (2 reasons × 4 marks = 8 marks)
1. Breads 2. Pasta 3. Breakfast cereals	1. Following low-carbohydrate diets 2. Coeliac cannot digest gluten products

(b) Give an account of the nutritive value of cereals.

(3 points × 5 marks = 15 marks)

- *Outer husk is rich in dietary fibre, aids digestion.*
- *High in starch, ideal energy food.*
- *Whole grains provide calcium, iron and are a rich source of B-group vitamins.*

(c) (i) Explain food fortification.   (5 marks)

*Food that has vitamins or minerals added to improve the nutritive value or to
replace nutrients lost in processing. Examples: Vitamins A and D are added to
low-fat or skimmed milk.*

(ii) Comment on the increasing consumption of fortified food products.

(5 marks)

Increasing intake of fortified foods helps consumers:

- *To reduce the risk of neural tube defects with the addition of folic acid.*
- *To prevent/reduce risks of osteoporosis by adding vitamins A and D to
milk.*

Fats and oils

Main characteristics:

LINK
- Lipids/fats in diet and nutrition (p. 23)

- **Fats:** mainly saturated, solid at room temperature.
- **Oils:** mainly polyunsaturated, liquid at room temperature.

Classification of fats and oils

Animal	Marine	Plant
Saturated fat: Dairy fat, meat, suet, lard, egg yolk	*Polyunsaturates:* ● Fish liver oils (cod, halibut) ● Oily fish (herring, salmon)	*Polyunsaturates:* Vegetable oils, nut oils, seed oils, vegetable suet

Nutritive value/nutritional significance of fats/oils

Protein	Insignificant levels of HBV protein (<1%)
Fat/lipid	Low-fat spread 40%; butter 82%; cooking oil 90%; suet 99%
Carbohydrates	Lacking in most oils, trace in flax oil
Vitamins	● Fat-soluble vitamins A, D, E and K – depends on product and if fortified ● Traces of B-group vitamins, no vitamin C
Minerals	Traces of calcium in butter and margarine
Water	Depends on the amount of fat present

Dietetic value

1. Concentrated source of heat and energy.
2. Provide fat-soluble vitamins A, D, E and K.
3. Source of essential fatty acids.
4. Polyunsaturates help reduce cholesterol build-up.
5. Protect delicate organs, e.g. kidneys.
6. Improve flavour of foods, e.g. dressings.

Revise the production of vegetable oil.

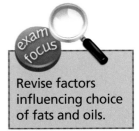

Revise factors influencing choice of fats and oils.

Margarine

Production of margarine

Oil extraction
(from vegetable sources)
↓

Hydrogenation
Hydrogen gas is forced through oil, in the presence of a catalyst,
to harden the mixture, converting it into saturated fats
↓

Blending
Blend of different oils depending on the properties of the final product
(low-cholesterol, vegetarian, plasticity, etc.)
↓

Ingredients added
Colourings, emulsifiers, flavourings, nutrients, salt,
skimmed milk, water and vitamins A and D
↓

Emulsification
Ingredients are churned with a rotator machine to regulate consistency, and
stabilisers are added
The temperature is lowered and the margarine kneaded, moulded and shaped
↓

Finishing the product
Margarine is weighed, wrapped, labelled and packed

exam focus

Investigate the producers of rapeseed oil in Ireland. It could form the basis of an investigation of a local food company for an exam question in Section B.

Types of margarine and dairy spreads

Spread type	Description and uses
Block margarine	Vegetable oils, high in saturated fat *Uses:* Frying, baking, spreading
Soft margarine (packed in tubs)	Vegetable oils, buttermilk/whey and water, high in saturated fats, a little less than block varieties *Uses:* Frying, baking, spreading

Low-fat spreads	Water, vegetable oil, milk proteins, emulsifiers, stabilisers, salt, colourings, vitamins A, D, E, trace protein, low in saturated fats *Uses:* Spreading
Spreadable low-fat butters	Water, cream, milk protein, salt, potassium sorbate, beta-carotenes, vitamins A, D, E *Uses:* Spreading
Functional dairy spreads	Sunflower oil, vegetable oil, buttermilk, plant stanol ester, water, salt, emulsifiers *Uses:* Spreading

Culinary uses of fats and oils

1. Creaming, flavouring, shortening and spreading.
2. As anti-staling agents, preventing food drying out.
3. In emulsions, e.g. mayonnaise, salad dressings.
4. Basting food, e.g. meat; sautéing foods, e.g. onions.
5. Frying foods (shallow/deep-fat).

LINKS
- Functional foods and spreads (p. 151)
- Food processing (p. 147)

Rules for storing fats and oils

1. Store fats in a fridge to prevent rancidity.
2. Cover fats to prevent absorption of odours, e.g. garlic.
3. Store oils in a cool, dark place.
4. Check the best before date.

Exam question and sample answer

Higher Level 2013, Section A, Q5 (6 marks)

Differentiate between the following dairy spreads and give **one** example of each.

Low-fat spread:
Contains less than half the fat of butter, ideal for low-calorie diets, low in saturates and high in monounsaturated fatty acids, (contains water, vegetable oil, milk proteins, emulsifiers, stabilisers, salt, colourings).

Example: *Dairygold Lighter*

Functional dairy spread:
No hydrogenated fatty acids and few trans-fats, plant sterols prevent absorption of cholesterol and proven to reduce cholesterol, useful in low-cholesterol diets, (contain sunflower oil, vegetable oil, buttermilk, plant sterols, water, salt).

Example: *Flora Pro-active*

Meal management and planning

When planning meals, consider:

- Current dietary guidelines
- Special dietary needs
- Life cycle stage of the individual
- Knowledge/skills of cook
- Resources available

- Time of year/season
- Occasion/number of people
- Aesthetics
- Religious beliefs

exam focus

Make sure you can elaborate on these points in the exam.

Guidelines for meal planning

1. Plan ahead: make a shopping list for a week's menus.
2. Plan to use all leftovers.
3. Buy foods in season (when they are cheapest).
4. Vary cooking methods.
5. Serve hot dishes in winter, chilled dishes in summer.
6. Choose fast methods of cooking if time is limited.
7. Plan accompaniments, garnishes/decorations to suit dishes.

exam focus

Revise the current Food Pyramid and the recommended dietary guidelines.

LINKS

- Dietary guidelines (p. 51)
- Food choices (p. 2)
- The Irish diet (p. 75)
- Family resource management (p. 207)
- Household technology (p. 234)

exam focus

In the exam you will be expected to demonstrate knowledge of current nutritional guidelines, balanced meal planning and correct menu formats.

Food preparation and cooking processes

LINK

- Cooking methods (Chapter 3: Extension 1, see www.moresuccess.ie)

Reasons for cooking food

1. To destroy micro-organisms and enzymes.
2. To make foods look appetising.
3. To improve the flavour of food.
4. To stimulate the appetite.
5. To make food more digestible.
6. To preserve some foods.

exam focus

Make sure you can explain and elaborate each of these points in an exam question.

Changes during food preparation – some examples

Physical changes	• *Tenderising meat:* using meat hammer or mincing to break down fibres • *Nutrient loss:* vitamin C is lost when food is cut, steeped or comes in contact with air • *Increase in size:* pulses absorb water • *Thickening:* whipping egg white or cream increases volume and traps air
Chemical changes	• *Enzymic browning occurs:* cut apples turn brown when enzymes react with oxygen in air • *Increase in size:* yeast dough expands • *Tenderising meat:* using proteolytic enzymes or marinades

Changes during cooking – some examples

Physical changes	• Colour changes • Micro-organisms are destroyed • Texture changes: food becomes digestible • Improved flavours, food is tastier • Loss of nutrients: at high temperatures or into cooking liquid • Decrease in size: meat shrinks • Increase in size: introduction of air in bread and cake-making • Thickening: adding flour to a sauce • Setting: gelatine sets desserts
Chemical changes	• Non-enzymic browning: Maillard reaction • Dextrinisation: toast • Caramelisation: sugar changes to a golden brown colour

Preventing nutrient loss during cooking

1. Prepare food just before cooking.
2. Use a sharp knife when cutting fruit/vegetables.
3. Use the minimum amount of cooking liquid.
4. Never steep overnight.
5. Cook vegetables for the shortest possible time.
6. Use cooking liquids for soups, stocks and gravies.

LINK

• Nutrients: properties (p. 2)

Principles underlying cooking methods

Heat is transferred in three ways:

1. **Conduction:** heat passes from one molecule to another. *Examples*: boiling, frying, stewing.
2. **Convection:** transfer of heat in currents. *Examples*: boiling, stewing, roasting.
3. **Radiation:** heat travels in straight lines from the heat source in the form of rays to the food. *Examples*: grilling, toasting, barbecuing.

Factors influencing cooking methods

• Composition of food: light or dense.
• Shape and size of food: joint, thin slices.
• Type of food: dense meat, spongy cake mixture.

- Personal taste: raw, medium or well done.
- Other factors: ingredients available, desired cooking results, skills of cook, time available, equipment, fuel economy.

Methods of cooking

Method	Examples	Effects of cooking
Dry heat	Grilling Barbecuing Baking Roasting	• Loss of B-group vitamins and vitamin C • Fat melts, sugar caramelises • Protein foods shrink • Maillard reaction • Foods become crisper
Moist heat	Boiling Braising Poaching Steaming Stewing Pressure cooking	• Loss of B-group vitamins and vitamin C • Collagen changes to gelatine • Cellulose softens • Food becomes more digestible • Overcooking causes food to fall apart • Flavours develop
Using fat/oils	Deep-fat frying Shallow frying Stir-frying Dry frying	• Increases fat content of food • Loss of vitamin A • Texture becomes crisper • Fried food can be soggy and greasy • More difficult to digest

Microwave cooking

LINK
- Microwave ovens (p. 242)

LINKS
- Maillard reaction (p. 8)
- Dietary guidelines (p. 53)
- Guidelines for meal planning (p. 123)
- Food safety and hygiene (p. 195)

Pressure cooking

Similar to steaming, but temperatures are higher than 100°C because of the pressure build-up in the appliance.

exam focus

Learn the changes to the nutritive value and the palatability of foods when using different cooking methods.

Application of principle	• By increasing pressure, food cooks at higher temperatures • Steam cannot escape, food cooks quickly
Advantages	• Saves time and energy • Little loss of nutrients • Little change in colour and flavour • Complete meal can be cooked in one pot

Disadvantages	● Danger of overcooking food
	● Needs constant attention
	● Danger of scalding from steam, steam must be released slowly
Suitable foods	Meat, poultry, preserves, vegetables, rice, complete meals, puddings

Basic structure of a pressure cooker

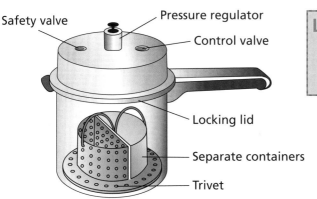

Safety valve
Pressure regulator
Control valve
Locking lid
Separate containers
Trivet

LINK

● Cooking methods – moist heat (Chapter 3: Extension 1, see www.moresuccess.ie)

Rules for using a basic pressure cooker

1. Follow the manufacturer's instructions.
2. Never overfill with liquids or solids.
3. Ensure a steady stream of steam before adding weights.
4. Time the cooking carefully.
5. Turn off heat, lift pressure cooker off hob.
6. Allow pressure to reduce to normal.
7. Remove lid carefully to avoid a burst of steam.

Sometimes the term 'guidelines' is used instead of 'rules' in questions.

Revise cooking methods, application of principles, advantages, disadvantages and suitable foods, soups, sauces and pastry.

Exam questions and sample answers

Higher Level 2010, Section B Q2 (b)

Recommend **one** dry method of cooking and **one** moist method of cooking suitable for fish.

In relation to each method recommended, state the underlying cooking principle and comment on the palatability of cooked fish.

It is useful to make a table for this answer.

(20 marks)

Method (2 × 2 = 4 marks)	State the underlying cooking principle involved (2 points × 3 marks) × 2 = 12 marks	Comment on the palatability of the cooked fish (2 marks × 2 = 4 marks)
Grilling (2 marks)	Cooking under radiant heat which seals the surface. Seals in moisture, flavour and nutrients.	Produces tasty easily digested foods but fish can overcook and dry out quickly.
Poaching (2 marks)	Cooking in liquid just below simmering point (80–90°C) for a short time. Conduction and convection currents.	Poached fish lacks flavour if herbs or other flavourings are not added to the cooking liquid.

Ordinary Level 2017, Section A, Q6   (6 marks)

Give **two** examples of different foods suitable for **each** of the following methods of cooking.

Methods of cooking	Example 1	Example 2
Grilling	Lamb cutlets	Tomatoes
Steaming	Fish fillet	Vegetables (broccoli)
Roasting	Chicken	Potatoes

Ordinary Level 2013, Section A, Q4   (6 marks)

Listed below are **three** different cooking methods. Name **two** examples of each.

Moist cooking methods	Dry cooking methods	Frying
Stewing	Grilling	Shallow-frying
Poaching	Roasting	Stir-frying

Raising agents and yeast cookery

Raising agents are used to introduce air into breads, cakes and pastries.

Classification of raising agents:

1. Natural/mechanical.
2. Chemical.
3. Biological.

Natural raising agents

1. **Air:** introduced by beating, creaming, folding, rolling, rubbing-in, sieving and whisking.
2. **Steam:** acts as a raising agent in batters and choux pastry.

Chemical raising agents

A chemical reaction occurs between an acid and an alkali in the presence of a liquid to produce CO_2, which raises the dough.

1. **Baking powder**

$$\text{Acid} + \text{Alkali} + \text{Liquid} \quad \rightarrow CO_2$$
$$\text{Baking Powder} + \text{Milk/Eggs} \rightarrow CO_2$$

2. **Bread soda**

$$\text{Acid} + \text{Alkali} \quad + \text{Liquid} \quad \rightarrow CO_2$$
$$\text{Buttermilk} + \text{Bread Soda} + \text{Buttermilk} \rightarrow CO_2$$

3. **Self-raising flour:** raising agent has been added during production.

Yeast – a biological raising agent

Yeast is a living organism which produces CO_2 due to fermentation. It needs warmth, moisture and food to multiply.

$$\text{Yeast} + C_6H_{12}O_6 + \text{Moisture} + \text{Warmth} \quad \rightarrow \quad 2C_2H_5OH + CO_2 + \text{Energy}$$
$$\phantom{\text{Yeast} + {}} \text{Glucose} \phantom{+ \text{Moisture} + \text{Warmth} \quad \rightarrow \quad} \text{Alcohol} \quad \text{Carbon}$$
$$\phantom{\text{Yeast} + C_6H_{12}O_6 + \text{Moisture} + \text{Warmth} \quad \rightarrow \quad 2C_2H_5OH + } \text{dioxide}$$

FERMENTATION

The actions involved in fermentation are:

Enzyme		Acts on		Produces
Diastase (flour)	→	Starch	→	Maltose
Maltase (yeast)	→	Maltose	→	Glucose
Invertase (yeast)	→	Sucrose	→	Glucose and fructose
Zymase (yeast)	→	Glucose and fructose	→	CO_2 + alcohol

- Gluten becomes elastic and holds the CO_2 produced during fermentation.
- CO_2 in the dough expands and raises the dough until double in size (happens outside the oven).
- Yeast is killed in the oven, dough stops rising and dough crust sets.
- Alcohol produced evaporates.

LINK

- Try this exam question:
  Higher Level 2009, Section A, Q6
  (www.examinations.ie).

exam focus

Revise the guidelines for using yeast.

Exam questions and sample answers
Ordinary Level 2011, Section A, Q6 (6 marks)

(i) Name a suitable raising agent for each of the following dishes.

Dishes	Raising agent
Bread	*Yeast*
Sponge cake	*Baking powder*
Muffins	*Bread soda and sour milk*

(ii) Explain the underlying principle of **one** of the raising agents named above.

Baking powder: Bicarbonate of soda (alkali) and cream of tartar (acid) in the baking powder react to produce CO_2 (gas) which raises the sponge cake or muffins, heat sets the baked product.

Higher Level 2017, Section A, Q7 (6 marks)

(a) Explain the process of fermentation.

Fermentation is the breakdown of organic substances by micro-organisms, e.g. yeast and bacteria in the presence of warmth, moisture and food to produce carbon dioxide, alcohol and energy.

(b) Name two by-products of fermentation.

1. Acids, e.g. vinegar.

2. Alcohol, e.g. wine.

Food preparation and cooking equipment

Preparation equipment	Cooking equipment
● Chopping board	● Cooker
● Sharp knives	● Microwave oven
● Food mixer	● Deep-fat fryer
● Food processor	● Sandwich toaster
● Liquidiser	● Doughnut maker
● Hand blender	● Bread maker
● Juice extractor	● Kettle
● Carving knives	● Contact grill

Selecting food preparation and cooking equipment

Consider:

1. Frequency of use.
2. Quality of the product.

3. Budget available.

4. Energy rating.

5. Storage space needed.

6. Guarantee and after-sales service.

Small electrical appliances

Examples: blenders (hand), food mixers, food processors and liquidisers.

Guidelines for safe use of small appliances

1. Follow the manufacturer's instructions.

2. Ensure hands are dry before operating appliance.

3. Remove/insert blades carefully, e.g. in a blender.

4. Fill to the recommended level.

5. Do not overfill small attachments: note level of contents.

6. Turn off and unplug electrical appliances after use.

Care of small appliances

1. Unplug appliance before cleaning.

2. Wash according to the manufacturer's instructions.

> **LINKS**
> - Household technology (p. 234)
> - Consumer choice (pp. 254)

3. Never wash the motor part, never immerse it in water.

4. Wipe outer casing with a hot soapy cloth.

5. Take care when cleaning blades, graters and discs.

6. Dry well before storing.

7. Wind flexes loosely to avoid damage.

8. Store appliance unplugged with its attachments.

Recipe balance and adaptation

Recipes are adapted or modified to:

- Improve nutritive value.
- Suit special dietary requirements.
- Alter the number of portions.
- Introduce variety in colour, flavour and texture.
- Implement current healthy eating guidelines.
- Make dishes/meals more economical.
- Use up leftovers and avoid waste.

> **LINKS**
> - Coeliac diets (p. 69)
> - Vegetarian diets (p. 66)
> - Dietary guidelines (p. 53)
> - Coronary heart disease (p. 64)

Modifications and some examples

Eat less salt	● Reduce/omit salt in dishes ● Avoid processed/convenience foods ● Replace salt with herbs/spices
Eat less sugar	● Reduce sugar in dishes ● Use artificial sweeteners ● Use dried fruits and fruit juices
Eat less fat	● Remove visible fat from meat ● Use poultry and lean cuts of meat ● Choose low-fat polyunsaturated spreads ● Use low-fat products ● Use low-fat methods of cooking
Eat more fibre	● Choose wholegrain products, e.g. oats, brown rice ● Increase intake of fresh fruit/vegetables ● Eat fruit/vegetables with skin on ● Add pulses to stews and casseroles

Exam questions – practising 'balancing menu' questions

Devise menus asked for in the following questions. The 'Note' states specific considerations.

- **Higher Level 2009, Section B, Q1** – A menu for a three course meal suitable for a vegan. *Note:* using Quorn mince.
- **Higher Level 2007, Section B, Q2** – A day's menu for a person with coronary heart disease. *Note:* include one functional food.
- **Ordinary Level 2017, Section B, Q2** – A day's menu for Paul and Lisa attending post-primary school. *Note:* they attend the school's Breakfast Club every morning.
- **Ordinary Level 2016, Section B, Q2** – A day's menu for a lacto-vegetarian. *Note:* current healthy eating guidelines.
- **Ordinary Level 2015, Section B, Q2** – A day's menu for a person who is obese. *Note:* current healthy eating guidelines.
- **Ordinary Level 2014, Section B, Q2** – A day's menu for a teenage girl. *Note:* healthy eating guidelines and adequate calcium.
- **Ordinary Level 2013, Section B, Q2** – A menu for one day for a person with high energy requirements. *Note:* include three meals and snacks.
- **Ordinary Level 2012, Section B, Q3** – A menu (3 meals) for one day for a family with teenagers. *Note:* current healthy eating guidelines and specific needs of adolescents.

HL **Higher Level 2015, Section B, Q1 (d)**

Discuss the role of parents in shaping their children's food choices.

(5 points × 4 marks = 20 marks)

In order to shape their children's food choices parents need to:

- *Act as good role models by choosing and eating a healthy balanced diet.*
- *Be aware of current healthy eating guidelines and the Food Pyramid.*
- *Consider the health status of family members, e.g. specific dietary needs.*
- *Serve one meal for the family rather than individual meals for everyone.*
- *Have regular family meal times which enables everyone to be present, e.g. dinner.*
- *Establishing healthy eating patterns, no fads, no distractions, e.g. TV, mobile phones.*

(Other points which could be used include the following:

- *Parents and children shopping for food together, menu planning.*
- *Opportunities for children to learn about nutrition and cooking.*
- *Serving one meal for family, it is not a restaurant with an extensive menu.*
- *Serving home cooked meals at home within the budget available.*
- *Cultural choices of parents/family.*
- *Religious beliefs of parents/family.)*

> **exam focus**
>
> Here is a **compulsory** question which requires you to apply your knowledge of roles and nutrition.

> **key point**
>
> Children learn from their parents about choices of traditional, ethnic and new foods

> **exam focus**
>
> List **five** points and then elaborate with examples related to children.

Aesthetic awareness of food

The **main aesthetic factors** which influence the **choice** of food are:

- Colour → sight
- Flavour → taste, smell, mouthfeel
- Aroma → smell
- Texture → touch
- Sound → hearing

Aesthetic awareness in food preparation

Appearance and **colour** are key indications of the freshness and quality of foods.

Appearance and colour (sight)

Sight enables us to judge colour, size, shape, appearance and presentation of dishes.

1. Key indicator of freshness and quality.
2. Linked to individual foods, changes during cooking.
3. Brightly coloured foods appeal to sense of sight.
4. Garnishes provide contrast.
5. Foods are expected to have a specific colour, e.g. peas.

key point

Foods are expected to have certain colours. Natural and artificial colours are used to replace colours lost during processing.

Flavour (taste)

Flavour involves a combination of smell, taste and mouthfeel. Nerves in the mouth react to the chemical characteristics and temperatures of foods.

To enhance flavour during food preparation:

1. Choose a variety of flavours for each menu.
2. Arrange flavours to suit the course: savoury to sweet.
3. Avoid strong overpowering flavours in every course.
4. Use only one strong flavour in the meal.

Aroma (smell)

The smell of food is an indication of quality, freshness, staleness. Smell receptors in the nose identify aroma. Smell intensifies food flavour.

To enhance the aroma of foods:

1. Add herbs/spices to improve aroma of bland ingredients.
2. Cook foods with aromas that stimulate the taste buds.
3. Overcooking foods produces 'burnt' aromas.
4. Prevent cross-flavours developing during preparation.
5. Avoid undercooking, which makes food bland.

key point

Shops use the aroma of baked goods and fresh coffee to attract customers.

Texture (touch, mouthfeel)

Texture is registered by sight and the taste/feel of food in the mouth, or consistency.

1. Add interest to menus by using a variety of textures, e.g. crispy salad with lasagne.
2. Individual foods produce expectations of what the textures will be, e.g. mayonnaise is smooth, apples are crunchy.
3. Texture of foods changes during cooking, e.g. roast potatoes.
4. Overcooking affects the texture of dishes, e.g. lumpy white sauces, curdled custards.

Sound (hearing)

The sounds made by food during preparation (e.g. popping, sizzling, fizzing) enhance our appreciation of individual foods, e.g. rashers frying, fizzy drinks, breaking a biscuit in two.

Aesthetic awareness in food presentation

The sight of food well presented is pleasing to the eye, and stimulates digestive juices and taste buds.

1. Foods should look attractive and be neatly arranged.
2. Serve cold or chilled food on cold plates.
3. Serve hot food piping hot on warmed plates.
4. Arrange food neatly on plates, do not overfill dishes.
5. Garnish or decorate dishes to improve presentation.
6. Wipe edges of plates/dishes before serving to remove drips.
7. Serve savoury foods on plain plates/dishes.
8. Serve sweet foods on more decorative plates/dishes.

> **LINK**
> - Meal management and planning (p. 123)

Word bank for describing/evaluating food

Colour (sight)	Colourful, pale, fresh, greasy, cloudy, overcooked, undercooked, burnt
Flavour (taste)	Sweet, sour, bitter, tasteless, bland, spicy, salty, smoky, creamy
Aroma (smell)	Sweet, sour, smoky, burnt, fresh, spicy
Texture (touch, mouthfeel)	Crisp, crunchy, hard, soft, nutty, brittle, smooth, chewy, lumpy, greasy
Sound (hearing)	Popping, sizzling, fizzing, crackling

HL Sensory analysis

Sensory analysis is used to determine the acceptability of a food product to consumers by measuring, analysing and explaining the characteristics of a food using the five senses: taste, smell, touch, sight and sound.

Sensory analysis is used to:
- Develop new products.
- Modify products, e.g. by reducing fat.
- Evaluate food products.

Types of sensory analysis tests

1. Preference tests

Purpose: to determine the acceptability of a food or food products.

Techniques:
- **Paired preference tests** (which product is preferred).
- **Hedonic test** (the degree of liking on a verbal scale).

2. Difference tests

Purpose: to identify differences in taste between two food samples.

Techniques:

- **Simple paired test** (to identify if two coded samples are the same or different).
- **Paired comparison test** (to determine differences in characteristics in pairs of coded samples).
- **Triangle test** (to determine which of three coded samples is different where two are the same).

3. Descriptive tests

Purpose: to rank specific organoleptic characteristics of food products, e.g. intensity of flavour, texture, odour and aftertaste, to identify the impact of a change in processing, packaging and storage on sensory quality of a product.

Techniques:

- **Descriptive ranking test** (to rank food samples in order by preference (hedonic ranking) or by specific characteristics).
- **Descriptive rating test** (to identify the extent of a person's like or dislike for a food or compare different aspects of quality of two or more foods).

Controlling test conditions

1. Timing of tests – mid-morning or mid-afternoon is best.
2. Avoid strong foods for 30 minutes before test.
3. Provide rinsing water for taster/s.
4. Temperature of food samples should be the same.
5. Same quantities of food in each sample.
6. Containers of same size, shape and colour – white or colourless.
7. Coding of samples (must not give information).
8. Sequence of samples (random, balanced or a combination).

Presenting results

Results are presented using pie charts, histograms or star diagrams, in order to determine the changes required.

Exam questions and sample answers

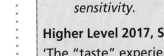

Higher Level 2009, Section A, Q8 (6 marks)

Name **two** uses of sensory analysis in the food industry.

1. *To analyse and evaluate food samples to improve food products*
2. *To compare similarities or differences in a range of products when developing 'own brands'.*

Name **one** sensory analysis test used to detect differences in food samples.

Simple paired test.

Higher Level 2015, Section A, Q6 (6 marks)

Outline **three** conditions necessary to ensure accurate results when carrying out sensory analysis tests.

- *Avoid eating strong flavoured foods for 30 minutes before test.*
- *Temperature of food samples should be the same.*
- *Timing of tests – mid-morning or mid-afternoon are best for taste sensitivity.*

Higher Level 2017, Section B, Q3 (a)–(c)

'The "taste" experience is an accumulation of multiple senses.'

(a) Discuss the influence of the senses when choosing, cooking and eating food.

(4 points × 4 marks = 16 marks)

Choosing: (summary of two points – develop selected points)

- *Sight is used to judge colour, shape, size, presentation (appearance).*
- *Specific foods are expected to be of a certain colour, e.g. green peas.*

Cooking: (summary of two points – develop selected points)

- *Develops and intensifies flavours, e.g. roasting, spicy, fruity.*
- *Texture changes, e.g. overcooking makes vegetables soggy.*

Choose one point for **each** area and **one** other point, elaborate and give examples.

Eating: (summary of two points – develop selected points)

- *Taste buds sense the sweetness, sourness, saltiness or bitterness of foods.*
- *Nerve endings react to thermal/chemical characteristics of foods, e.g. hot chilli.*

(b) Outline **four** conditions required for sensory analysis testing. (16 marks)

(4 conditions × 4 marks = 16 marks)

- *Location: Set up a quiet, brightly lit location with good ventilation and adequate space between the testers.*

- *Timing: Mid-morning or mid-afternoon is best for testing to ensure that the location is well-ventilated and free of aromas from other activities.*
- *Consistency: Samples should be uniform in shape, colour, quantity and temperature.*
- *Coding of samples: Samples can be coded using numbers, letters or geometric shapes. Arrange coded samples in the same sequence to eliminate bias.*

(c) Write a detailed account of **one** difference test used in the food industry. Refer to name of test, aim and implementation. (18 marks)

Name of test: *Triangle test* (3 marks)

Aim of test: *To identify the sample that is different* (3 marks)

Implementation: (6 points × 2 marks = 12 marks)

- *Set up trays with three coded samples using A, B, C, two foods the same, one different.*
- *Present coded samples in balanced order to ensure a combination of samples and that each food is presented the same number of times.*
- *Ask Testers to identify which one is different by tasting the samples in the order presented. Taste order ensures random tasting of samples.*
- *Testers fill out scorecards having tasted all samples presented.*
- *Responses are collated, presented (bar chart, pie chart, histogram) and analysed.*
- *Codes are revealed and results are evaluated.*

Higher Level 2013, Section B, Q2 (a), (b)

'Given the priority for population dietary change there is a need for a greater understanding of the determinants that affect food choice.' (European Food Information Council)

(a) Discuss the importance of aesthetic awareness in relation to the choice and presentation of food. (3 points × 4 marks = 12 marks)

- **Choice** *is affected by sight/appearance as it is used to judge freshness and quality of foods.*
- **Foods/dishes are evaluated by their presentation**, *colour, garnishes and decorations, e.g. grated cheese, dusted icing sugar on sponge cakes.*
- **Smell** *(through the nasal cavity) is used to determine the freshness or staleness of foods.*

Give **one** point on choice, **one** point on presentation plus **one** other.

(b) (i) State, giving examples, when sensory analysis tests are used in the food industry. (2 points × 4 marks = 8 marks)

- Product development: developing own brands, checking consumer response to new products.
- Matching other market products: comparing similar well-known branded food products.

(ii) Name **three** main categories of sensory analysis tests and state the main purpose of the tests in each category.

(3 × 6 marks: name = 3 marks and purpose = 3 marks)

Category of test	Main purpose
Preference test	To determine whether people like or dislike a product
Difference test	To detect small differences in food, do people notice the differences
Descriptive test	To describe the perceived sensory characteristics of a food product

The Irish food industry

Structure of the Irish food industry: government departments and food agencies

Department of Agriculture, Food and the Marine

Functions are to:

- Promote the agri-food/marine sector.
- Monitor and control aspects of food safety.
- Monitor and control animal health, plant health and animal welfare.
- Implement national and EU schemes/legislation.
- Operate the National Beef Assurance Scheme.
- Develop markets for Irish products.

Department of Health

Functions are to:

- Develop food safety policies and legislation.
- Develop health promotion strategies, implemented by HSE, education sectors and others.
- Work with agencies concerned with health, e.g. Food Safety Authority of Ireland (FSAI).

Bord Bia (Irish Food Board)

Functions are to:

- Promote Irish food, drink and horticulture nationally and globally.
- Provide quality assurance schemes for Irish meat, eggs, dairy products and horticulture.
- Provide consumer information via leaflets and website.

Bord Bia
Irish Food Board

The **Bord Bia Quality Mark** can be found on pre-packed bacon, beef, chicken, cooked ham, duck, pork, rashers, eggs, fruit and vegetables.

Bord Iascaigh Mhara

Functions are to:

- Promote the ongoing development of Irish mariculture, by providing technical expertise, business support and training to support innovation, sustainability and employment.

Teagasc (Agriculture and Food Development Authority)

Functions are to:

- Research agriculture and food production in Ireland.
- Provide services in partnership with various sectors of the agricultural and food industry.
- Provide advice and training to farmers on all aspects of farming.

Food Safety Authority of Ireland (FSAI)

Functions are to:

- Protect public health by raising food standards and creating a culture of excellence.
- Promote a collaborative approach to food safety.
- Protect consumers by providing accurate information.
- Co-ordinate the enforcement of food safety legislation.

Enterprise Ireland

Functions are to:

- Promote development and growth of Irish enterprises in world markets.
- Support start-ups and business expansion plans.
- Provide advice and financial support to help businesses increase their exports sales.
- Provide incentives to stimulate in-company research and development.

Food exports

Structure of the Irish food industry:

Dairy and ingredients, beef, lamb, pig meat, poultry, edible horticulture, mariculture, beverages, prepared consumer foods.

exam focus

Research the 'Love Irish Food' group.

The agri-food industry:

- 230,000 employed across this sector.
- Ireland exports to 180 countries.
- In 2016 exports were worth € 11.15bn.
- In the EU, Ireland is the net exporter of dairy ingredients, beef and lamb.

exam focus

Data for exports/imports are constantly changing. Check the latest data before the exams.

Irish Exports 2016

Category		Export (%)	Examples
Dairy produce and other ingredients		30%	Milk powder, butter, dairy spreads, cheese, yoghurt, ice cream, infant formula
Beef		21%	Beef
Prepared consumer foods		17%	Frozen, chilled, dried foods, e.g. confectionery, cooked meats, chocolates, snacks
Beverages		13%	Alcoholic (whiskey, liqueurs, cider, stout, ale) and non-alcoholic (water, juices)
Pig meat		6%	Bacon, pork and products *Main market is in UK*
Seafood		5%	Salmon, shellfish *Main market is in France*

Poultry		3%	Chicken, duck, ostrich
Sheep meat		2%	*France and UK are main markets (60% of export volume)*
Edible horticulture and cereals		2%	*Mushrooms to UK account for 75% of mushrooms grown in Ireland*
Livestock		1%	Cattle

Source: Bord Bia

Food imports

Types of food	Examples
Beverages	Beers, wines, spirits, juices, soft drinks, bottled water
Cereals	Barley, rice, pasta, maize, flour
Dairy	Milk, milk products, cheese, yoghurt
Fish	Canned, fresh, frozen, smoked
Fruit	Apples, citrus, bananas, grapes, kiwi, melons, pineapples, strawberries, tropical fruits (in fresh, frozen and dried forms)
Vegetables	Beans, garlic, lentils, tomatoes, peppers, soya
Other	Tinned products, tea, coffee, soya products, sauces, soups, pâté, speciality foods, olive oil, dried fruits

exam focus

Hint: Visit your local supermarket around March/April to check the countries of origin of produce on sale.

Small businesses and home enterprises

- Involve small numbers of people (some are family run).
- Produce speciality foods, e.g. cheese.
- Must implement EU hygiene and safety standards.

Reasons for growth of small businesses and home enterprises

1. Innovation, new ideas, desire to become self-employed.
2. Reduction in farm incomes, creation of value-added on-farm food enterprises
3. Potential for processing using new technology and skills.
4. State supports for new businesses and enterprises.
5. Recent unemployment, redundancy.
6. Development of entrepreneurial culture.

Benefits of small businesses and home enterprises

1. Create new employment opportunities.
2. Meet consumer demands for product variety.
3. Offer new exclusive ranges of food items.
4. Promote the use of quality local ingredients.
5. Identify and link into key markets.

Speciality food sectors

1. Bakery (bread, biscuits, gluten-free flour, spelt flour).
2. Beverages (beers, juices, smoothies, kefir, kombucha).
3. Condiments (dressings, sauces, mustards).
4. Confectionery (chocolate, sweets, desserts).
5. Dairy (cheese, yoghurt, cheesecakes).
6. Prepared foods (fresh/frozen ready meals, prepared vegetables/salads, desserts).
7. Preserves (chutneys, relishes, jams, marmalade, jellies).
8. Speciality meats and fish (smoked fish, puddings, sausages, ham).

exam focus

Investigate and write up a food industry in your local area using the following model.

Investigating a local food industry

Sample investigation: a local chocolate producer.

Name of producer: Gurteen Chocolate Company Ltd, Ireland.

When was it set up?	2011
Why was it set up?	● Owner became redundant from a food-related industry ● Owner wanted to start a small family-owned/run business
Research carried out	● Checked the Food Safety Authority of Ireland ● Investigated the Food Works Programme ● Investigated Bord Bia's Food Academy ● Checked the Companies Registration Office website
Does the business contribute to the area?	Five local families benefit from direct full employment
Are the suppliers local?	No. Some products are imported that are specific to the product
How many people are employed?	The company employs 10 people, 7 of whom are not family
Are there plans for expansion?	Not at present – it would cost too must financial investment in technology
Set up grants/grant aid?	None – redundancy money was used to set up business
What are its markets?	● Local specialist shop and country stockist ● A supermarket chain in Ireland ● On-line ordering in place since summer 2017
How do they market their product?	● In-store and marketing to retailers ● Online
Types of packaging used	Packaging that can protect chocolate from light, oxidation, moisture, insect infestation and excessive temperatures
What type of quality control is in place?	HACCP in accordance with EU legislation
What changes have been made since the business was established?	2011: All staff trained in HACCP 2012: Owner modified the business plan and production so that speciality products could be made at key times of the year, e.g. Christmas, Easter 2016: Owner investigated the export markets with the help of the support agencies 2017: Small order from specialist shop in UK

Career opportunities in food and related industries

Certificates, diplomas and degrees are offered by:
- Agricultural Colleges
- Teagasc
- Universities and Institutes of Technology
- Colleges of Education
- Fáilte Ireland.

LINKS
- Consumer responsibilities (p. 257)
- Food safety and hygiene (p. 195)
- HACCP (p. 198)

Career opportunities
- Creating new foods.
- Manufacturing/preparation in the food industry.
- Management and administration.
- Food technologists, biotechnologists, microbiologists.
- Non-designated crafts: bakers, butchers.
- Designated crafts: fitters, electricians, mechanics.
- Marketing and retailing.
- Product distribution and transport logistics.
- Suppliers of services and raw materials.

Careers in food production include: farming, fishing, horticulture and milling.

Careers in the catering/retail industry include:
- Chefs, bakers, butchers, confectioners, caterers.
- Deli counter staff.
- Hospitality assistants.
- Managers (hotel, restaurants, catering).
- Administrative staff (accountants, receptionists).

Check the careers guidance board/file in your school to see if there are new food courses/careers available.

Exam questions and sample answers

Higher Level 2017, Section A, Q3 (6 marks)

Outline the role of the Food Safety Authority of Ireland (FSAI) in the food industry.
The FSAI is responsible for co-ordinating the enforcement of food safety regulations in Ireland, protecting consumers by providing accurate food safety information, ensuring food is safe to eat (HACCP), advising the Minister and taking action when premises are in violation of food legislation/regulations.

Higher Level 2014, Section A, Q5 (6 marks)

Name and explain the primary function of **one** national agency involved in the Irish Food Industry.

Name: BIM – Ireland's Seafood Development Agency

Function: BIM develops and expands the Irish seafood industry by providing technical expertise, business support, funding, training and promoting responsible environmental practices in order to deliver on the government's targets for seafood and sustainable employment.

Examples could include Teagasc, BIM, An Bord Bia, FSAI. Choose only **one**.

Higher Level 2012, Section A, Q7 (6 marks)

Identify **three** major sectors of the Irish Food Industry

- *Dairy products: cheese, yoghurt*
- *Animals: beef, lamb, poultry, pigs*
- *Edible horticulture: fruits, vegetables*

Ordinary Level 2012, Section A, Q8 (6 marks)

Give **two** reasons why food production in small businesses and home enterprises is increasing.

- *Consumer demand for speciality foods and luxurious products.*
- *Food from small businesses/home enterprises has a healthy image as few additives are used.*

Name **two** major Irish food exports.

- *Dairy and ingredients (butter, cheese, etc.)*
- *Edible horticulture (mushrooms)*

Ordinary Level 2010, Section A, Q6 (6 marks)

Name **two** government departments or agencies that have a role in the food and drinks industry.

- *Department of Agriculture, Food and the Marine*
- *Food Safety Authority of Ireland (FSAI)*

List **two** career opportunities in the food industry.

- *Food manufacturer*
- *Agricultural scientist*

Higher Level 2017, Section B, Q2 (c)

(c) Discuss the role of artisan producers/small businesses in Irish food industry.

(4 points × 3 marks = 12 marks)

- *Produce speciality foods in small quantities using non-industrial traditional skills. Examples: jam-making, cheese-making.*
- *Use locally sourced quality ingredients containing few additives.*
- *Businesses are generally family run with a small local workforce.*
- *Create new employment opportunities in rural areas.*
- *Promote innovation in artisanal food production.*

exam focus

Choose any **four** points listed and elaborate in more detail.

3 Food Studies: Part Two

aims To learn and revise:
- Food processing
- Food profiles
- Functional foods
- Packaging
- Labelling
- Additives
- Microbiology
- Preservation
- Safety and hygiene legislation

Food processing and food profiles

Reasons for processing food:

1. To extend shelf life, provide variety and choice.
2. To improve nutritive value by fortifying food.
3. To create new food products and flavours.
4. To save time and energy used in preparing foods.
5. To make food safe to eat.

Categories of processing

Primary:

- Extensive processing of basic foods, e.g. milling, oil extraction.
- Extending shelf-life, e.g. pasteurised milk, pasteurised egg whites and egg yolks.

Secondary: Using basic processed foods to create new products of a higher value, e.g. margarine, oils, breads, cakes, dairy products, soups, sauces, stocks.

Types of processed/convenience foods

1. Bottled/canned foods

Examples	Preparation	Cooking
Fruit, vegetables, fish, soups, preserves, sauces	None	• Heating required • Saves time

LINKS
- The Irish food industry (p. 138)
- Food commodities (p. 81)

key point

Convenience foods also include fortified, functional and novel protein foods.

2. Cook-chill products

Examples	Preparation	Cooking
Fresh pasta, lasagne, soups, quiches, fish pies	None	Cook or reheat until piping hot

3. Dehydrated foods

Examples	Preparation	Cooking
Bread/cake mixes, soups, sauces, custard, stock cubes	• Some needed • Takes less time than making from scratch • Add a liquid (eggs, milk, water)	• Add liquid and cook as normal • Follow the manufacturer's instruction

→ 4. Frozen foods

Examples	Preparation	Cooking
Meats, poultry, fish, vegetables, cooked meals, prepared meals	None	• Cook from frozen • **But!** *Poultry should be fully thawed before cooking*

5. Instant/ready-to-serve foods

Examples	Preparation	Cooking
→ Takeaway foods, prepared salads, sandwiches, pastries, cakes	None	None required; serve as normal

processed

Advantages and disadvantages of convenience foods

Advantages	1. Save time and energy
	2. Less waste, easy to store and use
	3. Individual portions available, suit those living alone
	4. Low-fat varieties available, suit low-cholesterol diets
	5. Longer shelf-life, reduces shopping trips
	6. Good variety of products and flavours
	7. Little cooking skill required
Disadvantages	1. Some inferior to home-made varieties
	2. Expensive
	3. High in salt, sugar and fat
	4. Low in fibre
	5. Many contain artificial additives

LINKS
• Food choices (p. 2)
• The Irish diet (p. 75)

LINKS
• Food commodities (p. 81)
• Small businesses and home enterprises (p. 142)

Be able to present a profile of **three** types of processed foods:

1. A food that **undergoes extensive processing**. *Example:* milling of wheat to produce flour, production of vegetable oil from seeds and nuts.
2. A food **processed to extend shelf life**. *Example:* processing of milk.
3. A **value-added food**. *Example:* production of margarine, cheese or a cook-chill product.

Food profiles

Food profile 1. A food that undergoes extensive processing – Wheat/flour

Flour may be made from wheat, barley, rice, rye, etc.

Uses: baking, thickening sauces, coating food.

LINK

- Food commodities: cereals (p. 116)

THE MILLING PROCESS

Preparing Grains
Weighing and drying after harvesting.

Cleaning
Wheat is screened, sorted and washed to remove dirt, dust and straw; magnets remove metal particles if present in the grain.

Conditioning
Grains are dried and conditioned to adjust the moisture content. This softens the bran and aids the release of the white endosperm.

Blending
Wheats are mixed to form a 'grist' for the required type of flour.

Break rolling
Metal rollers are used to split open the grain (wholemeal flour).

Sieving/sifting
Flour is separated into 'first break flour', 'middlings' and 'coarse bran'. Germ and bran are removed during sieving.

Rolling and sieving
Endosperm is passed through a series of rollers until the germ and bran are removed.

Air classifying
Air is used to lighten the flour and control the protein quality.

Additives
Bleaching agents, improvers and nutrients are added.

Weighing, packing and distribution

Food profile 2. A food that undergoes processing to extend shelf life – Milk

Milk is a perfect medium for microbial growth. Processing delays spoilage and extends shelf life. Processing is carried out in two stages:

1. **Homogenisation** develops a uniform consistency.
2. **Heat treatments** destroy pathogenic bacteria and increase shelf life.

Homogenisation distributes fat globules evenly throughout the milk. Milk is heated to 60°C, forced through tiny valves to make the fat globules smaller and to suspend them evenly in the milk. Homogenised milk then undergoes a heat treatment.

Heat treatments to extend shelf life:

1. **Pasteurisation:** Milk is heated to 72°C for 25 seconds (HRST), cooled rapidly to below 10°C and sealed in sterilised containers. All pathogenic and some souring bacteria are destroyed. There is little change in texture and flavour.
2. **Sterilisation:** homogenised milk is bottled and sealed, heat-treated to 110°C for 30 minutes. Milk is sterilised in two ways: batch process; and continuous process. Milk will keep for months as all bacteria are destroyed. Milk is sweeter and creamier.
3. **Ultra-heat treated (UHT):** Milk is heated to 132°C for one to three seconds, cooled rapidly, packed into sterile containers and sealed. UHT milk keeps for months because all bacteria and their spores are destroyed. The flavour changes and vitamins C and B_1 are lost.
4. **Dehydration:** Milk is homogenised, pasteurised and evaporated to 60% of its volume, spray or roller dried and packed. Moisture is not present to support the growth of microbes. It has a reduced fat content, and loss of vitamins C and B.
5. **Evaporation:** Pasteurised milk is evaporated to half its volume, homogenised, sealed and sterilised at 115°C for 20 minutes in sealed cans. It keeps indefinitely, has a sweet cooked flavour and a creamy colour. There is a loss of vitamins C and B_1.
6. **Condensed:** Milk is homogenised, pasteurised, 15% sugar added, and its volume reduced to one-third; it is canned, sealed and sterilised at 115°C for 15 minutes. All bacteria, vitamins C and B-group are destroyed. The low moisture content and increased levels of sugar create an unsuitable environment for microbial growth.

> **LINK**
> - Food commodities: milk (p. 100)

> **exam focus**
> Revise the procedure involved in producing dehydrated milk.

Food profile 3. Processing food to add value – Cook-chill foodstuffs

Foods are prepared in **two** ways:

1. Cook-chill method.
2. Cook-pasteurise-chill method.

Advantages:

- Extends shelf life, saves time and energy.
- Low temperatures prevent microbial growth.

Disadvantage:

- Some loss of vitamin C.

Strict hygienic conditions are in place at all stages of the cook-chill method.

Cook-chill method

1. Ingredients are prepared and cooked immediately.
2. Food is divided into portion sizes in containers.
3. Containers are heat sealed.
4. Food is chilled rapidly to 3°C within 30 minutes of cooking.
5. Chilling is completed within a total time of 90 minutes.
6. Food is stored between −1°C and 3°C.
7. Food is transported in refrigerated conditions to the shop and stored in a chilled cabinet at ≤3°C.

Cook-pasteurise-chill method

1. Food is prepared, cooked and divided into portions.
2. Hot foods are put into flexible containers.
3. Containers are heat sealed and a partial vacuum forms.
4. Food is pasteurised to 80°C for 10 minutes.
5. Food is chilled to 3°C and stored between −1°C and 3°C.
6. Food is transported in refrigerated conditions.
7. Food is stored in a chilled cabinet in the shop.
8. Shelf life is between two and three weeks.

4. Functional foods

Functional foods contain an ingredient that gives a health benefit above the food's own nutritive value. They benefit the gut, bones, heart and immune system.

New ingredient	Examples	Health-promoting property/benefit
Plant sterols	Benecol, Flora Pro-activ	Reduce build-up of cholesterol and risk of CHD
Probiotics	Bio-yoghurt, yoghurt drinks, e.g. Activia, Vitality	Improve the digestive system and immune system health
Omega-3 fatty acids	Milk, e.g. Supermilk omega-3 enriched eggs, milk	May reduce risk of cholesterol build-up and CHD
Folic acid	Breakfast cereal, bread, milk (fortified food)	Reduces risk of neural tube defects, e.g. spina bifida

5. Genetically modified (GM) foods

- A GM food is one in which the DNA has been altered.
- A particular characteristic is isolated and transferred to another plant.
- Testing on GM foods is extensive.
- Potential to produce foods to benefit consumers.

GM foods are monitored by the Food Safety Authority of Ireland (FSAI) and European Food Safety Authority (EFSA). Some processed foods sold in Ireland may have GM ingredients, e.g. soya, maize, rapeseed oil.

LINKS

- Consumer responsibilities (p. 257)
- Food Safety Authority of Ireland (p. 139)
- Food legislation: EU (p. 204)

Exam questions and sample answers

Higher Level 2016, Section A, Q6   (6 marks)

Write a note on **two** of the following:

- Genetically modified food:
  Foods which have their DNA altered to change the characteristics of the food and benefits the producer and consumer e.g. resistance to disease. EU regulations apply. Food must be labelled GM if it has been produced from GM soya or maize, contaminated with more than 1% GM soya or maize or contains any ingredients GM modified.

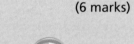

exam focus

Choose **two** of the three suggested in your answer.

- Organic food/produce:
  Food grown without the use of chemical fertilisers, pesticides or preservatives, organic farming rules must be implemented for an organic certificate to be awarded and symbols displayed on products. Organic products are more expensive than non-organic.

- Added-value food:
  Raw basic materials are processed to produce quality new products, e.g. cheese, breads, cook-chill products. It benefits producers, manufacturers and consumer demands for new products.

Higher Level 2014, Section A, Q7   (6 marks)

(a) Explain the term 'functional food'.

Foods made from natural ingredients with added ingredients to increase health benefits above the original nutritive value and when eaten have a specific function.

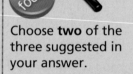

LINK

- Functional foods (p. 151)

(b) Outline **two** health benefits of including functional foods in the diet.
- *Reduces cholesterol levels (plant sterols in spreads)*
- *Improves the digestive system (probiotics in yoghurts)*

Ordinary Level 2008, Section A, Q7 (6 marks)

(a) Explain the term 'fortified' in relation to food processing.

Fortified foods have nutrients added to improve the food's nutritive value or to replace nutrients lost during processing.

(b) Name **two** fortified foods.
- *Milk – added vitamins (Supermilk)*
- *Breakfast cereals – added folic acid*

Higher Level 2011, Section B, Q3 (b) HL

(b) Profile a food of your choice that has undergone extensive processing.
(20 marks)

Give details of **each** of the following:
- Name of product (2 marks)
- Stages of production (5 points × 2 marks each)
- Packaging (2 points × 2 marks each)
- Labelling (2 points × 2 marks each)

> **LINK**
> - Milling of flour (p. 149)

Food of choice: *Wheat: extensively processed to produce flour.*

Food packaging

Packaging is used to:

1. Prevent dehydration, oxidation and contamination.
2. Prevent the transfer of flavours.
3. Extend shelf life of food, prevent waste and spoilage.
4. Prevent damage during storage and transportation.

> **OTHER FUNCTIONS OF PACKAGING:**
> - To improve marketing of products.
> - To provide consumers with nutritional information, use by dates, storage and cooking instructions.

Properties of good packaging

- Is safe, non-toxic, hygienic, easy to open/close.
- Looks attractive, is functional and economical to manufacture.
- Is environmentally friendly, biodegradable or recyclable.
- Is durable, strong, odourless, moisture/vapour-proof.
- Controls the movement of micro-organisms.

Types of packaging

Glass

Advantages	• Useful, hygienic, easily sterilised • Rigid/transparent, displays contents • Protects against contaminants, re-sealable • Suited to heat treatments, does not react with food • Easily moulded in a variety of colours, shapes, sizes
Disadvantages	Fragile, breaks easily, heavy to transport
Uses	Preserves, pickles, mayonnaise, sauces

Metal

Examples: aerosols, cans, aluminium foil, foil bags, foil containers.

Advantages	• Good variety of types and uses • Convenient, easy to store/transport • Foods can be sterilised in container • Internal lacquers may be applied • Protected from micro-organisms, gases, moisture
Disadvantages	Unsuitable for use in microwave ovens
Uses	**Tin:** fish, meat, fruit, vegetables **Aluminium cans:** beer, soft drinks **Aluminium foil:** for wrapping food, foil bags and foil containers

Paper

Advantages	• Variety of forms, weight and uses • Economical to produce and print on • Biodegradable, eco-friendly • Waxed cartons are strong and durable • Some are made heat-resistant and waterproof
Disadvantages	• Can be fragile • Absorbs moisture, falls apart • Most types cannot be resealed
Uses	**Waxed paper:** lining cake tins **Greaseproof paper:** wrapping foods **Paper bags:** flour, sugar **Cardboard:** outer covering for dry foods **Waxed cartons:** fresh soup, cream

Flexible packaging

Examples: cellulose films, polyethylene wrapping, polystyrene and PET bottles.

Advantages	<ul><li>Variety of weights, sizes, forms and uses</li><li>Some can be heat sealed</li><li>Moisture proof</li><li>Easy to handle, unbreakable</li></ul>
Disadvantages	<ul><li>Some plastics can contaminate foods</li><li>Not eco-friendly, non-biodegradable, limited recycling</li><li>Produced from non-renewable resource</li></ul>
Uses	To cover food, bottles, food trays, freezer containers, containers for custard, margarine, yoghurt, freezer bags, boil-in-the-bag foods

Research the dangers posed by micro-plastics entering the food chain.

Revise the suitability for purpose of each material used in packaging on the environment.

Environmental impact of packaging

1. **Glass:** reusable, recyclable, bottle banks save on materials, energy, landfill.
2. **Metals:** high production/transport costs, non-biodegradable; some are recyclable.
3. **Aerosols** with CFCs damage the environment (the ozone layer).
4. **Paper:** biodegradable, cheap to produce/transport, can be recycled.
5. **Plastics:** cause litter and pollution, limited recycling, plastic goes into landfill.

Problems caused by packaging

1. Use of non-renewable valuable resources.
2. High energy costs, e.g. production and transport.
3. Waste disposal and collection.
4. Litter in urban and rural areas, along roadsides.
5. Materials in landfills can be toxic.

Plastic pollution on land and in oceans is a danger to people and wildlife.

LINKS
- Consumer choice (p. 254)
- Food safety and hygiene (p. 195)

Reducing the environmental impact of packaging

- Reuse, recycle, and refuse excessive packaging.
- Buy unpackaged products, e.g. fruits/vegetables.
- Use cloth shopping bags instead of plastic bags.
- Bring bottles, etc. to recycling banks.
- Send paper for recycling (paper bins) – compost food waste and organic packaging.

Revise PET plastics.

LINK

- Consumer responsibilities (p. 257)

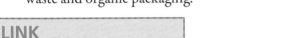

key point

Plastic bag usage reduced by approximately 90% due to introduction of plastic bag levy.

Exam questions and sample answers
Higher Level 2017, Section A, Q5 (6 marks)

Explain **each** of the following:

Modified atmosphere packaging (MAP)

- *Air is removed from package/container and replaced with a controlled mix of gases (carbon dioxide, nitrogen, oxygen).*
- *Pack is heat sealed. This action slows down the growth of food-spoiling micro-organisms.*
- *Shelf-life of food is improved and lengthened.*

Biodegradable packaging

- *Refers to the ability of the packaging material to break down into natural materials within a short time after disposal. Examples: paper bags, cardboard.*

LINK

- Food packaging (pp. 153)

Ordinary Level 2015, Section A, Q8 (6 marks)

List **two** desirable characteristics (qualities) of food packaging materials.

- *Easy to open and easy to re-seal to keep food in peak condition.*
- *Biodegradable or recyclable (environmentally friendly).*

Name **two** materials used to package food.

- *Glass (jars, bottles, food containers)*
- *Polystyrene (cups, food containers)*

Ordinary Level 2016, Section B, Q1 (d) (4 points × 5 marks = 20 marks)

Discuss **four** ways consumers can be environmentally aware when shopping and buying food for family meals.

- *Buy fruit and vegetables loose without plastic or netting.*

- Choose products in biodegradable or recyclable packaging with eco-friendly labels.
- Always use reusable shopping bags when shopping for food.
- Buy in bulk to reduce amount of packaging and shopping trips.

Ordinary Level 2012, Section B, Q1 (d)

(d) Explain the benefit to the consumer of each item included on food packaging.

(5 points × 4 marks = 20 marks)

List of ingredients:
Ingredients are listed in descending order to inform consumers of the main ingredients. It identifies ingredients that are allergens to allow consumers to cater for special dietary needs, e.g. vegetarian, diabetic, coeliac, etc., and lists additives, e.g. sweeteners and flavourings.

List the five points and explain each in more detail.

Weight:
Net weight is shown in metric measurements. Eggs are graded according to size. This enables consumers to plan for the number of servings and make comparisons with other brands of the same weight.

Nutritional information:
Claims on food must be true, e.g. low-fat, low-salt, gluten-free. Fortified foods must be clearly labelled listing the added nutrients, e.g. vitamin D, calcium. This allows consumers to make informed decisions regarding the nutritional value of meals.

Best-before date:
This is used on non-perishable foods with a long shelf-life (length varies) and must be clearly labelled. Consumers can buy food when it is at its best and plan meals in advance.

Country of origin:
Consumers may decide to choose Irish-produced food rather than products transported over long distances; an absence of name, address of manufacturer, producer and seller can mislead consumers.

Food labelling

Reasons for labelling food

1. To provide information to consumers (informed choices).
2. To give nutritional information.
3. To identify ingredients relevant to dietary conditions, e.g. coeliac and allergies.
4. To identify additives and methods of processing.
5. To outline storage and cooking instructions.
6. To sell products.

New EU regulations in December 2014 established general principles, requirements and responsibilities regarding information, labelling and nutritional information.

Labelling regulations (packaged and non-packaged foods)

Pre-packed foods	

Labels must be easy to see, clear, truthful, not misleading, legible and indelible, written in the language of country of origin. | ● Name of product/food
● List of ingredients in descending order of weight
● Allergens, if present in the finished product (e.g. gluten, nuts)
● Additives including flavourings and sweeteners
● Quantity of specific ingredients, e.g. % of meat in sausages
● Date indication:
 – Best before: for non-perishable long shelf-life foods
 – Use-by date: for highly perishable foods
● Storage conditions/conditions of use
● Business name and address of food manufacturer/producer in the EU
● Place of origin: mandatory (an omission might mislead consumers)
● Instructions for use: cooking, reheating, preparation, thorough cooking of minced meat, etc.
● Nutritional information |
| **Non-packaged or loose foodstuffs** | Information must be displayed at the point of sale:
● Name of food
● Origin, class and variety
● Metric unit price, e.g. price per kg |

Nutritional labelling

1. Provides consumers with information regarding energy value, nutritive value, amounts of each nutrient, sugar, salt and supplementary nutrients.
2. Nutritional content is shown per 100 g/100 ml to allow for easy comparison between products.

key point

Nutritional declaration for pre-packed food became mandatory in December 2016.

LINKS

● Dietary guidelines (p. 53)
● Special diets (p. 55)
● Food commodities (p. 81)
● Family resource management (p. 207)

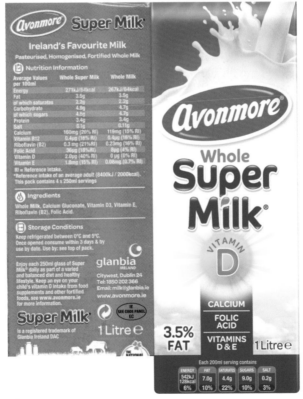

Price and labels

- Selling price must be displayed.
- For pre-packaged foodstuffs, unit price and selling price must be included.
- Unit price per kg/per litre must be displayed beside loose foodstuffs.

Bar codes

A bar code is a series of lines and spaces which contains product information (name, price, brand name) that can be read by a scanner. This information is printed on the customer's receipt and the shop's stock records are adjusted.

Exam questions and sample answers

Ordinary Level 2014, Section B, Q3 (c)

(c) Evaluate the role of food labelling in assisting the consumer when purchasing convenience soups. (3 points × 4 marks = 12 marks)

- *Informs consumers if any of the ingredients have been genetically modified or irradiated.*
- *Informs consumers if any allergens are present, e.g. eggs, milk, nuts, fish, wheat.*
- *Labels provide information on storage, preparation and cooking of products.*

Higher Level 2017, Section B, Q2 (b)

(b) Describe the production, packaging and labelling of cheese. (18 marks)

Cheese production: (7 stages × 2 marks = 14 marks)

LINK
- Cheese (p. 106)

Note the allocation of marks in this question. Most marks are awarded for the stages of production.

Packaging: *Wrapped in waxed paper, plastic tubs* (2 marks)

Labelling: *Type of cheese; brand, nutritional information, quantity, date-stamp* (2 marks)

Higher Level 2016, Section B, Q 3 (c)   (18 marks)

(c) Evaluate the role of packaging/labelling in relation to the following:

Suitability for purpose: (2 points × 3 marks = 6 marks)

- *Protects foods from moisture, micro-organisms, cross-contamination.*
- *Some containers may be printed on, removing the need for extra labels.*

Environmental impact: (2 points × 3 marks = 6 marks)
- *Plastic is made from a non-renewable resource and is non-biodegradable.*
- *Paper is from a sustainable resource, is biodegradable and recyclable.*

Note equal marks are allocated to each area.

Source of consumer information: (2 points × 3 marks)
- *Product labels display ingredients, nutritional value and allergy information.*
- *Social media advertising, electronic newsletters from retailers.*

Food additives and food contaminants

Food additives

Additives are ingredients added to food to improve colour, flavour, texture, shelf life and nutritional value. They must fulfil acceptable and useful functions.

This section could be examined in Section A or Section B.

- **Direct additives** are added to foods for specific beneficial reasons, e.g. nutritive value.
- **Indirect additives** become part of a product due to handling, packaging or storage.

Main types and sources

Natural	Plants and animals, e.g. chlorophyll
Nature identical	Identical to a natural substance but synthetically made, e.g. ascorbic acid
Artificial	Synthetically made, e.g. esters

Advantages of additives

1. Enhance colour, flavour and texture.
2. Inhibit action of enzymes and micro-organisms.
3. Improve or increase shelf life of food.
4. Maintain or supplement nutritional value.
5. Increase the variety of foods available throughout the year.

Disadvantages of additives

1. May deceive consumers (colours, flavours, textures).
2. Side effects (allergies, hyperactivity, toxin build-up).
3. Cumulative effects on humans not known.
4. Bitter aftertaste left by some additives.

LINKS
- Food choices (p. 2)
- Consumer choice (p. 254)

Classification and examples of additives (direct)

Antioxidants (E300–E399)
Functions:

1. To prevent oxidative rancidity (fats and oils).
2. To prevent oxidative discolouring (fruits/vegetables).

Type	Examples: sources and uses
Natural	Vitamin C – from fruits/vegetables. *Uses:* fruit products, jams Vitamin E – from seeds, nuts. *Uses:* vegetable oils
Synthetic	Butylated Hydroxytoluene (chewing gum) – BHT Butylated Hydroxyanisole (stock cubes) – BHA

Colourings (E100–E199)
Functions:

1. To improve the natural colour of food.
2. To improve the colour of processed/preserved foods.
3. To replace colours lost during processing.
4. To respond to consumer demand.

Class	Source	Use
Natural		
Cochineal (red) E120	Cactus insects	Ketchup, red jelly
Chlorophyll (green) E140	Plants	Canned vegetables
Carotene (orange) E160	Carrots	Soft drinks
Caramel (brown) E150	Caramelised carbohydrates	Sauces, gravies
Artificial		
Amaranth (purple) E123	Coal tar	Blackcurrant products
Tartrazine (yellow) E102	Coal tar	Soft drinks
Sunset yellow E110	Coal tar	Sweets, chewing gum

Flavourings (no E numbers)

Functions:

1. To enhance/improve the flavour of food.
2. To change the flavour of food.
3. To replace/add flavour lost in processing.

Class	Source	Use
Natural		
Sugar	Beet, cane, fruit	Tinned beans, cereals, jams
Salt	Rock or sea salt	Butter, cheese
Spices	Seeds, fruit, bark, roots	Convenience foods
Herbs	Leaves, seeds, flowers	Stocks, soups, sauces

Sweeteners

Function:

To sweeten food.

Class	Source	Use
Natural		
Fructose	Fruit	Tinned peas
Sucrose	Beet, cane	Tinned fruit, sweets, biscuits
Glucose	Fruit, honey	Tinned fruit
Artificial – Intense sweeteners, used in small amounts		
Aspartame E951	Produced in laboratories	Sweeteners (e.g. Canderel), diet drinks and desserts
Saccharin	Produced in laboratories	Sweetener (e.g. Hermesetas), diet drinks
Artificial – bulk sweeteners, used in large quantities		
Mannitol E421	Produced in laboratories	Sugar-free confectionery, chewing gum
Sorbitol E420	Produced in laboratories	Sugar-free confectionery, jam
Xylitol	Produced in laboratories	Sugar-free chewing gum

Preservatives (E200–E299)

Functions:

1. To inhibit growth of enzymes and micro-organisms.
2. To increase/extend shelf life of foods.
3. To increase the variety of foods available.
4. To provide food 'out of season'.
5. To prevent waste.

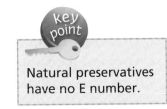

key point

Natural preservatives have no E number.

Class	Source	Use
Natural		
Salt	Rock salt, sea salt	Bacon, preserves (e.g. pickles)
Sugar	Beet, cane	Sweets, preserves (e.g. jams)
Spices	Seeds, fruits, bark	Cakes, biscuits, preserves
Vinegar	Fermentation	Preserves (e.g. pickles, chutneys)
Alcohol	Fermentation	Cakes, fruit
Smoke	Burning wood	Fish, meat, cheese
Artificial		
Sorbic acid E200	Produced in laboratories	Cheese, dried fruit, baked goods
Sulphur dioxide E220	Produced in laboratories	Dried fruit, fruit juice
Benzoic acid E210	Produced in laboratories	Coffee, acidic fruit juices

Nutritional supplements

Functions:

1. To improve the nutritive value of food.
2. To replace nutrients lost during processing.
3. To satisfy consumer demand for healthier products.

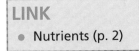

LINK

- Nutrients (p. 2)

Nutrient	Uses – added to:
Vitamins A and D	Low-fat milk, super milk, margarine
B-group vitamins	Breakfast cereals, flour, TVP
Vitamin C	Fruit drinks
Iron	Breakfast cereals
Calcium	Flour, milk

Physical conditioning agents (E400–E499)

HL

Main agents	Functions and uses
Anti-caking	Prevents lumps forming in dried foods *Uses:* cake mixes, powdered milk
Anti-foaming	Prevents foaming and a scum forming *Uses:* packet soups
Buffers	Control pH in a food
Bulking agents	Add bulk (but not energy value) to food *Uses:* sauces, baked goods
Emulsifiers	To make permanent emulsions, e.g. lecithin, alginates, pectin *Uses:* desserts, ice cream, mayonnaise
Glazing agents	Give a shiny appearance, seal and prevent food drying out *Uses:* confectionery
Humectants	Prevent foods drying out, e.g. sorbitol, mannitol *Uses:* confectionery, sweets
Stabilisers	Prevent emulsions separating, e.g. carrageen, guar gum *Uses:* baked goods, ice cream

Legal control of food additives

1. Approved substances undergo testing for safety.
2. Allocation of an E number confirms safety of additive.
3. The EU controls the use and amounts of additives.
4. EU directives do not include flavourings or nutritive additives.
5. Food additives must:
   - Perform a useful purpose.
   - Be safe.
   - Not reduce the nutritive value of the food.
   - Not mislead the consumer.
   - Not disguise faulty processing.
   - Comply with the regulations.

Indirect additives – contaminants

Contaminants are substances which accidentally enter the food chain and can potentially cause damage to humans.

LINKS

- Lipids (p. 23)
- Vitamins (p. 32)
- Food processing (p. 147)
- Food packaging (p. 153)
- Food safety and hygiene (p. 195)

exam focus

Revise the effects of contaminants on humans.

Classification, sources and examples

Class	Sources and examples
Endogenous plant toxins	● *Cyanide:* traces in beans, peas ● *Protease inhibitors:* kidney beans, chickpeas
Endogenous animal toxins	● Fish with poisonous tissue (fish poisoning) ● Shellfish contaminated with toxic algae (paralytic)
Microbial toxins	**Bacterial toxins** and **mycotoxins** from moulds
Toxic residues	● Metal residues: aluminium, lead ● Industrial residues: dioxins ● Agricultural residues: antibiotics, pesticides ● Radioactive residues: fallout, waste
Chemicals from food processing	● Carcinogens: smoked food products, by-product of cooking methods ● Fumigants: used in the sterilisation of food

LINKS

- Food spoilage – microbiology (p. 167)
- Food safety and hygiene (p. 195)
- Consumer protection (p. 263)

OTHER CONTAMINANTS INCLUDE:

Insecticides, herbicides, fungicides, plastics from packaging, metals from soil, water and cooking equipment, dust, dirt, human hair and skin, broken glass, etc.

Exam questions and sample answers

Higher Level 2011, Section B, Q2 (b), (c)

(b) Classify artificial sweeteners and give **one** example of each. (12 marks)

Classification	Example
Bulk sweeteners	*Sorbitol (used in diabetic foods)*
Intense sweeteners	*Aspartame, e.g. Canderel sweetener*

(c) Outline the uses of sweeteners in food manufacture.

(2 points × 4 marks = 8 marks)

- *Production of diabetic foods and confectionery*
- *Used instead of sugar in low-calorie and slimming foods/products*

Ordinary Level 2017, Section A, Q8 (6 marks)

Indicate with a tick (✓) whether each of the following statements is true or false.

	True	False
Food additives prolong (increase) the shelf-life of foods.	✓	
Artificial colourings are permitted in baby foods.		✓
The use of food additives is regulated by EU legislation.	✓	

Ordinary Level 2012, Section A, Q7 (6 marks)

(a) Explain the term food additive.

Any natural or artificial substance added to food during the manufacturing process to improve nutritive value, colour, flavour, texture and shelf-life.

(b) State **two** disadvantage of using additives in food.
- *May deceive consumers into thinking food is of a higher quality and fresher.*
- *May destroy nutrients, e.g. vitamins.*

Higher Level 2011, Section A, Q6 (6 marks)

Complete the following table in relation to food additives.

	Example	Function	Example of use
Antioxidants	*Vitamins A, C, E*	*Prevents oxidation*	*Cooking oils*

Food spoilage – microbiology

There are **three groups** of micro-organism: fungi, bacteria and viruses.

Factors influencing the growth of micro-organisms

Only fungi and bacteria are examined in detail.

Temperature	Mesophiles: optimum 25–45°C
	Psychrophiles: optimum −5 – +20°C
	Thermophiles: ideal above 45°C
	Danger zone = 5–65°C
Food/nutrients	• Saprophytes feed on decaying or dead matter, e.g. food/soil
	• Parasites feed on living matter, e.g. humans/animals
	• Micro-organisms need food for energy and growth
	• Yeasts need carbohydrate-rich foods
	• Nutrients are absorbed via cell walls

Oxygen	*Aerobic:* need oxygen for growth
	Anaerobic: do not need oxygen
	Facultative: grow with or without oxygen
	Microaerophilic: grow in a reduced oxygen environment
Correct pH level	● Bacteria prefer a neutral pH
	● Moulds and yeasts prefer a slightly acidic pH
Moisture (needed to dissolve foods for use)	● Prefer high-water food sources
	● Cannot use ice, frozen or dried foods
	● Grow best in foods with a water activity above 0.61aw
Time	In favourable conditions, bacteria will multiply every 20 minutes
Light	● Grow best without light
	● Destroyed by sunlight

Moulds – multicellular fungi

Characteristics

- Simple plants.
- Cannot manufacture own food; do not contain chlorophyll.
- Saprophytic fungi survive on dead matter, e.g. bread.
- Parasitic fungi feed on living matter, e.g. ringworm.

Competitive effects: when bacteria compete with each other for food, oxygen and moisture.

Mutualism: when two organisms benefit from growing near each other.

Classification

Class	Examples
Ascomycetes	Aspergillus, Penicillium
Phycomycetes	Mucor, rhizopus
Basidiomycetes	Mushrooms – large fungi
Saccharomycetes	Yeast

Moulds are multi-cellular, spore-forming fungi.

Consisting of many cells

Conditions needed for growth of moulds

Food	Most are saprophytes; grow on a variety of foods
	Examples: bread, fruit, cheese
Moisture	Prefer moist, humid conditions and moist foods
Oxygen	Aerobic; grow on surface of food, e.g. bread
Warmth	Most are mesophiles; freezing inactivates growth; moulds destroyed by cooking above 75°C

pH level	pH 4–6 (slightly acidic), growth inhibited by very alkaline or acidic environment
Time	Need time to grow and multiply
Light	Most grow best without light

Basic Structure

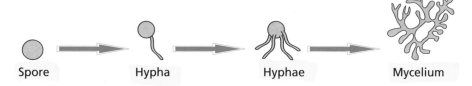

Spore — Hypha — Hyphae — Mycelium

Asexual reproduction

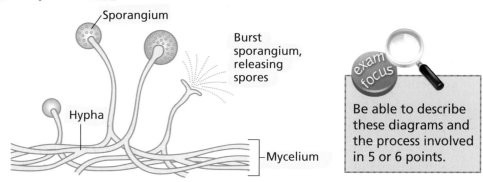

Sporangium

Burst sporangium, releasing spores

Hypha

Mycelium

> **exam focus**
>
> Be able to describe these diagrams and the process involved in 5 or 6 points.

Sexual reproduction

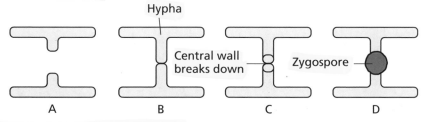

Hypha

Central wall breaks down

Zygospore

A   B   C   D

Common food spoilage moulds

Classification	Example	Details	Food sources
Ascomycetes 20°C to 25°C Septate (cross walls)	Aspergillus	• Saprophytic • Asexual • Conidia • Green-grey or black	• Cereals • Fruit • Black rot on fruit and vegetables
	Penicillium (several species)	• Saprophytic • Asexual • Conidia • Green-blue • *Uses:* blue cheese, antibiotics	• Cheese • Fruit • Bread

Phycomycetes 30°C most favourable Non-septate	Mucor	• Saprophytic • Asexual/sexual • White hyphae • Grey sporangium	• Bread • Meat • Cheese • Soil
	Rhizopus	• Saprophytic • Asexual • White hyphae • Black sporangium	• Bread • Rot on fruits and vegetables

Large fungi – basidiomycetes

Fungi are visible to the naked eye. Some are edible; others are poisonous. *Examples:* commercial varieties (button, oyster, porcini), wild field mushrooms, truffles (grow underground).

Development of a mushroom

- A single spore develops hyphae, which form a mycelium.
- Organic material underneath the soil provides food.
- A stalk develops and pushes out of the ground.
- A closed cap forms on top of the stalk with gills underneath.
- Cap swells and bursts open, and pink gills become visible.
- Gills darken, basidia form and spores are released from between gills onto the ground and into the air.

Yeast – saccharomycetes

Single one cell
- Unicellular facultative, saphrophytic fungi, destroyed by high temperatures.
- Found in air, on fruit skins, in slightly sweet and acidic foods.
- Important source of B-group vitamins, used in health products, food supplements.
- Used to produce bread, vinegar, wine and beer.

Environmental conditions for growth

Food	Feed on carbohydrate foods, e.g. sugars
Moisture	Need moisture/moist conditions to grow
Oxygen	Facultative, survives with or without oxygen
Warmth	Ideal temperature range is 25–30°C, killed above 60°C, inactivated at low temperatures
pH level	Prefers acid environment
Time	Needs time to multiply

Basic structure

Thin, single outer cell walls, filled with cytoplasm containing a nucleus, one vacuole and food storage granules.

Reproduction

Yeast reproduces asexually by the process called **budding**.

Parent cell · Bulge · Nucleus moves toward bulge · *splits in 2* · Nucleus Nucleus · Parent cell Bud

Bulge grows · *cell membrane cell* · *food storage* · *cell membrane* · *2 new cells form* · Wall

Wall · Nucleus · Vacuoles · *leus* · *food storage* · *cytoplasm cell wall* · *vacuole* · Granular Cytoplasm · Bud · Nucleus divides

LINK
- Fermentation (pp. 128, 190)

key point

The bud separates completely from the parent cell.

Uses of fungi

Food production, brewing and bread-making, antibiotics, supplements, novel protein foods, cooking.

Disadvantages of fungi

1. Cause food spoilage.
2. Some are poisonous, e.g. amanita.
3. Cause plant diseases, e.g. potato blight.
4. Cause human diseases, e.g. ringworm, athlete's foot.

Bacteria

Bacteria:

- Are small, single-celled micro-organisms.
- May be parasites or saprophytes, pathogenic or non-pathogenic.

Sources: air, animals, foods, plants, soil and water.

exam focus

Revise the guidelines to prevent food spoilage by moulds and yeast.

Environmental conditions for growth of bacteria

Food	*Parasitic bacteria* feed on living matter *Saprophytic bacteria* feed on dead or decaying matter
Moisture	Need a good supply of moisture in liquid form for growth, e.g. milk, stew, cream
Oxygen	Needs vary; most are aerobic, some are anaerobic, others facultative
Warmth	Extensive range of temperature. Each has a maximum, minimum and ideal range (psychrophile, mesophile, thermophile)
pH level	Most prefer a near neutral pH range
Time	Bacteria double every 20 minutes but rapid growth is limited by the extent of the food sources available
Light	Need darkness; destroyed by ultra-violet rays of the sun

Structure of bacterial cells

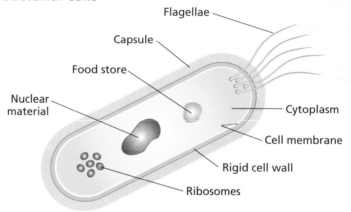

Reproduction

- Bacteria reproduce asexually by binary fission.
- Cells grow and divide into two separate parts.
- A cell wall is formed and the two cells separate.
- Rapid growth ends when bacteria run out of food, oxygen, moisture and space.
- Waste toxins build up and prevent further growth.

Growth curve

The time between each division is referred to as **generation time** (about 20 minutes). Overcrowding results in bacteria competing for food, oxygen and moisture, and death eventually results.

The **growth curve of bacteria** is divided into four phases:

- Lag phase: bacteria are adapting to new environment (little growth).
- Log phase: bacteria multiply rapidly, exponential growth.
- Stationary phase: overcrowding, no increase.
- Decline phase: toxins building up, bacteria numbers reducing and dying off.

Growth curve of micro-organisms

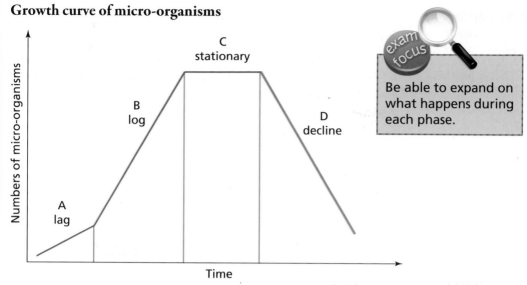

Be able to expand on what happens during each phase.

Classification

Bacteria can be classified according to shape or gram staining.

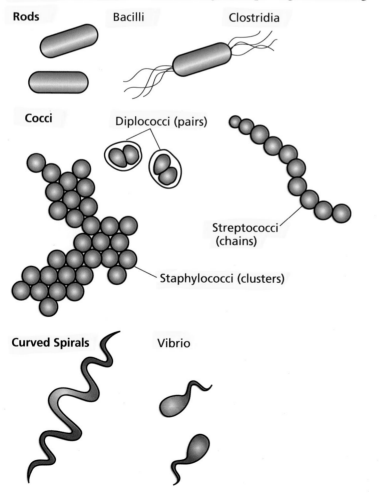

Bacillus (rod-shaped)	1. *Bacilli* – arranged singly, e.g. *Salmonella, E. coli, Listeria*
	2. *Clostridia* – arranged in chains, e.g. *Clostridium botulinum, Clostridium perfringens*
Coccus (round)	1. *Coccus* (single), e.g. meningitis
	2. *Diplococci* (pairs), e.g. pneumonia
	3. *Streptococci* (chains), e.g. tonsillitis
	4. *Staphylocci* (clusters), e.g. food poisoning
Curved	1. *Vibrios* – short, comma-shaped, e.g. cholera
	2. *Spirilla* – long, spiral, e.g. syphilis

Gram-staining results

Bacteria can be classified into two groups:

1. Gram-positive (*Clostridia, Streptococci*).
2. Gram-negative (*E. coli, Salmonella*).

exam focus

Revise the method for gram-staining.

Gram-positive bacteria	Gram-negative bacteria
Blue-black colour	Reddish, the colour of iodine
Thick single-cell wall	Cell wall has two thin layers
2% lipid in cell wall	20% lipid in cell wall
Generally aerobic	Aerobic and anaerobic
Non-mobile (no flagellae)	Mobile – have flagellae
Spore forming	Do not produce spores
Little resistance to antibiotics	High resistance to antibiotics

Advantages of bacteria

1. Provide starter cultures for cheese, yoghurt, vinegar.
2. Produce vitamins B and K in human gut.
3. Involved in breaking down waste matter.
4. Used in production of food supplements.

LINK
- Food spoilage and food poisoning (p. 177)

Disadvantages of bacteria

1. Responsible for food poisoning.
2. Cause diseases in plants, animals and humans.
3. Involved in food spoilage (e.g. sour milk).
4. Cause of dental caries/tooth decay.

LINKS
- Cheese (p. 106)
- Yoghurt (p. 104)
- Alternative protein foods – novel proteins (p. 98)

▷ Endospores

- Tough dormant cells produced by bacilli and clostridia.
- Form when conditions are unfavourable for growth.
- Formed within bacterial cells, surrounded by a thick protein wall.
- Resistant to cold, heat and some chemicals.
- Destroyed by dry heat (150°C for one hour) or steam (121°C for 15 minutes).

Toxins (cause food poisoning)

- Endotoxins
- Enterotoxins
- Exotoxins
- Mycotoxins

LINK

- Indirect additives – contaminants (p. 165)

Viruses

Viruses are small non-cellular micro-organisms that are responsible for a range of diseases.

Examples:

- SRV – small round structured viruses: shellfish.
- BSE (bovine spongiform encephalopathy) – affects cattle.
- NvCJD (new variant Creutzfeldt-Jakob disease) – human form of BSE.

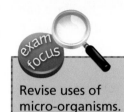

Revise uses of micro-organisms.

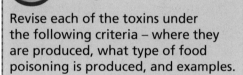

Revise each of the toxins under the following criteria – where they are produced, what type of food poisoning is produced, and examples.

Exam questions and sample answers

Higher Level 2014, Section A, Q8 (6 marks)

Complete the table below in relation to the use of micro-organisms in food production.

Micro-organisms	Use
Lactic acid bacteria	*Cheese, yoghurt*
Lactobacillus bulgaricus	*Yoghurt*
Yeast	*Bread, brewing, wine making*

Ordinary Level 2013, Section A, Q7 (6 marks)

Identify **two** conditions required for the growth of micro-organisms.

   1. Food

   2. Moisture

State **one** use of micro-organisms in food production.

Lactic acid bacteria are used in cheese making.

Higher Level 2015, Section B, Q3 (a)–(c)

(a) Discuss **four** conditions necessary for the growth of moulds.

(4 points × 4 marks = 16 marks)

   1. Food: Most are saprophytes, feed on dead organic matter e.g. bread, cheese, jam, fruit.

2. *Warmth: Most are mesophiles, inactivated by freezing (–18°C), retarded growth below 15°C and in fridge at temperatures below 5°C.*

3. *Oxygen: Aerobic, need oxygen to grow on food surface (jam) or through a structure (bread).*

4. *pH levels: Prefer slightly acidic conditions of pH 4–6, either end of the pH scale inhibits growth.*

The example answers given are only summaries – make sure you can write an answer in full.

(b) Write a detailed account of **one** type of mould with reference to the following:

Name (4 marks)	Description/characteristics (2 × 3 marks)	Asexual Reproduction (4 × 3 marks)
Aspergillus	1. Saprophytic mould 2. Black or green mould 3. Reproduces asexually	1. Mycelium spread out and establish on food source. 2. Hyphae grows upwards out of the mycelium. 3. Conidia (chains of spores) develops at head of hyphae. 4. When ripe, conidia burst, releasing spores into the air to find suitable conditions for new mould growth.

(c) Outline the uses of micro-organisms in food production.

(3 uses × 4 marks = 12 marks)

Choose any **three** from the examples given.

Micro-organism	Use
Yeast	Fermentation: bread-making (yeast breads, sourdough), brewing (beer), winemaking, vinegars
Edible fungi	Truffles are used in the gourmet food production industry Mushrooms in convenience foods, sauces, soups, pre-prepared meals
Bacteria	Meat products (salami, chorizo, pepperoni), fermented dairy products (yoghurt, kefir, buttermilk, sour cream), pickled vegetables, functional foods (probiotic yoghurts), supplements, soya sauce
Moulds	Cheese-making, e.g. blue cheese
Fungi – Fusarium venenatum	Mycoprotein novel protein foods, e.g. Quorn

Food spoilage and food poisoning

The main **causes of food spoilage** are:

1. Loss of moisture.
2. Micro-organisms (moulds, yeasts, bacteria).
3. Action of enzymes.

Loss of moisture:

- Mainly affects fruits and vegetables after harvesting.
- Results in shrinkage, wrinkling and a limp appearance.

exam focus

- Be able to discuss and give examples for each of the causes of food spoilage.
- Revise bacterial and fungi spoilage.
- Revise the guidelines for controlling the action of enzymes on food.

Chemical food poisoning: *caused by* pesticides, antibiotics, chemical contamination of the water supply, accumulation of metals, insecticides and residues from farming and horticulture.

Biological food poisoning: *caused by* poisonous substances found in some foods (e.g. oxalic acid in rhubarb leaves), solanine in green potatoes.

Bacterial food poisoning: *caused by* pathogenic bacteria in food due to unhygienic handling, cross-contamination, contaminated water, etc..

Types of bacterial food poisoning

Go to Higher Level 2014, Section B, Q3 (c); 2013, Section B, Q3.

High-risk foods

Milk, eggs, cooked meats, poultry, reheated food, gravy.

Common pathogenic or food poisoning bacteria

Toxic food poisoning bacteria

1. Clostridium botulinum

Characteristics	• Rod-shaped
	• Gram-positive
	• Forms spores
	• Causes toxic food poisoning – very rare but potentially life-threatening
Habitat/sources	• Soil, decaying fruit and vegetables, untreated water
Environmental factors	• Anaerobic bacteria
	• Optimum temperature 30–37°C
	• Destroyed at 121°C for 15 minutes

High-risk foods	• Low-acid canned foods, improperly canned foods
	• Vacuum-packed foods
	• Smoked fish, fermented fish
Incubation and duration	*Incubation:* 12–36 hours
	Duration: 1–8 days (toxic illness)
	• Mortality rate 5–15%
	• Recovery takes months
Symptoms	Blurred vision, diarrhoea, dizziness, headache, slurred speech, paralysis, death

2. Staphyloccus aureus

Characteristics	• Spherical in shape
	• Arranged in clusters
	• Gram positive
	• Non-spore forming
Habitat/sources	• Nose and throat
	• Unwashed hands
	• Infected skin
Environmental factors	• Facultative
	• Optimum temperature 30–40°C
	• Salt tolerant
High-risk foods	• Unpasteurised milk
	• Cream, milk, custard
	• Cold meats
Incubation and duration	*Incubation:* 2–6 hours
	Duration: 24 hours
Symptoms	Cramps, vomiting, diarrhoea

Infectious food poisoning bacteria

1. Listeria monocytogenes

Characteristics	• Rod-shaped
	• Gram-positive
	• Non-spore forming
	• Multiplies at low temperatures, can survive heat treatments
Habitat/sources	Soil, human and animal waste

Environmental factors	• Facultative
	• Optimum temperature is 30°C (mesophile), can grow at 4–43°C
	• Slightly acidic pH range
	• High moisture content
	• Salt tolerant
High-risk foods	Raw meat and poultry, unpasteurised milk, soft cheese, prepared salads, pâté, cook-chill products, raw vegetables
Incubation and duration	*Incubation:* 1–70 days
	Duration: several days
Symptoms	Fever, diarrhoea, septicaemia, meningitis in newborn babies, may cause miscarriage

2. Escherichia Coli (E. coli)

Characteristics	• Rod-shaped
	• Gram-negative
	• Non-spore forming
	• Causes infectious food poisoning
Habitat/Sources	• Unwashed hands
	• Animal and human intestines
	• Excreta
	• Contaminated water
Environmental factors	• Aerobic
	• Optimum temperature 30–40°C
High-risk foods	• Unpasteurised milk
	• Raw meats
	• Undercooked mince, burgers, salami
Incubation and duration	*Incubation:* 12–24 hours
	Duration: 1–5 days
Symptoms	Abdominal cramps, bloody diarrhoea, fever, nausea, vomiting
	Serious cases: kidney failure, death

3. Salmonella

Go to Higher Level 2017, Section A, Q6 for detailed account of Salmonella. (page 181)

LINKS

• Food commodities (milk, dairy products) (p. 81)
• Protein (p. 3)

Controlling the microbial spoilage of food

To control microbial spoilage of food, focus on personal, kitchen and food hygiene, and the cooking and chilling of food.

Core principles

1. Remove the factors that contribute to food poisoning.
2. Use good hygiene practices to avoid cross-contamination.
3. Store foods at low temperatures.
4. Cover foods when not in use.

LINK
- Food safety and hygiene (p. 195)

Personal hygiene

See page 197.

Kitchen hygiene

1. Keep kitchen well ventilated.
2. Check fridge daily; keep fridge clean and dispose of stale foods.
3. Disinfect food preparation and serving areas.
4. Use separate knives to prepare raw meat and raw fish.
5. Use separate chopping boards for raw and cooked foods.
6. Wipe up spills as they occur, wash up as you go along.
7. Wash kitchen cloths, tea towels and hand towels daily.
8. Empty, disinfect and wash kitchen bin daily.
9. Sweep, wash and disinfect kitchen floor daily.

Food hygiene, cooking and chilling

LINK
- HACCP (p. 198)

1. Store foods at the correct temperature.
2. Store chilled and frozen food correctly.
3. Label home-prepared frozen foods before freezing.
4. Store raw and cooked meats separately.
5. Use tongs or forks when handling food.
6. Cook foods to a core temperature of 70°C for two minutes.
7. Reheat leftovers only once – heat until piping hot.
8. Follow instructions on package of pre-prepared foods.
9. Cook meat until juices run clear, use a meat thermometer.

Role of micro-organisms in food spoilage

- Souring of foods (cream, milk, yoghurt).
- Spoilage of food (breads, cheese, fruits and jams).
- Produce slime and 'rotten' smells.

Role of enzymes in food spoilage

Enzymes cause spoilage of food through:

1. Ripening in fruit and vegetables.
2. Browning (enzymic browning).

Controlling enzymatic spoilage of food

Enzymatic spoilage can be controlled using heat, cold temperatures, blanching before freezing, using acids to prevent fruits browning and the addition of preservatives, e.g. sulphur dioxide.

Exam questions and sample answers

Higher Level 2017, Section A, Q6 (6 marks) HL

Name **and** describe **two** common food poisoning bacteria using the headings below.

Food poisoning bacteria	Description/ characteristics	Habitat
Listeria	Rod-shaped, gram positive, non-spore forming, asexual reproduction, facultative	Soil, human and animal waste
Salmonella	Rod-shaped, bacilli, gram negative, non-spore forming, asexual reproduction, facultative	Gut of humans and animals, human and animal waste, unwashed hands, vermin, high-risk foods, e.g. poultry, eggs

Higher Level 2016, Section A, Q7 (6 marks)

Name parts A, B and C, as shown on the diagram of a yeast cell.

A = vacuole

B = nucleus

C = food reserve
/granular cytoplasm
/food vacuole

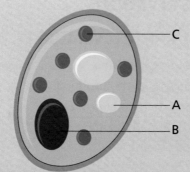

Higher Level 2014, Section B, Q3 (c) (6 marks)

(c) Differentiate between toxic food poisoning and infectious food poisoning.

(2 points × 3 marks = 6 marks)

Toxic food poisoning:

- Caused by eating food contaminated by waste products, exotoxins, released by bacterial cells.

- Some bacteria produce exotoxins before and after the food is eaten.
- They are difficult to destroy, boiling for 30 minutes is essential. Symptoms develop quickly. Examples: Clostridium botulinum, staphylococcus aureus.

Infectious food poisoning:

- Caused by eating food contaminated with pathogenic bacteria which produce endotoxins within their cells. Endotoxins are released when bacteria die.
- Easily destroyed with correct cooking and reheating. Examples: Salmonella, Listeria.

Higher Level 2013, Section B, Q3 (a)   (15 marks)

'The shelf-life of a product is critical in determining both its quality and profitability'.

(a) Discuss the causes of food spoilage in relation to the action of enzymes.

              (3 points × 5 marks = 15 marks)

Enzymes bring about food spoilage in three ways, over-ripening, enzymic browning and enzymic deterioration.

1. *Over-ripening: enzymes speed up the ripening process so that foods become over-ripe. Example: unripe bananas contain starch which converts to sugar, bananas sweeten, soften, skin colour changes from yellow to black and bananas become over-ripe.*
2. *Enzymic browning: when specific foods are exposed to oxygen in the air they turn brown as the cut surface releases oxidase, e.g. apples, bananas.*
3. *Enzymic deterioration: oxidase in the cell walls of plants is activated by oxygen in the air and destroys some vitamins B-group, C and A; vegetables will deteriorate if they are not blanched.*

Food preservation

Principles of food preservation

1. To destroy micro-organisms.
2. To prevent their re-entry into food.
3. To inhibit the activity of enzymes.
4. To maintain colour, flavour, texture and nutritive value of food.

LINKS

- Nutrients (p. 2)
- Food processing (p. 147)
- Food spoilage – microbiology (p. 167)

Reasons for preserving foods (advantages)

1. To extend the shelf life of food.
2. To destroy micro-organisms and prevent food spoilage.
3. To avoid waste by preserving garden produce when it is plentiful.
4. To save money by using foods in season.
5. To provide food for emergencies in a convenient form, e.g. frozen fruits, vegetables, meats.

Methods of preservation

Home methods	Commercial methods
• Freezing	• Freezing: plate, flow, blast
• Heat treatments:	• Heat treatments: canning, bottling, UHT
– jams and jellies	• Dehydration: freeze, air, roller
– chutneys, pickling	• Chemical preservation: salt, sugar, acids, alcohol, antioxidants, sulphur dioxide
– bottling	• Fermentation: vinegar, brewing
• Dehydration/drying	• Irradiation
• Chemical preservation:	
– jams and jellies	
– chutneys, pickling	

Preservation involves controlling microbial growth conditions:

Heat treatments: high temperatures destroy enzymes and micro-organisms.

Freezing: low temperatures inactivate enzymes and micro-organisms.

Chemicals: chemicals inhibit enzymes and micro-organisms.

Dehydration: bacteria cannot multiply without moisture.

Vacuum packing: some bacteria cannot survive without oxygen; sealing food prevents their re-entry.

> **LINKS**
> • Nutrients: properties (p. 2)
> • Food processing (p. 147)
> • Food spoilage – microbiology (p. 167)

Home freezing

Principles of freezing

1. Warmth and moisture are removed.
2. The source of liquid used by bacteria is removed.
3. Blanching vegetables inactivates enzymes.
4. Wrapping foods prevents re-entry of micro-organisms.

Quick freezing (fast-freeze section of the freezer): converts water into small ice crystals at −25°C, causes little damage to cell walls, little loss of liquid on thawing, maintains nutritive value, colour and flavour.

Slow freezing (ice box in fridge): converts water into large ice crystals at 0°C to −25°C, extensive damage to cell walls, loss of nutrients and increased loss of liquid on thawing.

Advantages of freezing

1. Good method of preserving a variety of foods.
2. Bulk freezing saves fuel, time and money.
3. Foods are available out of season; prevents waste.
4. Food can be cooked and frozen in useable quantities.
5. Little loss of flavour, colour and nutritive value.
6. Useful in emergencies.
7. Avoids waste as leftovers can be frozen.

Disadvantages of freezing

1. Freezers are expensive – initial outlay, running costs.
2. Bulk cooking/freezing requires time and work.
3. Danger of buying too many convenience foods/meals.
4. 'Freezer burn'.
5. Keeping the freezer full needs careful planning.

General guidelines for freezing

Preparation	• Choose fresh, high-quality foods
	• Turn on fast-freeze switch 2–3 hours in advance
	• Divide food into useable quantities
	• Blanch vegetables before freezing
	• Cool food before freezing
	• Freeze only one-tenth of the capacity of the freezer in 24 hours
Packaging	• Use suitable packaging material (moisture-proof, vapour-proof)
	• Pack food in small quantities (portions/servings)
	• Remove as much air as possible
	• Allow headspace for expansion of liquids
	• Seal food correctly
	• Label food with name, quantity and date
Freezing	• Freeze in fast-freeze section for the required time at –25°C
	• Open freeze foods that stick together, then pack into containers
	• Freeze food according to type
	• Remove frozen food from the fast-freeze section and put in storage area
	• Turn off fast-freeze switch, return freezer to –18°C
Storing	• Keep a diary of what is in the freezer
	• Store same food types together, use in rotation
	• Store for the recommended time
	• Keep freezer full to reduce running costs

Rules for thawing food

1. Thaw foods slowly and completely in the fridge.
2. Some foods do not require thawing but do require thorough cooking, e.g. commercial ready-prepared meals.
3. Cook all thawed foods fully to prevent food poisoning.
4. Never re-freeze frozen foods: cook and use quickly.
5. Avoid 'thaw drip' from meat contaminating other foods.

key point

Cook vegetables from frozen to maintain nutrients, colour and texture.

Foods suitable for freezing	Foods unsuitable for freezing
Cooked and fresh meats, poultry, fish, sauces, soups, fruits, vegetables, cakes, bread and pastries, sweet and savoury dishes	Foods with high water content, e.g. whole tomatoes, salad greens, whole eggs, mayonnaise, whole potatoes
Commercial products, e.g. pizza, ready meals	Bananas, dairy produce and foods containing gelatine

Packaging materials for freezing
See food packaging (p. 153).

Heat treatments

1. Jam-making

Underlying principles of jam-making:

- Enzymes and micro-organisms are destroyed at 100°C.
- Fruits are softened in the process.
- Sugar (65%) inhibits the growth of micro-organisms.
- Pectin and acids help jams to set.
- Sealing jars prevents the re-entry of micro-organisms.

> **key point**
>
> Sugar acts as a preservative by surrounding the bacterial cells and drawing out the water (by a process called osmosis) from the cells.

Fruit, pectin, acid and sugar

Fruit	Choose:
	● good-quality ripe acidic fruits
	● fruits with a high pectin content
	● acidic fruit (apples, blackcurrants)
Pectin	● A polysaccharide found in fruit
	● Present in cell walls of fruit
	● Essential for setting jam and jelly
	● Some fruits are richer in pectin than others
	● To get a good set, combine fruits low in pectin with fruits rich in pectin
	● Liquid pectin is available
Acid	● Helps draw out the pectin from cell walls
	● Many fruits are acidic
	● Some recipes add lemon juice (acid)
	● Use of acids improves colour and flavour
	● Helps prevent crystallisation
Sugar	● Acts as the preservative
	● Sugar must be measured accurately (65%)
	● Warm sugar before use
	● Commercial jam sugar with added pectin has a shorter boiling time

> **key point**
>
> Over-ripe fruits do not produce a good set.

The stage of maturity of the fruit influences the amount of pectin present:

Fruit	Contains	Setting quality
Under-ripe fruits	Pectose	Poor
Ripe fruits	Pectin	Good
Over-ripe fruits	Pectic acid	Poor

Pectin content of fruit (some examples):

Rich in pectin	Apples, blackcurrants, gooseberries
Medium pectin	Apricots, plums, raspberries
Low in pectin	Late blackberries, rhubarb, strawberries

Results of test for pectin (methylated spirits)

- High in pectin → large single clot
- Medium pectin → two or three soft clots
- Low pectin → several small soft clots

Fruits with medium or low pectin levels must have pectin added by using fruits rich in pectin, liquid pectin or preserving sugar.

Setting tests for jam

1. Temperature test.
2. Cold plate test.
3. Flake test.

Revise the method of making jam.

Jam-making problems

Crystallisation	Too much sugar (over 65%), sugar not dissolved before boiling, insufficient boiling, insufficient acid, overcooking
Fermentation	Too little sugar (less than 65%), poor quality fruit, insufficient boiling
Mould growth	Too little sugar, unsterilised containers, damp storage conditions
Poor set	Incorrect ratio of pectin, sugar and acid, insufficient boiling
Shrinkage	Cellophane cover loose on jar, warm storage conditions

2. Chutney making

Chutneys are made from a mixture of fruits, vegetables, salt, sugar (brown), spices (whole, in a muslin bag) and vinegars (5% acetic acid).

Chutney has a consistency similar to jam. The flavour of chutneys improves with storage. Leave for about three months before use.

Underlying principles of chutney making:

1. High temperatures destroy micro-organisms and enzymes.
2. Vinegar acts as a preservative by lowering the pH level; prevents microbial growth.
3. Sugar acts as a preservative by dehydrating the bacterial cells (osmosis).
4. Sealing jars prevents the re-entry of micro-organisms.

> **EXAMPLES OF CHUTNEY:**
> apple, pear and walnut, tomato, beetroot.

Commercial preservation

Examples: freezing, bottling, canning, pasteurisation, sterisilisation, UHT, dehydration, chemical preservation, fermentation and irradiation.

> **LINKS**
> - Food commodities (p. 81)
> - Food profiles (p. 147)

1. Canning/bottling

Underlying principles of canning/bottling:

1. High temperatures destroy enzymes, micro-organisms and spores.
2. Food is sterilised in cans or glass.
3. Airtight containers prevent re-entry of micro-organisms.

The canning process – a summary

1. Food is prepared.
2. Vegetables are blanched.
3. Meat/fish is cooked.
4. Cans are filled with food, sauce/brine/oil/syrup.
5. Air is removed from cans.
6. Cans are hermetically sealed (airtight).
7. Cans and contents are sterilised.
8. Cans are cooled and labelled.

Aseptic canning process – a summary

1. Cans and foods are sterilised separately.
2. Food is sterilised for a short time at 120–150°C.
3. Food is placed into sterile cans and sealed hermetically.
4. Cans are cooled and labelled.

Canning high- and low-acid foods

Canning temperatures and times differ depending on the acid content of foods.

High-acid foods	Heated to 100°C for less than 30 minutes to destroy pathogenic bacteria
Low-acid foods	Heated to 115°C for more than 30 minutes to destroy bacterial spores

Effects of canning

1. Micro-organisms and enzymes are destroyed.
2. Loss of heat-sensitive vitamins – B-group and C.
3. Changes in colour, flavour and texture.
4. Food may have salt, fat and sugar added.

key point

Cans are lacquered on the inside to prevent reactions between foods and metal.

2. Commercial dehydration

Underlying principles of dehydration:

1. Removing moisture to prevent microbial growth.
2. Enzymes are inhibited.

key point

Vegetables need to be blanched before commercial dehydration and freezing.

Methods of dehydration – a summary

Sun drying	• Drying fruits and vegetables in hot countries
	• Food prone to contamination and attacks from animals, birds and insects
Accelerated freeze drying (AFD)	• Food is frozen quickly at –30°C
	• Water is converted to ice crystals
	• Food is passed through a heated vacuum cabinet
	• Ice crystals change to a vapour by the process of sublimation
	• Food is packed, labelled, stored and transported
	• Food is reconstituted with the addition of liquid
	Uses: coffee, dried fruits and vegetables, meat
	Effects of AFD:
	• Loss of vitamins B and C
	• Change in shape and weight of food
	• Oxidative rancidity (foods containing fat)
	Advantages:
	• Longer shelf-life
	• Good flavour
Fluidised bed-drying	• Warm air is circulated around food to remove moisture and prevent it sticking
	• Food is agitated to prevent sticking
	• Temperature, humidity and air flow are monitored until the moisture level is reduced
	• Food is packed, labelled, stored and transported
	Uses: vegetables

Roller drying	• Prepared food is poured over revolving heated rollers, dried and scraped off in powder or flakes, cooled and packed • Moisture reduced to 10–14% *Uses:* breakfast cereals, dried milk
Spray drying	• Liquid is sprayed through fine nozzles into a heated chamber (165°C) • Dried powder falls to the bottom of the chamber • Powder is cooled, packed and labelled *Uses:* powdered eggs and milk

> **exam focus**
> Revise the advantages and disadvantages of dehydration.

3. Commercial freezing
Underlying principles of commercial freezing

1. Low temperatures are used to prevent growth of micro-organisms.
2. Moisture in food is converted to ice.

Methods of commercial freezing

> **LINK**
> • Properties of protein (denaturation) (p. 8)

> **LINK**
> • Home freezing (p. 183)

Blast freezing	Cold air (−30°C to −40°C) is blown over food as it moves through a tunnel on a conveyor belt *Uses:* meat, vegetables
Contact or plate freezing	Packaged food or liquid is arranged between two cold metal surfaces. Food freezes in a short time *Uses:* burgers, fish, fish fingers, meat
Cryogenic freezing	Food is sprayed with liquid nitrogen to freeze foods in a short time *Uses:* prawns, strawberries
Flow freezing or fluidised freezing	Cold air (−30°C) is blown under foods, keeping them moving and preventing them sticking together, and freezing them in the process *Uses:* berries, peas, sweetcorn

4. Commercial chemical preservation
Underlying principles of chemical preservation

1. Chemicals dehydrate and destroy microbial cells by osmosis.
2. Acids lower pH levels, inhibit enzymatic activity and micro-organisms.
3. Alcohol denatures bacterial cell protein.
4. Antioxidants inhibit enzymatic action and prevent rancidity.

> **exam focus**
> Chemical preservation could form part of a question with food legislation and food additives.

Common chemical preservatives

Preservative	Uses
Anti-oxidants	Fruits, fats, oils
Acids	Chutneys, pickles, relishes
Nitrates/nitrites	Cured meats
Salt	Cheese, bacon, sausages, foods in brine
Smoking	Meats, poultry, fish, cheese
Sugar	Jams, jellies, canned or bottled fruit
Sulphur dioxide	Dried fruits, wines

5. Fermentation

Underlying principles of fermentation

1. Carbohydrates and sugars are broken down by the action of yeast or bacteria to produce alcohol and carbon dioxide.
2. By-products of fermentation are in themselves preservatives, e.g. alcohol, vinegar.

LINKS
- Yeast (p. 128)
- Yoghurt (p. 104)

Examples of fermentation in action

Food	Raw ingredient	Organism
Bread (baking)	Flour, sugar	Yeast
Wine (brewing)	Grapes	Yeast
Yoghurt	Milk (lactose)	Lactic acid bacteria
Pickles	Vegetables	Yeasts and bacteria
Vinegar	Wine, cider	Yeasts and acetobacter bacteria
Blue cheese	Milk	Lactic acid bacteria and mould

6. Irradiation

Underlying principles of irradiation – ionising gamma radiation is passed through food to:
- Sterilise it.
- Delay ripening.
- Destroy pathogenic and food spoilage bacteria.
- Kill insects/parasites.
- Prevent sprouting.

Irradiated foods carry an internationally recognised label/symbol, Radura.

Advantages of irradiation

Revise the principles of irradiation and add the following:
- Reduces use of chemicals.
- Increases shelf-life.

Disadvantages of irradiation

1. Unsuitable for foods with a high fat content.
2. Loss of nutritional value, e.g. vitamins.
3. Consumer concerns over impact of irradiated foods on health.
4. Concerns over using irradiation to hide inferior products.

Effects of preservation on food

> ## LINKS
> - Freezing (pp. 183, 189)
> - Commercial dehydration (p. 188)
> - Canning/bottling (p. 187)

Comparative evaluation of methods of preservation

Use the approach suggested for **comparative evaluation questions.** Include 'Areas to Investigate' and use a table format to present your answer.

Evaluation of frozen and canned peas – a summary

Areas to investigate	Freezing	Canning
Ingredients	Fresh peas	Fresh peas Water, additives Colouring
Type of packaging	Plastic bags	Metal cans
Labelling information	- Name of product - Weight of product - Number of servings - Ingredients - Nutrition information - Storage instructions (star rating) - Cooking instructions - Best before data - Commitment to quality - Customer care data - Address of producer	- Name of product - Ingredients - Nutrition information - Cooking instructions - Storage instructions - Customer care data - Weight - Symbols (low GI, recycling, guaranteed Irish)
Shelf life	Up to one year	- Unopened product has a long shelf life - Once opened eat within two days

Effects of processing	• Micro-organisms are inactivated • Enzymes are inactivated • Nutritional value is close to that of fresh peas	• Micro-organisms are inactivated • Enzymes are inactivated • Loss of water-soluble vitamins B and C • Loss of colour, flavour and texture • Increase in salt content
Risks of spoilage	Repeated defrosting and refreezing can lead to microbial growth	Dented, pierced or damaged cans/food may result in food poisoning
Cost: fill in current costs	€1.69 (450 g)	€1.24 (410 g); drained weight 250 g
Culinary use	• Easy to use • Quick to cook	• Easy to use • Quick to cook

LINKS

- Food commodities (vegetables) (p. 112)
- Food safety (p. 195)

Exam questions and sample answers

Higher Level 2015, Section A, Q8 (6 marks)

Explain how **two** of the following assist in the control of enzymic food spoilage.

Blanching	Prepared vegetables are placed into boiling water to inactivate enzymes, plunged into ice-cold water for the same amount of time to stop the cooking process.
Cold temperatures	Enzymic activity is slowed down by cold temperature in the fridge at 4°C or inactivated in the freezer at −18°C.
Acids	Using an acid, e.g. lemon juice, inactivates enzymes in food as the pH is changed.

Higher Level 2013, Section A, Q7 (6 marks)

In relation to freezing, explain **each** of the following:

Quick freezing:
Food is frozen quickly at −25°C in the fast-freeze section of a freezer, small ice crystals form causing little damage to the cell walls of the foods; nutritive value, colour, flavour and texture are retained.

Slow freezing:
This happens at 0°C to −24°C causing large ice crystals to form which damage cell walls, loss of nutrients, texture, colour, flavour, increased loss of vitamins and liquid on thawing.

Higher Level 2011, Section A, Q5 (6 marks)

In relation to freezing vegetables, explain how loss of vitamin B$_1$ and vitamin C may occur.

- *Blanching results in loss of vitamins as vitamins B$_1$ and C are water-soluble.*
- *Slow-freezing results in large ice-crystals forming cell walls being damaged and loss of vitamins on thawing.*
- *Thawing of vegetables, before cooking, causes loss of vitamins B$_1$ and C into thawed liquid.*

Ordinary Level 2016, Section A, Q7 (6 marks)

Indicate with a tick (✓) whether each of the following statements is true or false.

	True	False
Quick freezing at −25°C forms ice crystals within the food cells	✓	
Bananas and lettuce are suitable foods for freezing		✓
Vegetables are blanched before freezing to destroy enzymes	✓	

Ordinary Level 2015, Section A, Q6 (6 marks)

Indicate with a tick (✓) whether each of the following statements is true or false.

	True	False
Enzymes present in food cause it to decay.	✓	
Chutney making is a method of preventing food spoilage.	✓	
The Food Safety Authority of Ireland is responsible for promoting Irish Food nationally and internationally.		✓

Ordinary Level 2011, Section A, Q5 (6 marks)

In relation to the preservation of food match the following with its function.

(3 points × 2 marks = 6 marks)

Pectin   **Blanching**   **Sugar and vinegar**

Function	Substance
Used as a preservative when making chutney	*Sugar and vinegar*
Used to set jam	*Pectin*
Used to inactivate enzymes when freezing food	Blanching

HL

Higher Level 2016, Section B, Q3 (a), (b)

(a) Outline the benefits of incorporating frozen foods in meal planning.

(4 points × 3 marks = 12 marks)

- *Prevents waste by freezing food when inexpensive and plentiful.*
- *Bulk cooking and freezing saves time and money.*
- *Increases shelf-life of perishable foods and are useful in emergencies.*
- *Frozen foods are convenient, always available and safe to eat.*

(b) Set out details of one method of freezing fresh vegetables. (20 marks)

Description of method chosen (11 marks)

Name: Home freezing of vegetables (name = 2 marks)

Description/process: (description = 3 points × 3 marks)
1. Prepare and blanch vegetables.
2. Place blanched vegetables in a moisture-proof freezer bag/container, removing the air in the process.
3. Place in the fast freeze section (–25°C) of the freezer, then when frozen store at –18°C.

Choose from home, plate or contact, air blast, or flow freezing.

Underlying principle involved (2 points × 3 marks)
- *Blanching the vegetables destroys or inactivates the enzymes present.*
- *Removing moisture and warmth prevents the action of micro-organisms.*

Effect of freezing on food (1 point × 3 marks)
Freezer burn discolours food through oxidation, dries out and toughens protein foods.

Choose from quick freezing, freezer burn or slow freezing.

Higher Level 2014, Section B, Q2 (c)

Set out details of **one** process used to extend the shelf-life of meat.

Name of process: Commercial freezing (2 marks)

Process: (3 points × 3 marks)
- *Meat is boned and trimmed*
- *Blast frozen at –30°C*
- *Sealed in moisture proof packaging.*

Effect of the process on meat: (1 point × 4 marks)
- *Freezing helps retain nutrients, colour and texture. Some loss of minerals and B vitamins.*

Higher Level 2013, Section B, Q3 (c)

(c) Assess irradiation as a method of food preservation.

$\qquad$ (3 points × 5 marks = 15 marks)

- *Destroys insects, parasites and micro-organisms.*
- *Prevents germination, sprouting and slows ripening process (fruits and vegetables).*
- *Causes loss of vitamins.*

Include advantages and disadvantages when answering this question.

Higher Level 2012, Section B, Q3 (b) $\qquad$ (16 marks)

(b) Name **one** method of home preservation that involves the application of heat and explain the principle involved.

Method: *Jam/chutney making* $\qquad$ (4 marks)

Principles involved: $\qquad$ (3 points × 4 marks = 12 marks)

- *Heat: High temperatures soften fruits, destroy enzymes and micro-organisms and sterilise storage jars.*
- *Acid: Acid draws pectin out of the fruits, improves colour and flavour and helps prevent crystallisation.*
- *Sugar: Sugar helps set jam and acts as a preservative by forming a concentrated solution, which draws water out of the microbial cells by osmosis. This dehydrates and kills the microbial cells.*

Choose from jam/chutney, bottling or drying.

Food safety and hygiene

Safe food preparation

To avoid contamination and prevent food poisoning:

1. Follow strict hygiene practices.
2. Prepare foods in hygienic conditions.
3. Separate raw and cooked foods.
4. Maintain correct temperatures when storing, preparing and cooking foods.

LINKS

- Food spoilage and poisoning (p. 177)
- Food spoilage – microbiology (p. 167)

The aims of good food hygiene practices/systems are to:

- Destroy any micro-organisms.
- Prevent their re-entry into the food.
- Prevent contamination and cross-contamination.
- Prevent carriers of food poisoning bacteria (humans) causing an outbreak of food poisoning.

Reducing the risk of food contamination

During food preparation	During cooking
1. Handle food as little as possible	1. Keep equipment and cooker spotlessly clean
2. Wash fruit and vegetables	2. Thaw frozen meat, fish and poultry fully before cooking
3. Prepare raw and cooked foods separately	3. Ensure that meat, fish and poultry are cooked fully (check internal temperatures)
4. Prepare meat, fish and poultry separately	4. Do not handle cooked foods (use serving forks, etc.)
	5. Avoid reheating foods

Guidelines for food storage

(a) Non-perishable and dry foods (cupboards)

1. Store foods in clean, dry, well-ventilated cupboards.
2. Store dry goods in a clean, dry, well-ventilated place.
3. Use in rotation, check stocks, replace as required.
4. Store opened dry foods in airtight containers.

Examples: flour, rice, cans, jars.
Hazards: insects, microbial contamination.

key point

The danger zone for contamination is between 5°C and 65°C.

(b) Frozen foods (freezer)

Examples: meat, fish, convenience meals, vegetables.
Hazards: microbial growth (incorrect temperature).

LINK

- Guidelines for home freezing (p. 184)

(c) Chilled foods (fridge)

1. Store chilled foods in the fridge at below 4°C.
2. Allow for circulation of air in fridge.
3. Cover all food in the fridge.
4. Store foods in the recommended areas in the fridge.
5. Check use-by date; use food in date order.
6. Place raw foods below cooked foods.

Examples: convenience meals, fresh soup, yoghurt.
Hazards: mould growth, microbial growth.

key point

Check the storage instructions on food labels.

(d) Fresh fruit and vegetables

Examples: apples, pears, carrots, onions, salads.

Hazards: enzyme activity, mould growth, microbial contamination, pests.

<table>
<tr><td>

LINKS
- Food spoilage – microbiology (p. 167)
- Food spoilage and food poisoning (p. 177)

</td><td>

LINK
- Fruit and vegetables (p. 109)

</td></tr>
</table>

(e) Perishable foods

Store perishables in fridge for 1–3 days.

Examples: dairy products, eggs, meat, fish.

Reheating procedures – guidelines

1. Cool quickly, cover and store leftovers in the fridge.
2. Use leftover foods within two days.
3. Reheat foods only once.
4. Reheat to 100°C for 10 minutes to destroy micro-organisms.
5. Follow food producer's instructions if using a microwave oven.

Personal hygiene

1. Wash hands using disinfectant soap, hot water and a nail brush.
2. Wash hands before handling all foods, after using the bathroom, after sneezing and coughing, after handling pets and waste.
3. Remove jewellery, tie back/cover hair, wear an apron.
4. Keep nails cut short and clean (no nail varnish).
5. Do not touch hair or face when preparing food.
6. Cover all cuts with a waterproof dressing.
7. Do not smoke near food, do not cough over food.
8. Do not handle food if ill, e.g. diarrhoea, vomiting.

Kitchen hygiene

High standards of kitchen hygiene require:

- Durable, smooth, non-absorbent, easy to clean surfaces.
- Effective lighting, ventilation, waste and recycling systems.
- Colour-coded chopping board system.
- Clean water supply and effective drainage system.

Work surfaces	Wash and disinfect daily
Floors	Sweep, wash and disinfect daily
Wall surfaces	Wash regularly
Equipment	Wash, dry and store in clean cupboards
Food storage	• Clean cupboards regularly • Check and wash out fridge weekly
Chopping boards	• Use separate boards for raw and cooked foods • Wash boards each time they are used
Kitchen cloths	• Use different cloths for different purposes • Wash, disinfect and change daily or on completion of tasks
Kitchen bins	• Bins must be covered, lined and operated by foot • Empty daily • Wash, disinfect and dry daily • Keep covered when not in use
Spills	Wipe up immediately
Pets	Never let pets into the kitchen

LINKS

- Food spoilage – microbiology (p. 167)
- Food preparation and cooking processes (p. 123)

Hazard analysis and critical control points (HACCP)

The HACCP system:

1. HACCP is a **system of analysis** that identifies, evaluates and controls potential hazards that might occur at specific points in all areas of food production.
2. These **'danger points'** can be identified, monitored and controlled in order to prevent contamination.
3. Hazards can be identified as chemical, microbial or physical contaminants.

Setting up a HACCP system – a summary

1 Set up a HACCP team
Members representing all areas involved with relevant knowledge and training.

↓

2 Develop a flow chart for all aspects of food production

↓

3 Identify and analyse potential hazards
Identify anything that might cause harm to consumers. This can occur at any stage of production, from purchase of raw materials to point of sale.

Main hazards/contaminants	Examples
Biological	Moulds, yeasts, bacteria
Chemical	Pesticides, cleaning agents
Physical	Glass, human hair, metal

Analyse hazards and examine implications for consumer safety.

↓

4 Carry out a risk assessment
A **risk** is the probability of a hazard occurring during food production. The risks present can be high, medium or low.

↓

5 Identify critical control points (CCPs)
A **critical control point** is a step in the food production process where hazards must be controlled.

Controls can be applied in order to eliminate, prevent or minimise hazards.

The CCP is the final opportunity to correct a hazard.

LINK
- Go to the food production areas table on the next page to see who/what might be involved.

↓

6 Decide on control measures to eliminate or reduce risk
What has to be done, when, by whom.

↓

7 Implement control measures

↓

8 Monitor and record control strategies as they are implemented

↓

9 Implement further action at control points if necessary

↓

10 Evaluate the HACCP system regularly (especially when production systems change)

↓

11 Comply with legislation by establishing a recording system that is always available

Food production areas and who/what is involved

Purchase of raw materials	Suppliers, deliveries, premises, records, sampling
Delivery of raw materials	Delivery vehicles, temperatures, unloading
Storage of raw materials	Chilled, frozen, dry, in suitable covered containers
Preparation of food product	Cleaning, monitoring, equipment, environment
Application of baking, cooking or heating methods	Times, temperatures
Cooling food product	Times, temperatures, storage
Assembly of food product	Equipment, monitoring, staff, hygiene
Storage	Temperatures, containers, time
Display	Temperatures, dates
Reheating	Core temperatures above 75°C, reheat only once
Delivery/sale	Vehicles, temperatures, unloading, records, date stamps

People involved include suppliers and delivery, production and distribution staff.

Advantages of HACCP

1. Identifies potential hazards.
2. Eliminates or reduces potential hazards.
3. Focuses employees on food safety and food hygiene.
4. Records implementation of food safety legislation.
5. Provides an accurate summary of food production.

exam focus
Be able to apply the above information to a HACCP system for the production of any food or dish.

International Organisation for Standardisation (ISO)

- An independent, non-governmental international organisation formed by national standard bodies from over 162 countries that sets standards of quality to ensure consumer needs are met.
- ISO scheme for food companies is operated by the National Standards Authority of Ireland.
- ISO 22000 sets standards for food safety management across international food supply chains and, if compliant, certificates are awarded.
- All food businesses must comply with Irish and EU food hygiene legislation.

key point
ISO 22000 enables companies to show customers that they have a food safety management system in place.

exam focus
Check for new revisions to the ISO 22000 standard in advance of your exams.

Check out these government departments and agencies:

- Department of Agriculture, Food and the Marine (www.agriculture.gov.ie)
- Department of Health (health.gov.ie)
- Department of Environment, Community and Local Government (www.housing.gov.ie)
- Health Service Executive (www.hse.ie)
- Food Safety Authority of Ireland (www.fsai.ie)
- Public Analyst's Laboratory (www.publicanalystdublin.ie)
- National Standards Authority of Ireland (www.nsai.ie)
- Competition and Consumer Protection Commission (www.ccpc.ie)
- Safefood (www.safefood.eu)

LINK

- Food legislation (p. 204)

Exam questions and sample answers

Higher Level 2013, Section A, Q6   (6 marks)

Complete the table below in relation to food contamination.

Contaminant	How contamination occurs	Possible effect on the body
Pesticides	*Crops are sprayed with insecticides, fungicides and herbicides, sprays contaminate air and soil where they seep into the ground; contaminated water is taken up by plants and soil organisms.*	*1. Respiratory problems* *2. Heart and circulatory problems* *3. Birth defects* *4. May cause cancer*
Metal residues	*Transferred to food from soil, contaminated water, water pipes, cooking equipment, food cans, humans consume contaminated water and foods*	*1. Headaches* *2. Stomach cramps* *3. Kidney and liver damage* *4. Immune system damage*

Higher Level 2016, Section A, Q8   (6 marks)

In relation to the Hazard Analysis Critical Control Point (HACCP) system, explain **each** of the following terms. Give **one** example in each case.

Hazard:

A hazard is a food contaminant that could cause injury to consumers, e.g. physical, chemical or microbial. Example: cross-contamination between meat and other perishable foods.

Control measure:

A control measure is put in place to minimise or control a hazard which might occur in areas of food production systems, e.g. delivery, storage, preparation, cooking, chilling, staff/kitchen hygiene. Example: storing products at the correct temperatures at all stages of the food production system, e.g. limiting time of preparation, storage after preparation, at point of purchase, after purchase.

Ordinary Level 2011, Section A, Q7 (6 marks)

How should raw meat and chicken be stored in the home in order to prevent cross-contamination? Give **two** points. (2 points × 3 marks = 6 marks)

- *Remove meat and chicken from wrapping, place on separate plates, cover to prevent drying out and danger of drips falling onto other foods.*

- *Place raw meat and chicken on a shelf below cooked foods to reduce risk of contamination.*

exam focus

Give one point on preparation, one point on cooking plus four other points.

Higher Level 2014, Section B, Q3 (a)–(c)

'Outdoor dining is a great way to savour good food, company and the great outdoors.'

(a) Outline a HACCP system that should be followed when preparing and barbecuing food. (6 points × 4 marks = 24 marks)

LINK
- Setting up a HACCP system (p. 199)

Stages	Potential hazards	Control measures
Preparation	Bacterial contamination: - *cross-contamination* - *growth of bacteria*	- *Wash hands with antibacterial soap before and after handling food, wash hands frequently (hygiene standards)* - *Use colour-coded chopping boards to prevent cross-contamination* - *Keep raw and cooked foods separate, ensure foods are within date* - *Frozen foods should be fully thawed in the fridge before barbecuing*
Barbecuing *(cooking and serving)*	*Cross-contaminations, growth of bacteria, dirty utensils/equipment*	- *Correct temperatures and clean equipment/utensils* - *Turn food regularly to ensure high temperatures are reached to eliminate food poisoning risk* - *Ensure food is thoroughly cooked before serving e.g. poultry, skewered meats*

Serving	Survival of bacteria, contamination by food handlers, dirty utensils, food poisoning	• Food handlers must follow hygiene rules • Serve immediately on clean plates • Do not keep warm or reheat • Marinades used on meats in advance of barbecuing must not be used as dips or sauces.

(b) Assess grilling/barbecuing as a method of cooking. Refer to:

Cooking/underlying principle   (3 points × 3 marks = 9 marks)

   1. *Quick method of cooking food over or under radiant heat (grill or hot coals).*

   2. *Seals the surface of the food maintaining moisture, flavour and nutrients.*

   3. *Food must be turned regularly to ensure food cooks evenly.*

Guidelines to follow   (3 points × 3 marks = 9 marks)

   1. *Pre-heat the grill or barbecue.*

   2. *Seal surface of food to reduce nutrient and moisture loss.*

   3. *Marinade meats in advance to develop flavour and retain moisture.*

Effect on the nutritive value of the food   (1 point × 2 marks = 2 marks)
Fat content is reduced due to melting of fat during cooking.

(c) Differentiate between toxic food poisoning **and** infectious food poisoning.

> **LINK**
> • Microbiology (p. 167)

Higher Level 2012, Section B, Q3 (a)   (24 marks)

'Food safety is a right not a privilege.' (Safefood, 2007)

(a) To ensure that food is safe to eat, discuss the importance of each of the following: Food storage, cooking and reheating procedures, kitchen hygiene.

                        (6 points × 4 marks = 24 marks)

Food storage:
   • *Store frozen food in the freezer at −18°C.*
   • *Remove plastic coverings from fruits and vegetables on returning home.*

Cooking and reheating procedures:
   • *Defrost frozen poultry thoroughly in the fridge before cooking.*
   • *Reheat foods quickly above 100°C to ensure they are safe to eat.*

Kitchen hygiene:
   • *Bins should be emptied, washed and dried daily.*
   • *All work, wall and floor surfaces should be easy to clean to reduce risks of microbial growth.*

exam focus

Two points are required under each heading.

Food legislation

The purposes of food legislation are to:

1. Protect human health.
2. Inform consumers.
3. Prevent fraud.
4. Facilitate trade.

Food Hygiene Regulations (1950–89)

The regulations:

1. Prohibit the sale of food that is diseased, contaminated or unfit for human consumption.
2. Require that adequate precautions are taken to prevent food contamination at all stages of production.
3. Allow the seizure and destruction of unfit food.
4. Require specific food businesses to be registered.
5. Require that food stalls are licensed annually.

HL European Communities (Hygiene of Foodstuffs) Regulations 2006

These EU regulations require that food businesses:

1. Operate and maintain hygienic practices at all stages of production.
2. Ensure that staff are trained in hygiene practices.
3. Ensure that HACCP is implemented.

Hygiene regulations apply to all stages of production and sale: premises, delivery areas, storage, preparation, transportation, water supply, staff training and personal hygiene.

Food Information to Consumers (FIC) Regulations 2011

It is enforced by Food Safety Authority of Ireland. It outlines requirements regarding the provision of nutritional information; regulations cover labelling, presentation and advertising of foodstuffs. The regulations state that labels:

1. Should be clear, legible and indelible.
2. Should be written in a language understood by consumers.
3. Must not mislead the consumer.
4. Should not be covered or hidden by pictures or written information.
5. Should be impossible to remove from the product.

Sale of Food and Drugs Acts (1875, 1879, 1899, 1936)

These Acts protect consumers against fraud and adulteration of foodstuffs, which may be damaging to human health.

It is illegal to:

- mix, colour, stain or powder any article of food with an ingredient which would damage health
- sell food items that are not of the nature, substance and quality demanded by the consumer.

Health (Official Control of Foodstuffs) Regulations 1991

In order to prevent danger to public health, these regulations set out guidelines for:

- general food hygiene from production to retail sale
- HACCP as part of quality assurance
- the setting of food composition standards
- penalties for breaking the regulations.

The Act allows for inspection of food premises by enforcement officers, who may prescribe penalties.

Agencies concerned with the regulation of food additives

- European Food Safety Authority (www.efsa.europa.eu)
- World Health Organisation (www.who.int) – Joint Expert Committee on Food Additives (JECFA)
- Food and Agriculture Organisation (www.fao.org) – Codex Alimentarius Commission (CAC): established by FAO and WHO to maintain food standards.

Revise food labels, nutritional information provided on packaged and non-packaged food labels.

In Ireland

- Food Safety Authority of Ireland (www.fsai.ie)
- Department of Agriculture, Food and Marine (www.agriculture.gov.ie)

Exam question and sample answer

Higher Level 2011, Section B, Q3 (c)   (10 marks)

(c) Outline the protection provided to the consumer by the Sale of Food and Drugs Acts (1875, 1879, 1899 and 1936).

- *Protects consumers against fraud and adulteration of foodstuffs damaging to health.*
- *It is illegal to:*
  - *mix, stain or powder any food with ingredients which would damage health.*
  - *sell food items which are not of the nature, substance and quality demanded.*
- *Consumers have the right to have a food tested by the Public Analysis Laboratory (fee applies).*

4 Family Resource Management and Consumer Studies

aims To learn and revise:

- Family resource management
- Management of household financial resources
- Housing finance
- Household technology
- Textiles
- Consumer studies

Family resource management

Resource management terms

Management – the effective use of resources to manage or run something, e.g. managing a home, people, money, etc.

Resources – anything that people use to achieve goals, e.g. time, people, skills, equipment and money.

Resource management – using resources wisely to achieve goals.

Family resource management – planning, controlling and evaluating the use of resources in order to achieve goals and improve the quality of family life.

The topics in this chapter are examined in **Sections A** and **B** and are **integrated** across questions.

Purposes of family resource management

1. To use resources wisely to achieve goals.
2. To improve the quality of family life.
3. To help individuals achieve goals.
4. To reduce waste and achieve maximum use of resources.
5. To cope with changing family circumstances.

Factors affecting family management systems include: resources available, needs, wants, goals, decision-making and evaluation of goals.

Management systems – three basic types

Open system	Depends on, and interacts with, systems outside the family to achieve goals, e.g. health, education, protection
Closed system	All activities occur within the family or community
Contingency system	A change in one area of a system affects another, e.g. unemployment

The family as a managerial unit

The family uses an **open managerial system**, which interacts with other, external, systems.

Management skills are needed in different aspects of family life:

Areas	Some examples of knowledge and skills involved
Financial management	Knowledge, management skills (budgeting, saving, bills), decision-making, problem-solving, negotiation skills, IT skills
Meal planning	Knowledge of nutrition, specific diets, decision-making, budgeting, shopping, consumer information, planning menus
Childcare	Decision-making, planning skills, schedule of care, safety, hygiene, health, education, time management, homework, school lunch and extra activities (sports, drama), negotiation skills
Cleaning and maintenance	Decision-making re: cleaning, laundry, maintenance and gardening, management, organisational skills, problem-solving, negotiation skills

Components of management

There are **three** components of management: **inputs**, **throughputs** and **outputs**.
Inputs are made up of demands and resources.

Inputs	Examples
(a) Demands	• *Needs:* food, clothing, shelter • *Wants:* non-essentials, luxuries • *Values:* what we believe to be right and wrong • *Goals:* what we aim to achieve (short term etc.) • *Events/family commitments:* vary between families
(b) Resources	• *Human resources:* people, skills, time • *Material resources:* money, equipment • *Environmental resources:* water, land/space, energy • *Social resources :* education, health, welfare, protection

Throughputs involve processing the inputs. Throughputs link inputs and outputs. **Throughputs consist of:**

Planning

Clarifying goals, gathering information, considering options and consequences, setting standards and sequencing activities

Examples: contingency, directional or strategic plans

↓

Organising

Allocating tasks and resources: may be task-centred or person-centred

↓

Implementing

Putting a plan into action, being in control, adjusting plan as necessary, evaluating the process

---

Outputs are the **end results** of the inputs and throughputs. They are obvious in:

- Goals achieved or demands met/not met.
- Resources used.
- Plan followed and completed.
- Satisfaction that the plan has worked.
- Changes in family values and/or goals.

Evaluation and feedback: evaluation of inputs, throughputs and outputs provides feedback, which is useful for future input stages.

The decision-making process

Decision-making involves examining two or more alternatives and making a choice between them based on personal values and goals.

Decision-making is influenced by **primary** (family and friends) or **secondary reference groups** (other people).

Basic steps in the decision-making process:

1. Define the decision to be made or identify the goal.
2. Examine the alternatives or possible solutions.
3. Consider the consequences of each solution.
4. Make a decision: choose a solution.
5. Draw up a list of resources.
6. Develop an action plan.
7. Implement the plan.
8. Evaluate the outcome.

Types of family decisions:
- Accommodation
- Consensual
- 'De facto'

Communication

Communication:

- Is the process of exchanging information.
- May be verbal or non-verbal.
- Is a two-way process.

key point

Effective communication is essential for harmony and understanding.

Characteristics of effective communication:

1. Message sent is clear to the sender and the receiver.
2. Receiver hears and understands the full message.
3. Receiver understands the verbal/non-verbal aspects of the message.
4. Receiver relates to the message and responds to the sender of the message.

Key factors affecting family management – a summary

1. Family members' stages in the life cycle.
2. Size and composition of family.
3. Employment pattern.
4. Management of dual roles.
5. Gender roles.
6. Culture.
7. Values/standards.
8. Socio-economic status.

exam focus

Be able to elaborate on each of these points in exam questions.

exam Q

Exam questions and sample answers

Higher Level 2017, Section A, Q9   (6 marks)

Name **three** components/stages in family resource management.

- *Inputs*
- *Throughputs*
- *Outputs*

Give **two** examples of family life which require management skills.

- *Budgeting (financial management)*
- *Meal planning (decision-making)*

Higher Level 2013, Section B, Q4 (a)–(c)

(a) Discuss **four** factors that can influence the management of family resources.

(20 marks)

1. *Size and composition of family: number in family, ages, decision-making process, special needs.*
2. *Employment pattern: number working, dual incomes, employment type, hours worked.*

3. *Management of dual roles: sharing tasks, childcare, lone-parent, demands as earner and parent.*

4. *Stages in life-cycle: priorities depending on family member, children, aging parents, income.*

(b) You have been elected as chairperson of your school's graduation committee. Using the management framework (inputs, throughputs, outputs), set out the plan for the event. (18 marks)

exam focus

Elaborate on each of the areas outlined. Refer to the components of management. Use Higher Level 2006, Section B, Q4 below as a model answer.

Components	Application of management system – a summary
Inputs (demands and resources)	1. *Demands: needs, goals, wants, values*
	2. *Resources available: human, economic, material environmental*
Throughputs (planning, organising and implementing)	1. *Planning: goals, resources*
	2. *Organising and allocating tasks and resources*
	3. *Implementing the plan, putting the plan into action as agreed*
Outputs (goals met, resources used, plan followed)	1. *Were the goals achieved?*
	2. *Any changes for the next graduation?*

(c) Give an account of the importance of decision making in family resource management. (3 points × 4 marks = 12 marks)

1. *Essential for the sharing of household tasks and financial management.*

2. *Involves the whole family in sharing of ideas and information.*

3. *Provides opportunities for current and future planning to achieve goals.*

Higher Level 2006, Section B, Q4 (b)

Case study

> Colm and Jane Brown live with their teenagers – David aged 15 and Yvonne aged 17. Monday is a hectic day in the household. Colm leaves for work at 7.30 a.m. and returns at 5.30 p.m. Jane works from 9.00 a.m. to 4.00 p.m. David and Yvonne have training for the local swimming team from 4.30 p.m. to 5.30 p.m. Yvonne also goes to guitar lessons at 6.30 p.m. As they live in a rural area transport is necessary for all activities. The family try to apply a management system to ensure that everything runs smoothly.

(b) Using the components of management explain how the Brown family could apply a management system to ensure that Mondays run smoothly in the household. (18 marks)

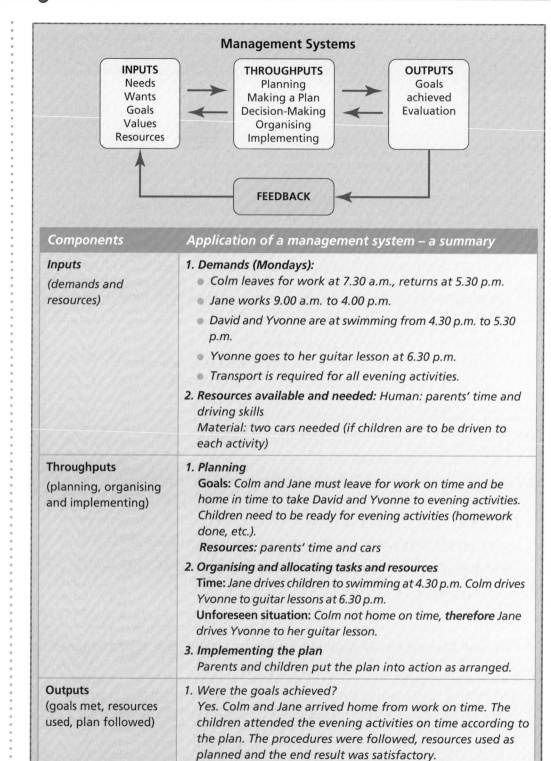

Management Systems

INPUTS
Needs
Wants
Goals
Values
Resources

THROUGHPUTS
Planning
Making a Plan
Decision-Making
Organising
Implementing

OUTPUTS
Goals
achieved
Evaluation

FEEDBACK

Components	Application of a management system – a summary
Inputs *(demands and resources)*	**1. Demands (Mondays):** • *Colm leaves for work at 7.30 a.m., returns at 5.30 p.m.* • *Jane works 9.00 a.m. to 4.00 p.m.* • *David and Yvonne are at swimming from 4.30 p.m. to 5.30 p.m.* • *Yvonne goes to her guitar lesson at 6.30 p.m.* • *Transport is required for all evening activities.* **2. Resources available and needed:** *Human: parents' time and driving skills* *Material: two cars needed (if children are to be driven to each activity)*
Throughputs *(planning, organising and implementing)*	**1. Planning** **Goals:** *Colm and Jane must leave for work on time and be home in time to take David and Yvonne to evening activities. Children need to be ready for evening activities (homework done, etc.).* **Resources:** *parents' time and cars* **2. Organising and allocating tasks and resources** **Time:** *Jane drives children to swimming at 4.30 p.m. Colm drives Yvonne to guitar lessons at 6.30 p.m.* **Unforeseen situation:** *Colm not home on time, **therefore** Jane drives Yvonne to her guitar lesson.* **3. Implementing the plan** *Parents and children put the plan into action as arranged.*
Outputs *(goals met, resources used, plan followed)*	1. Were the goals achieved? *Yes. Colm and Jane arrived home from work on time. The children attended the evening activities on time according to the plan. The procedures were followed, resources used as planned and the end result was satisfactory.* 2. Any changes for next Monday? *None, but there is a back-up plan if Colm does not arrive home on time from work; Jane drives the children to activities.*

Ordinary Level 2011, Section B, Q4 (c)

(c) Discuss how **each** of the following may affect a
family when managing the home:

State each factor and
elaborate with examples.

(i) Stage in life-cycle   (2 points × 3 marks = 6 marks)

- *Priorities for different age groups e.g. adults, children.*
- *Financial resources, demands and commitments.*

(ii) Employment patterns   (2 points × 3 marks = 6 marks)

- *Dual-incomes, unemployed.*
- *Employment hours: shift work, flexi time, job sharing.*

(iii) Sex/gender roles   (2 points × 3 marks = 6 marks)

- *Egalitarian roles and attitudes, individual roles less defined.*
- *Household management and tasks involve all family members.*

Management of household financial resources

The household as a financial unit

LINK

- Functions of the family
  (p. 276)

1. Families contribute to the national economy.
2. Family spending generates revenue for the
   government.
3. Taxes paid are used for state services.
4. Income provides the family's financial resources.
5. Income provides for needs, wants and luxuries.
6. Families may be self-sufficient or dependent on the
   state.

Check the latest statistics
on employment, homeless
families, poverty figures,
etc. on government
websites before your exam.

Factors affecting household income

1. Age	• Changes in patterns of employment
	• Income may increase due to promotion, new job
	• Teenagers often work part-time to contribute to family finances
	• Income reduces in retirement
2. Culture	Cultures may value income differently with regard to how family income is spent:
	• Disposable income spent on luxuries
	• Most income spent on basic needs

3. Gender	• Pay equality legislation (Anti-Discrimination Pay Act 1974, Employment Equality Act) guarantees equal pay and conditions for men and women • More men than women are in paid work • Few women are in senior positions
4. Socio-economic status	• Parents' socio-economic group, education and salary influence a person's opportunities and income • Lower socio-economic groups spend less income on luxuries • Higher socio-economic groups have better opportunities and higher incomes

Sources of household income – some examples

1. Wages and salaries.
2. Social welfare allowance and benefits.
3. Pensions.
4. Investments and savings (dividends/interest).

key point

Other sources of income could include farming subsidies and benefits.

Financial terms

Gross income – income *before* any deductions are made.
Net income – income *after* deductions are made.

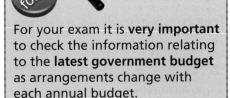

exam focus

For your exam it is **very important** to check the information relating to the **latest government budget** as arrangements change with each annual budget.

Deductions from wages/salary

Compulsory (statutory)	Voluntary (non-statutory)
1. Pay As You Earn (PAYE)	1. Pension contribution
2. Pay Related Social Insurance (PRSI)	2. Private health insurance
3. Universal Social Charge (USC)	3. Trade union subscriptions
	4. Saving schemes

Statutory/compulsory deductions

PAYE (income tax)
- Tax is deducted from each employee's salary/wages.
- The tax deducted is sent directly to the government by the employer.
- Each citizen has a Personal Public Service Number (PPSN).
- Self-employed people are responsible for their own tax returns.

key point

The Revenue Commissioners collect taxes on behalf of the government.

Tax credits

Tax is calculated on gross income and tax credits are applied.

The **annual tax certificate**, *'Notification of determination of tax credits and standard cut-off-point'*, provides taxpayers with information on tax credits and tax liability.

Check the **current** tax rates, tax credits, allowances, levies and any other pay-related deductions. Use a table like the one below to record the tax rates and credits for the current year.

Tax liability in Ireland – standard rate cut-off points

	2018	Exam Year
Single/widowed/surviving civil partner without qualifying children	€ 34,550 @ 20% Balance @ 40%	
Single/widowed/surviving civil partner qualifying for one parent Family Tax Credit	€ 38,550 @ 20% Balance @ 40%	
Married couple/civil partners, one income	€ 43,550 @ 20% Balance @ 40%	
Married couple/civil partners, two incomes	€ 69,100 @ 20% Balance @ 40%	

Universal Social Charge (USC)

The USC is a tax payable on gross income from all sources, but before pension contributions.

Standard rates for 2018	Examination Year	Exempt groups/ reduced rates
€ 0 – € 12,012 @ 0.5%		
€ 12,013 – € 19,372 @ 2%		
€ 19,373 – € 70,044 @ 4.75%		
Balance @ 8% (over € 70,045)		

Some groups are exempt from USC, others pay reduced rates of USC.

Exempt groups 2018: All DEASP payments, similar type payments, incomes of €13,000 or less, etc.

Reduced rates 2018: Holders of full medical cards and individuals aged 70 years and over whose income is €60,000 or less pay 0.5% on €0 - €12,012 and 2% on the balance.

PRSI (Pay Related Social Insurance) – paid into the National Social Insurance Fund

- A compulsory deduction (over 16 and under 66 years).
- Cost of PRSI is shared between employers and employees.
- PRSI is based on a percentage of employee's income.
- To claim benefits employees must have made 39 contributions.
- Benefits: maternity, unemployment, disability, contributory pension.
- Different rates apply and some groups are exempt from PRSI contributions.

Since 2014, unearned income is liable for PRSI, e.g. rents, investments, dividends, deposit interest.

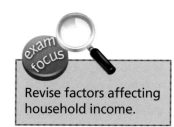

Revise factors affecting household income.

Pensions

Types of pension

Types	Conditions
1. Contributory old age pension (state pension)	State pension age is 66 in 2018, but will change thereafter. Minimum number of contributions Not means tested
2. Non-contributory old age pension (state pension)	People over 66 who do not qualify for contributory pension (age 67 from 2021, age 68 from 2028) Means tested
3. Occupational pension	Workers pay percentage of salary into a pension fund set up by employers
4. Personal/private pension	Individuals pay into private pension fund

Additional allowances/benefits for pensioners who qualify

- Living Alone Allowance
- Household benefits package
- Fuel Allowance
- GP Visit Card (subject to conditions)
- Free travel in Ireland

Social Welfare and Pensions Act 2005

This Act is based on the EU Pensions Directive. It protects the consumer and may investigate pension schemes.

Social welfare payments

There are **three categories** of social welfare payment:

1. Social insurance payments (contributory).
2. Social assistance payments (non-contributory).
3. Universal payments.

The Social Welfare and Pensions Act 2011 made changes to retirement ages.

Check for current social welfare, social assistance and universal payments on www.welfare.ie.

Household expenditure

Essential expenditure	Discretionary expenditure
Money used for essentials: 1. **Fixed:** mortgage/rent, insurance, electricity 2. **Irregular:** food, clothes, education, health, household maintenance	**Disposable income:** money spent by individuals according to personal choice, e.g. holidays, savings

Budget planning

A budget is a plan for spending money over a specific period of time. It involves balancing income and expenditure.

Reasons for budgeting

1. To develop good money management habits.
2. To control spending and reduce financial stress.
3. To plan for irregular and regular bills.
4. To identify areas where economies can be made.
5. To set short-term and long-term saving goals.

Budgets need to be

- Re-organised as family needs/priorities change.
- Examined as income changes, e.g. employment/unemployment.
- Checked annually or more often if circumstances change.

LINK

- Functions of the family (p. 276)

Personal budgets **and** family budgets can be calculated using the same method. Complete your own example based on a variety of circumstances, e.g. single adult, student, adults with or without children, pensioner living alone.

Sample budget and allocations

Expenditure	Allocation	Example: € 400 per week (net) Single adult	Two adults, two children, one income	Two adults, no children, one income	Pensioner on their own
Food	25%	€ 100			
Housing	25%	€ 100			
Household	15%	€ 60			
Education/childcare	10%	€ 40			
Transport	5%	€ 20			
Health/medical	5%	€ 20			
Clothing	5%	€ 20			
Savings	5%	€ 20			
Entertainment/holidays	5%	€ 20			

Areas of expenditure and some examples dependant on individual needs

- **Food and housekeeping:** weekly grocery bill, lunches, cleaning, toiletries.
- **Housing:** rent/mortgage, insurances, property tax, repairs, maintenance.
- **Household:** energy, bin charges, internet, telephone, TV licence.
- **Education and childcare:** books, uniforms, contributions, childminding, crèche.
- **Transport:** work, school, activities via bus, train, car.
- **Health:** insurance, doctors, dentist, optician, prescriptions.
- **Clothing and personal:** casual, work, school, grooming products, services.
- **Savings:** short-term, long-term, emergencies, special events, gifts.
- **Entertainment:** extra-curricular, family events/hobbies, club memberships.

Preparing a household budget

1. List all regular net income (omit irregular income).
2. List planned expenditure (fixed, irregular).
3. Add up the totals, divide by 52 to calculate weekly expenditure.
4. Always allocate money in budgets to short-term and long-term savings.
5. Make provision for special events, e.g. birthdays.
6. Keep receipts and evaluate the budget regularly.

LINK
- Meal management and planning (p. 123)

key point

Decide to budget on a weekly, monthly or annual basis.

Money Advice and Budgeting Service (MABS)

- Set up by the state.
- Provides advice to those in financial difficulties/worried about personal debt.
- Free, confidential, independent service, has a helpline and operates nationwide.
- Helps people analyse their financial situation and plan realistic budgets/repayments.
- Negotiates with creditors on behalf of individuals, agreed protocols are in place.

Examples of personal debt: Mortgage/rent arrears, credit card loans, utilities arrears, bank loan arrears

Methods of paying for goods and services

Method and use	Advantages	Disadvantages
Cash	Convenient, quick and easy, no extra costs, less risk of overspending	Dangers of carrying cash, paying for large items, cannot use online or over the phone
Cheque	Safe, convenient, interest-free, records on cheque stubs and receipts	Charges for cheque and cheque book
Debit Card (Visa or Mastercard)	Safe (chip and pin system), convenient, cash-back facility, widely used and accepted, cannot overspend, money taken directly from account	Government charge for card; may be a transaction charge, account must have sufficient funds
Credit card (banks, building societies)	Set credit limit, Chip and Pin system for security, convenient, readily acceptable, useful for expensive items, online and telephone purchases	High interest rates, danger of overspending, high penalty charges, repossession of goods
24-hour banking	Pay bills over the phone, convenient, transfer money between Irish accounts	Transaction charges may apply
Online banking/ mobile banking	Pay bills over the Internet, accessible 24 hours, can be accessed from virtually anywhere	Transaction charges may apply
Direct debit/standing orders	Safe, easy to set up, convenient, bills paid on time	May involve setting-up and transaction charge, risk of stress if several bill payments due at same time
ATMs	Easy to use, convenient, can pay bills and withdraw money	Transaction charges apply
Money transfer/giro	Easy to use, convenient, all details on giro form	Transaction charge, must go to bank or post office
BillPay (An Post's free payment service)	No handling fees, easy to use, convenient, good tracking system	Limited to Post Office opening hours

Credit: 'buy now, pay later'

Credit allows consumers to buy goods or services and to repay the money along with interest and other charges on a regular basis.

Forms of credit include mortgages, personal/term loans, car loans, overdrafts, credit cards, charge cards, store cards, hire purchase, in-store interest-free credit.

> **LINK**
> - Consumer choice (p. 254)

>
> **exam focus**
>
> Check the latest information relating to conditions of use for **each** of the methods of paying for goods and services before your exam.

Advantages and disadvantages of credit

Advantages	Disadvantages
1. Consumer has use of goods while paying for them	1. High interest rates
2. Useful for large items or luxury items, e.g. home, car	2. Easy to get into debt, impulse buy and overspend, encourages spending
3. Do not need to save	3. Borrowers might not maintain repayments
4. Little need to carry cash	4. Repossession of goods if repayments are not made
5. Interest-free period on credit cards	5. Goods not owned by consumer until final instalment is paid

Points to check before entering into a credit agreement

1. Is it a need, a want or a luxury?
2. Repayment arrangements (cost, when and for how long).
3. Rates of interest charged (APR); other hidden charges.
4. Consequences or penalties for non-payment or late payment.
5. When do you own the product?

Consumer legislation

1. Hire Purchase Acts (1946, 1960)

Hire purchase agreements must state the following:

- Names, addresses, signatures of parties involved.
- Description of goods.
- Cash price and total hire purchase price of goods.
- APR – Annual Percentage Rates of interest.
- Initial deposit paid.
- Cost of credit, repayment arrangements, due dates.

>
> **exam focus**
>
> Revise hire purchase, and its advantages and disadvantages.

- Termination of agreement, repossession, penalty clauses.
- Details of the 10-day 'cooling-off period'.

Note: conditions for hire purchase are now part of the Consumer Credit Act 1995.

2. Consumer Credit Act 1995

- Consolidates all consumer credit legislation (from advertising to contracts or written agreements).
- Provides protection for consumers (the borrowers) in relation to consumer loans and credit agreements, hire purchase, overdrafts, leasing, mortgages, etc.
- Monitors credit advertisements: must show APR, cost of credit, security or deposit required, details of penalties, etc.
- Is implemented by the Competition and Consumer Protection Commission (see note).

Note: In 2014, the National Consumer Agency was amalgamated with the Competition Authority to form the Competition and Consumer Protection Commission.

Savings

Advantages of regular saving

1. Provides security for emergencies, holidays and family events.
2. Establishes a good financial record/rating for future borrowing.
3. Encourages planned saving and paying for goods in cash.
4. Reduces the need for loans and credit agreements.
5. Reduces stress associated with debts.
6. Savings earn interest.
7. Reduces paying interest and charges on loans.

Keep focused!
Savings options available are liable to change. **Check** the latest information and draw up a summary table of five saving schemes.

Methods of saving

When considering saving schemes, check:

- Rate of interest (shop around).
- Ease of access to funds/withdrawal.
- Risk/return (terms and safety of scheme).
- Tax payable (tax-free or DIRT applied).

Summary table of saving schemes – an example

Type of account	Risk/terms	Interest rates	Ease of access	Tax
1				
2				

Bank/building societies – examples

Demand deposit accounts	• Short-term savings
	• Savings are guaranteed
	• Variable low interest rates
	• Easy to access
	• Withdraw money any time (ATM)
Notice accounts	• Short-term deposits
	• Higher interest rate
	• Subject to DIRT
	• Access depends on type of notice, e.g. 30 days
Special term accounts	• One-off lodgement invested for a fixed term, e.g. 2–5 years
	• Penalties apply if withdrawals made before end of agreement

An Post

Deposit account (various types on offer)	• Easy to access, safe
	• No fees, minimum deposit
	• Interest payable
	• Subject to DIRT
Instalment savings	• Fixed monthly instalments
	• Minimum/maximum investment limit
	• No transaction fees
	• Save for 1 year, leave for 5 years, interest calculated annually
Savings certificates	• State guaranteed
	• No fees charged
	• Minimum/maximum investment limit
	• Invested for 5 years
	• Interest calculated every 6 months
	• 7 working days' withdrawal notice
Savings bonds	• State guaranteed
	• No fees charged
	• Minimum/maximum investment limit
	• Interest over 3 years
	• Interest calculated each year
	• 7 working days' withdrawal notice

key point

Other An Post products include National Solidarity Bonds, Childcare Plus, Post Office Savings Bank Deposit Account.

Insurance

- Insurance provides financial protection against a risk.
- The risk is shared with an insurance company.
- Premiums are paid (terms and conditions apply).

Insurance terms

Insurance: protects against something that **might** happen.
Assurance: protects against something that **will** happen.
Broker: an agent who sells insurance policies and receives commission on a sale.
Policy: written details of the terms and conditions.
Premium: the money paid to the company in monthly instalments or annually.
Claim: request/demand for compensation.

Categories of insurance

- **Obligatory insurance:** PRSI, car insurance.
- **Voluntary insurance:** salary protection, health, home and contents, life.

Guidelines for choosing insurance

1. Check family needs and circumstances.
2. Seek independent advice.
3. Shop around and compare policies on offer.
4. It is important to check what insurance cover is already in place and stage of life of family members.

key point

Factors affecting price of insurance include age, smoking, work and lifestyle.

Life assurance

- Life assurance is taken out on an individual's life.
- Provides financial security for the family.
- May include an element of saving (check policy).

Types of life assurance

exam focus

Revise advantages/ disadvantages of term assurance.

1. Term life assurance

- Cheap form of assurance, provides security.
- Insured person's life is covered for set period.
- No payment if insured person survives term.
- Terms vary greatly across schemes.

2. Whole of life assurance

- More expensive.
- No time limit: covers person for entire life.
- Payment made to family if insured person dies.

3. Endowment assurance

- Most expensive form of assurance.

- Combines savings element and whole-life cover.
- Agreed monthly premium payments for a set period, and a lump sum is paid at the end of this period.
- Lump sum is paid to dependents if insured person dies within the set time.

Mortgage protection policy

- Type of term assurance taken out alongside a mortgage.
- Conditions set down by institution when granting mortgage.
- Loan is repaid if the borrower/either spouse dies (if it is a joint mortgage).

Property insurance

A fixed sum is paid monthly with mortgage repayments or annually to the insurance company.

Types include:

- House and building insurance.
- Contents insurance.
- All-risk insurance.

Others:

Travel insurance, motor insurance, events insurance, pet insurance, funeral cover, IT cover.

Private health insurance

Types of health-related insurance:

1. Income protection/health insurance.
2. Serious/critical illness cover.
3. Private medical insurance.

Benefits of private health insurance

1. Variety of schemes.
2. Options of semi-private or private rooms.
3. Covers medical treatment abroad.
4. Tax relief available.
5. In-patient/day patient options.
6. GP visits.
7. Limited dental and optical checks.
8. Alternative treatments may be included.
9. Access to nurse/GP via phone/internet.

Salary protection insurance

If a person has to retire from work due to illness or injury, an income based on a percentage of the original salary is paid until the person reaches retirement age.

Exam questions and sample answers

Higher Level 2017, Section A, Q11 (6 marks)

Name **three** social welfare payments available to individuals.

- *Contributory old age pension*
- *Family Income Supplement*
- *Supplementary welfare allowance*

Ordinary Level 2015, Section A, Q11 (6 marks)

Explain why loyalty schemes, used by retail outlets, encourage consumers to purchase goods.

Enable consumers to accumulate reward points based on money spent, points can later be exchanged for reductions on items or put towards other rewards, e.g. hotel stays.

Name **one** shopper loyalty scheme.

SuperValu Real Rewards Card

Ordinary Level 2016, Section B, Q4 (a)–(c)

Case Study

'Saoirse is a first year college student living away from home and sharing a house with two other students. She has a weekly allowance of € 220, for all her college expenses including rent, and she cycles to college.'

(a) Discuss **four** reasons why Saoirse should set out a budget.

(4 reasons × 5 marks = 20 marks)

1. *To prevent overspending and keep within her financial resources.*
2. *To provide for emergencies, e.g. visit to the dentist.*
3. *To avoid debt by avoiding reliance on credit.*
4. *To reduce stress by knowing bills will be paid on time, e.g. rent.*

(b) Set out a weekly budget plan showing how Saoirse should allocate her money to ensure her needs and wants are met. (5 points × 4 marks = 20 marks)

Using a calculator work out exactly how € 220 is allocated to each area. Make a chart to present your answer.

Area of spending	Percentage of income	Approximate allocation
Rent	25%	€ 55
Food	25%	€ 55
Household bills (utilities)	15%	€ 33
College (books, etc.)	10%	€ 22
Leisure	5%	€ 11
Clothes	5%	€ 11
Savings	5%	€ 11
Health	5%	€ 11
Personal spending	5%	€ 11

(c) Suggest **one** suitable savings account that you would recommend for Saoirse. Give **one** reason for your choice.   (2 points × 5 marks = 10 marks)

Savings account: *An Post Deposit Account.*

Reasons for choice: *Ease of access, e.g. many branches and open on Saturdays.*

Higher Level 2015, Section B, Q4 (a)–(c)

(a) Analyse **three** social factors that affect household income.

                 (3 factors × 6 marks = 18 marks)

| Analyse and elaborate on factors giving examples. |

LINK
- Factors affecting household income (p. 213)

Socio-economic group:

1. *Parent's socio-economic group, education and salary affect an individual's opportunity and income.*

2. *Individuals from low-socio-economic backgrounds tend to leave school early without qualifications leading to work in low-paid jobs, little career advancement or unemployment.*

3. *Higher-income groups have educational opportunities, leading to qualifications which result in high incomes and career prospects.*

Gender: *Numbers of women in the workforce have increased due to educational opportunities, Employment Equality Act and 'Back to Work' schemes. Managerial positions continue to be male dominated in Ireland.*

Age: *Income increases with age due to promotions and salary increases. Outgoings increase due to mortgages/rent, childcare, college fees. Income decreases during unemployment and on retirement unless savings and pensions are in place.*

(b) Design a family budget (two adults and two children) where the net weekly income is € 650. Give a reason for the proposed allocation of income for each area of expenditure. (6 points × 3 marks = 18 marks)

Area of expenditure	%	Amount	Reason
Housing	25%	€ 162.50	Rent/mortgage, insurance, repairs, property tax
Food	25%	€ 162.50	Meals at home, lunches, eating out, celebrations
Household expenses	15%	€ 97.50	Bills for services and utilities
Education	5%	€ 32.50	Books, uniform, extra-curricular, planning for college
Childcare	5%	€ 32.50	Crèche, after school, childminder
Travel	5%	€ 32.50	Work, school, activities, car insurance, fuel, NCTs, servicing
Clothing	5%	€ 32.50	For school, work, leisure
Medical	5%	€ 32.50	Doctor, dentist, prescriptions
Savings	5%	€ 32.50	Short-term/long-term, emergencies, special celebrations
Entertainment	5%	€ 32.50	Leisure activities, socialising with family and friends

(c) Recommend **one** type of savings scheme suitable for a family. (14 marks)

Institution (2 marks) Saving scheme (1 mark)	Interest paid (1 point × 3 marks)	Ease of access to funds (1 point × 3 marks)	Tax payable (1 point × 3 marks)
An Post 6-year Instalment Savings	Save for 1 year, leave for five years, Interest 5.5%, AER 0.98%	7 day notice for withdrawal. Less interest if withdrawn early	Less interest if withdrawn early Tax free to Irish residents

Higher Level 2014, Section A, Q9 (6 marks)

What is Pay Related Social Insurance (PRSI)?

A compulsory deduction from income applied by government (related to pay, shared by employer and employee) and used to provide social welfare, etc.

Name **two** PRSI benefits.

- *Carer's benefit*
- *Disability benefit*

Higher Level 2016, Section A, Q10 (6 marks)

Explain **each** of the following.

Life assurance:
An agreed premium is paid throughout life by the insured person with no time limit on the policy. An agreed sum is paid on the death of the insured person.

Mortgage protection policy:
Term assurance taken out by those getting a mortgage to protect the insured person for the life of the mortgage in case of death prior to the full repayment of the mortgage.

Ordinary Level 2015, Section A, Q10 (6 marks)

Name **two** types of credit available to consumers when buying household goods.

1. *Credit card payment*
2. *Term loan from financial institution*

State the main advantage of **one** of the types of credit named.
Allows expensive large goods to be purchased for immediate use, e.g. cooker, fridge.

Housing finance

Mortgages

A mortgage is a loan from a lending institution to buy a home, which must be repaid over a set time, e.g. 20–30+ years.

Sources of mortgages: banks, building societies, local authorities.

> **exam focus**
>
> Revise the additional costs involved when arranging a mortgage and buying/building a home.

> **LINK**
> - Higher Level 2017, Section B, Q4 (p. 232)

General conditions

1. Amount of money borrowed	Check current Central Bank guidelines
2. Borrower's deposit	10% of the purchase price for first time buyers (LTV)
3. Credit history/rating (creditworthiness)	Savings record – shows ability to repay loan, no bad debts
4. Proof of income	P60; self-employed people must show audited accounts and a tax clearance certificate
5. Length of mortgage	Age of applicant influences length of loan
6. Type of property	Must be surveyed, in reasonable condition, value for money
7. Building insurance	Required by lender as a condition

The **mortgage agreement** states the amount of each payment, interest payable, date due each month, term of mortgage.

Types of interest rate

1. Variable – rise and fall in line with ECB rates.
2. Fixed – for a set time.
3. Tracker – tracks the ECB rate.
4. Split – variable and fixed rates are applied to different portions of the mortgage.

Types of mortgage

1. Annuity
2. Interest-only (pension-linked endowment policy)
3. Deferred start

Local authority housing

Check out the types of mortgages available during your exam year.

Local authorities provide housing for individuals who are unable to provide a home from their own resources.

- Houses are provided according to eligibility and need.
- Applicants must be unable to get a mortgage from a financial institution.
- Household income is assessed (income thresholds apply).
- Assessment includes family size, current housing and special needs.
- Points are allocated and houses assigned.

Summary of current local authority schemes

Mortgage to Rent Scheme 2017 – a summary	
	• Government initiative to assist homeowners at risk of losing their home
	• Homeowner must be unable to make repayments to a private lender
	• Applicants complete a Mortgage Arrears Resolution
	• Local Authority Areas set the maximum value of homes acceptable
	• Must not own other property, cash limits apply, qualify for social housing
	• Annual income levels applied depend on the area of the country
	• Option to buy back home after five years if circumstances improve
	• Housing associations responsible for property maintenance (tenancy agreement)
	• Must have a right to remain in Ireland long-term

Rental Accommodation Scheme (RAS) – a summary	• Short or long-term leases arranged with private landlords • Applicants in receipt of rent supplement, living in private rented accommodation • Terms and conditions apply if transferring to RAS in the current accommodation • Local authority pays full rent to landlord, tenant pays part of rent to local authority • Houses must be registered with the Residential Tenancies Board (RTB) • Increases in income results in higher rent contributions • Regular payments of mortgage and rent: outgoings are lower than regular mortgages
Housing Assistance Payment (HAP) – a summary	• Local authorities pay landlords directly within 'rent limits' • Tenants pay the local authority a weekly HAP rent based on income • HAP available in all local authority areas since March 2017 • Accommodation must meet minimum standards for rented housing • Landlords must be tax compliant
Other schemes	• Incremental Purchase Scheme (IPS) (Tenant Purchase Scheme) • Tenant Purchase of Apartment Scheme (TPAS) • Local Authority Mortgages (annuity loans with variable interest rates) • Mortgage Allowance Scheme

The Housing Agency

Supports and works with local authorities, approved housing bodies and the Department of Housing, Planning and Local Government in delivering housing and housing services. Underwriter of the House Purchase Loan (HPL) and Home Choice Loan (HCL).

Factors affecting housing choices

> **LINK**
> • Family Home Protection Act 1976 (p. 297)

(a) Socio-economic factors

1. Life cycle and ages of family members.
2. Special needs, e.g. wheelchair access, no stairs.
3. Budget available, family income.
4. Proximity to amenities, transport, school, shops.
5. Proximity to work, family, friends.

(b) National housing policy

- Formulated by the Department of Housing, Planning and Local Government.
- Aims for housing to be accessible, affordable and of good quality.
- Social housing supports to individuals, families and vulnerable people.
- Encourages builders to create schemes of high quality for those buying homes.

- Legislation for rented accommodation, improvement/restoration grants.
- Supports and develops sustainable communities.
- Supports housing association provisions.

(c) Trends in housing development

- Increases in numbers unable to buy their own home.
- Reduction in the numbers of houses to rent at affordable prices.
- Mix of housing types and home-ownership schemes.
- Inner city renewal developments, commercial and residential.
- Increase in expensive and small exclusive gated-communities.
- Smaller house and garden sizes in cities, larger homes in satellite towns.
- Increase in energy friendly homes, e.g. A-rated homes.

> **key point**
>
> Policies address provision for the homeless, people with disabilities, travellers, regulating building standards and rented accommodation, and the sale of local authority housing to tenants.

(d) Property tax

An annual Local Property Tax (LPT) is charged on all residential properties in Ireland.

(e) Availability of housing

- Demand for buying and renting homes has increased.
- Demand for rented accommodation exceeds supply.
- Individuals unable to get a mortgage due to salaries and employment.
- Demand for social housing exceeds supply of local authority housing.

> **exam focus**
>
> Be able to describe the latest National Housing Policy for your exams. Check for updates on www.citizensinformation. ie, and Local Authority and Revenue Commissioners websites.

> **LINKS**
>
> - Key factors affecting family management (p. 210)
> - Family structures (p. 272)
> - Functions of the family (p. 276)
> - Making a Will (p. 297)

> **exam focus**
>
> Review the availability of housing nearer the exam.

Exam questions and sample answers

Higher Level 2014, Section A, Q10   (6 marks)

State **two** features of current National Housing Policy in Ireland

- *Provision of social affordable housing through different social housing schemes.*
- *Promotion of energy efficient homes through building regulations, BER ratings, grant schemes.*

Higher Level 2017, Section B, Q4 (a)–(c)

'Everyone needs a home: a secure, comfortable place in a pleasant and sustainable community: a place to rear family if they so wish and to grow old in serenity.' (Social Housing Strategy 2020)

> **exam focus**
> Analyse and elaborate on the key points and give relevant current examples.

(a) Analyse the factors that influence housing choices. Refer to:

  (i) Socio-economic factors   (2 factors × 3 marks)

- *Cost of housing: determines if one rents or buys, the size, location and condition of the house (newly built or in need of renovation). Other costs include on-going service charges and utility bills.*
- *Location and amenities: determines house prices, future investment potential and access to family and friends, transport, travel time, cost and access to work, schools, entertainment, and leisure.*

  (ii) Availability of housing   (2 factors × 3 marks)

- *Social housing: extreme shortage as demand is higher than supply, long waiting lists.*
- *Private housing: shortage as demand exceeds supply in cities and towns, house prices are increasing and young people find it difficult to get a mortgage.*

  (iii) National housing policy   (2 factors × 3 marks)

- *Promotes quality housing at affordable prices in sustainable communities.*
- *Promotes energy efficient homes through grants, BER ratings and building regulations.*

(b) Outline the conditions that are required in order to qualify for mortgage approval.

              (4 conditions × 4 marks = 16 marks)

> **exam focus**
> Refer to **current** terms for mortgage approval. Terms and conditions can change.

  1. *Excellent credit history: Regular savings habit, no bad debt and acceptable spending habits. Regular savings show that one is capable of making regular mortgage repayments.*

2. Income: *Applicants must show proof of a regular income, e.g. P60 and provide salary slips.*

3. Deposit: *Central Bank regulations – 10% deposit for first-time buyers, 'loan-to-value' ratio, second-time buyers must have a 20% deposit.*

4. Terms of loan: *Decided on at time of application, varying from 20–40 years. Shorter term for older applicants. Terms may be shortened at a later date if financial circumstances improve.*

(c) Name and describe one type of mortgage available to house purchasers.

(16 marks)

Rebuilding Ireland Home Loan/available from local authorities, February 2018

- *Available for first-time buyers to buy a new or second-hand house or build a house.*
- *One can borrow up to 90% of the market value of the property (location determines value).*
- *Applicant must be in continuous employment for two years (must show evidence).*
- *Applicants income is assessed, € 50,000 as an individual or € 75,000 joint income.*

Ordinary Level 2014, Section B, Q4 (a)–(c)

Paul and Geraldine are responsible consumers planning to buy a new home.

(a) Explain how **each** of the following could influence Paul and Geraldine when planning to buy their new home.   (4 points × 5 marks = 20 marks)

Cost:

Income determines budget available for deposit, purchase, mortgage and all associated fees, location, size of home, resale value, initial furnishings, ongoing services and utilities.

Give relevant examples for each of the points listed in the question.

Size and type of house/apartment:

Personal preference, variety of styles available, adequate for current and future family needs and activities, energy efficiency, garden space or balcony, etc.

Location/environment:

Rural or urban, easy access to work, shops, leisure, schools, transport systems, safe and secure neighbourhood, no risks of flooding, subsidence, pylons, pollution, factory emissions, etc.

Trends in housing developments:

Variety of designs and developments available, A-rated energy efficient homes with passive heating and solar energy systems, small gated communities, redeveloped city/town residential areas, mixed housing estates, increased apartment living in cities and towns, living in satellite towns near large cities and commuting to work and college.

(b) (i) Name **two** different types of pollution that can cause problems for householders. (2 types × 5 marks = 10 marks)

(ii) State the effect on the environment of **each** type of pollution named. (2 effect × 5 marks = 10 marks)

Types	Effect on the environment
Water pollution	Destroys fish, plants, landscape, destroys drinking water, affects tourism
Noise	Headaches, lack of sleep, anxiety, rows between neighbours

(c) Identify and give details of **one** initiative aimed at promoting a clean green environment.

Name: Green Dot

Details:
An international symbol showing that suppliers have contributed financially to the cost of recovery and recycling of packaging materials of consumer goods. Trademark is used by Repak.

exam focus

Name = 5 marks, details = 5 marks, total = 10 marks.

Household technology

Examples of technological developments

- **Food preparation:** blenders, food processors, liquidisers, mixers, juice extractors, kettles.
- **Cooking:** fan ovens, steam ovens, induction hobs, dual grills, microwave ovens, contact grills.
- **Cleaning:** vacuum cleaners, dishwashers, steam cleaners, central vacuuming systems.
- **Laundry:** washing machines, dryers, irons, trouser presses.
- **Household surfaces:** stainless steel, ceramic, plastic.
- **Entertainment:** TVs, DVDs, PCs, tablets, surfers, smart phones
- **Security:** alarms, lights, automatic gates, CCTV systems.
- **Communication:** Internet, mobile phones, Skype, video calling, emails, texting.
- **Automation:** lighting, timers on water, lighting, heating, smart appliances.
- **Maintenance:** electric drills, garden equipment.
- **Computer packages:** budgeting, accounts, spreadsheets.

Contribution of technology to home management

1. Reduces workload; tasks completed quickly.
2. Improves quality of home life; more leisure time.

3. Energy-efficient appliances and systems save money.

4. Appliances are fitted with safety devices.

5. Higher standards of food and kitchen hygiene.

Guidelines for choosing household appliances

LINK
- Food preparation and cooking equipment (p. 129)

Cost	<ul><li>Consider budget available</li><li>Shop around, compare costs, get value for money</li><li>Buy the best you can afford</li><li>Check purchase, installation and running costs, length of warranty</li></ul>
Brand	<ul><li>Choose a reliable, well-known brand</li><li>Buy from a reputable dealer</li><li>Check for quality symbols</li></ul>
Energy	Check energy-efficiency rating (A to G)
Design and construction	<ul><li>Durable, must be easy to use</li><li>Easy to care for/clean and maintain</li><li>Colour and shape should suit the home</li><li>Check whether extra services are needed, e.g. power points, plumbing, ventilation</li></ul>
Safety	Check safety symbols and features
Size	<ul><li>Family needs, size of household</li><li>Space available, check measurements</li></ul>
Guarantee	<ul><li>Check terms of guarantee (parts, time, labour) and warranty</li><li>Check after-sales service if a fault develops</li></ul>

LINKS
- Consumer choice (p. 254)
- Consumer responsibilities (p. 257)
- Consumer protection (p. 263)

Household appliances

Types of appliance

With a motor	With a heating element	With a motor and a heating element
Food processor, vacuum cleaner, smoothie maker, juice extractor, refrigerator	Coffee maker, electric cooker, slow cooker, kettle, deep-fat fryer, sandwich maker, iron	Fan heater, washing machine, tumble dryer, dishwasher, bread maker

Small appliance with a motor – food processor

A food processor is a versatile motor appliance that saves time and energy, speeds up food preparation and is easy to use and maintain.

Construction

Food processors are made up of:

1. A **base unit**, containing:
   - A motor enclosed in a strong metal or plastic casing.
   - A flex and three-pin plug with appropriate fuse.
   - A variable speed button/switch with on/off switch.
2. A plastic, glass or metal **bowl unit**, containing:
   - A lockable funnelled lid.
   - A central spindle to hold blades and discs.
   - A feed tube and pusher.
3. **Attachments**: a selection of metal and plastic blades and discs.

Attachments and uses

Steel chopping blade	Puréeing fruits, soups, sauces; chopping parsley, vegetables, meats; making breadcrumbs, mayonnaise
Grating discs (fine, medium, coarse)	Slicing, dicing, grating cabbage, carrot and potatoes
Whisk attachment	Meringues, sponge cakes, sauces
Juice extractor	Fresh orange juice, lemon juice
Liquidiser	Soups, sauces, purées
Dough hook	Breads, pastry, cake mixtures

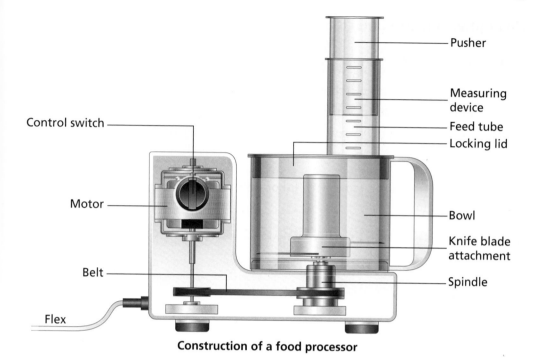

Construction of a food processor

Working principles of a food processor

- A blade or disk is placed carefully on the spindle in the bowl.
- Ingredients are placed in the bowl and the lid is locked securely into place.
- Push food through the feed tube when the food processor is turned on.
- Plug the food processor into the electric socket.
- The motor (powered by electricity) causes the spindle and discs/blades to rotate.
- Rotating disc/blades beat, chop, liquidise, slice or whisk ingredients.
- Use the various speed controls as required.

Standard capacity: Standard size is two litres, smaller and larger capacities are available.

Guidelines for use

- Follow the manufacturer's instructions and hygiene guidelines.
- Never operate appliance with wet or damp hands.
- Choose correct attachments and fix correctly in place.
- Use food pusher when feeding small pieces of food through feed tube, never use spoons or fingers.
- Do not overload the bowl, stop occasionally to scrape down the sides of the bowl.
- Never force switches or locking mechanism.

Guidelines for care and cleaning

1. Unplug the food processor before cleaning, allow motor to cool.
2. Be careful when removing, washing and drying discs and blades.
3. Wash all removable parts in hot, soapy water and dry thoroughly.
4. Never immerse motor in water, wipe outside and flex with a damp cloth.
5. Never use abrasives, they may cause odours and damage to the surfaces.

Storage

Dismantle food processor, store with lid off in a well-ventilated kitchen unit to allow good air circulation.

Small appliance with a heating element – electric kettle

Construction

- Available in a variety of colours, shapes and sizes.
- Made in chrome, stainless steel or coloured plastic.
- Most have fitted lids (easily opened or removed).
- Pouring spout with filter to remove limescale.
- Heat-resistant handles.
- Water level indicator.
- Vents for steam to escape.
- On/off switch.
- Indicator light.
- Concealed heating element.
- Thermostat which turns off kettle at 100°C.

Standard capacity: 1.7 litres

key point

Cordless kettles sit on a separate base unit with a plug. Newer kettle models have indicator switches for other temperatures.

— Lid

— Heat-resistant handle

— Water level indicator

— Indicator light

— On/off switch

— Concealed heating element

— Lead

Construction of an electric kettle

Working principles

1. Kettle is plugged in and turned on.
2. Electricity causes element to heat up.
3. Element heats water by conduction and through convection currents.
4. Thermostat automatically switches the kettle off when water reaches boiling point.
5. 'Boil-dry' safety switch is a feature of most kettles.

Guidelines for use

1. Follow the manufacturer's instructions.
2. Switch on using dry hands.
3. Unplug and switch off before filling.
4. Ensure that the element is covered with water.
5. Never overfill.
6. Allow the kettle to cool before refilling.
7. Use only for heating water.

Guidelines for care and cleaning

1. Switch off and unplug before cleaning.
2. Never immerse the kettle in water.
3. Clean filters in spout daily.
4. Descale if necessary.
5. Wipe outside with a warm, damp cloth.
6. Dry with a clean cloth.
7. Never use abrasives to clean kettles.

Large refrigeration appliance – a refrigerator

The function of a refrigerator is to keep perishable food fresh for a specific length of time under cold conditions by preventing the action of micro-organisms.

Types of refrigerator

1. Standard refrigerator (fits under the counter).
2. Larder refrigerator (no ice box).
3. Fridge-freezer (different capacities).

Design and construction

- A variety of types, designs, colours and finishes.
- Outer layer of insulated enamelled steel.
- Inner lining of moulded polystyrene.
- Layer of insulating material between the steel and polystyrene.
- Door with magnetic catch and rubber door seals.
- Thermostat to control temperatures.
- Selection of adjustable plastic-coated shelves.

- Storage drawers.
- Adjustable door bottle rack and moulded compartments.
- Icebox at the top of refrigerator.
- Automatic light inside the cabinet.

Size/capacity: average is 150 litres; ranges from 50 litres to 280 litres

Special features of modern refrigerators

1. Compartments, adjustable shelves and storage areas.
2. Chilled drinks dispenser for water and/or fruit juices.
3. Internal ice maker and/or external ice dispenser.
4. Automatic defrosting.
5. Zoned refrigeration.
6. Frost-free refrigerators.
7. Digital temperature displays.
8. Integrated fridge doors for kitchen cabinets.

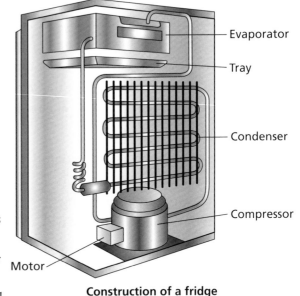

Evaporator

Tray

Condenser

Compressor

Motor

Construction of a fridge

Working principles

- A **compressor** at the base of the refrigerator is activated by an electric motor. This forces a gaseous refrigerant into the condenser.
- The **condenser** cools the refrigerant and it changes to a liquid.
- The liquid refrigerant passes into the **evaporator**, where it evaporates by removing heat from inside the refrigerator.
- The evaporated refrigerant returns to the compressor where the cycle begins again.

Exam questions and sample answers

 Higher Level 2015, Section A, Q11 (6 marks)

State the function of **each** of the following parts of the refrigerator.

Thermostat: *Controls and maintains the internal temperature at or below 5°C.*

Refrigerant: *Liquid refrigerant evaporates by removing heat from within the fridge and as a result cools the internal storage area.*

Ordinary Level 2016, Section A, Q11 (6 marks)

Indicate with a tick (✓) which of the following household appliances has a motor or an element.

Household appliance	Element	Motor
Kettle	✓	
Food processor		✓
Toaster	✓	

Ordinary Level 2017, Section B, Q4 (a)–(c)

'Refrigerators are designed to keep food fresh and assist in reducing food waste.'

> **LINK**
> - Refrigerator (p. 239)

(a) Discuss **four** factors that should be considered when choosing a refrigerator for a family (4 factors × 5 marks = 20 marks)

1. *Costs involved: initial costs and running costs.*
2. *Energy efficiency: an A+ rated energy-efficient appliance lowers running costs.*
3. *Space available: appliance must fit into existing space.*
4. *Dealer: buy from a reputable store with a good after-sales service.*

> exam focus
>
> Choose the most important factors and elaborate on your answer.

(b) Set out the result of a study you have carried out on a refrigeration appliance. Refer to:

Type of refrigeration appliance (1 type × 2 marks)

Larder fridge

Guidelines for use (3 guidelines × 4 marks = 12 marks)
1. *Follow the manufacturer's instructions for use, cleaning and maintenance.*
2. *Store raw and cooked food separately to prevent cross-contamination.*
3. *Cool cooked foods before placing them in the refrigerator.*

Modern features (2 features × 3 marks = 6 marks)
1. *Automatic defrost*
2. *Zonal refrigeration*

(c) Outline **two** sources of consumer information available to consumers when purchasing household appliances. (2 sources × 5 marks = 10 marks)

1. *Media e.g. magazines, television, online.*
2. *Word of mouth: family and friends.*

Methods of defrosting

1. Automatic.
2. Manual.
3. Push-button.

Star rating		Temperature	Storage time
*	1 star	−6°C	1 week
**	2 star	−12°C	1 month
***	3 star	−18°C	3 months
****	4 star	−18°C to −25°C	Up to 1 year

Guidelines for use

1. Open refrigerator only when necessary.
2. Cool warm/hot food before storing in the fridge.
3. Cover foods to stop drying out and transfer of flavours.
4. Store foods in the recommended area.
5. Store raw and cooked meats separately.
6. Store foods for the recommended time; use in rotation.
7. Allow for circulation of air around food.

Guidelines for care and cleaning

1. Position fridge away from any heat source.
2. Clean regularly, i.e. weekly.
3. Wash with a solution of warm water and bread soda.
4. Wipe the outside of the fridge daily.
5. Avoid build-up of ice.
6. Wipe up spills immediately.
7. Keep the back of the appliance free of dust.
8. When not in use, unplug and leave door open.

> **LINK**
> • Food safety and hygiene (p. 195)

Microwave ovens

Types of microwave oven

1. Conventional microwave oven: cooking, reheating and defrosting.
2. Combination microwave oven: combines microwave, oven and grill, browns food.
3. Microwave oven with grill: cooking, reheating, defrosting and browning.

Foods suitable for microwave cooking

• Evenly shaped food without sharp corners.
• Foods for re-heating, e.g. meals, sauces, soups.

- Ready-made meals and individual dishes.
- Fish, meat, poultry, fruit, vegetables.

Design and construction of a microwave oven

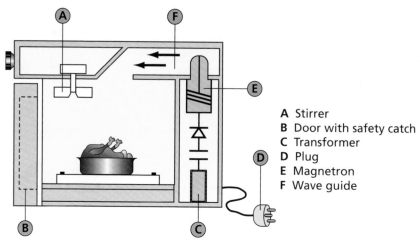

A Stirrer
B Door with safety catch
C Transformer
D Plug
E Magnetron
F Wave guide

Working principles

1. Microwave oven is turned on.
2. Transformer steps up the standard voltage.
3. Magnetron converts electrical energy to electromagnetic energy or waves.
4. Electromagnetic energy enters the oven via the wave guide.
5. Wave stirrer directs microwaves around the oven.
6. Electromagnetic waves are (a) reflected off the walls of the oven, (b) transmitted through the containers and (c) absorbed by the food to a depth of 2–4 cm.
7. Water molecules vibrate rapidly, creating heat, which cooks, re-heats or defrosts the food. Heat travels to the centre of the food by conduction.
8. Water comes to the surface and prevents the food crisping or browning.

> **LINK**
> - Methods of cooking (p. 125 and Chapter 3: Extension 1, www.moresuccess.ie)

Guidelines for use

1. Follow the manufacturer's instructions.
2. Never turn on the microwave when empty.
3. Use recommended cooking containers, **never** metal.
4. Arrange food in a circle, cover food.
5. Pierce foods with skins to prevent from bursting.
6. Allow recommended 'standing time' before serving.
7. Use recommended heat-resistant cling film.
8. Never leave unattended – overcooking can cause a fire.

exam focus

Revise the safety rules to follow when using a microwave oven.

9. Use oven gloves to remove dishes.

10. Stir liquids to prevent 'hot spots'.

Care and cleaning of a microwave oven

1. Follow manufacturer's instructions.

2. Unplug microwave oven before cleaning.

3. Avoid abrasives, use hot soapy water.

4. Wipe door seal and interior of oven, rinse and dry.

5. Remove turntable, wash, rinse and dry.

6. Wipe up spills immediately.

7. Get oven serviced by a qualified engineer.

Advantages

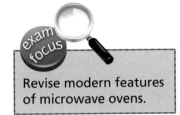

- Economical method of cooking.
- Cooks foods quickly, defrosts foods quickly.
- Food retains natural colour, flavour and nutrients.
- Saves on washing up, saves time and energy.
- Foods can be served in dishes in which they were cooked.

Revise modern features of microwave ovens.

Disadvantages

- Foods do not brown satisfactorily in basic models.
- Tough cuts of meat cannot be used (will not tenderise).
- Unsuitable for fried and roast foods, cakes and batters.
- Foods/dishes need standing time before serving.
- Extra time needed when cooking larger amounts of food.

Containers and microwave ovens

	Examples
Suitable	Glass, Pyrex, plain china, earthenware, heat-resistant plastic, oven-proof dishes
Unsuitable	Foil containers, metal dishes, metal-trimmed dishes, thick dishes, glazed pottery

Exam questions and sample answers

Ordinary Level 2017, Section A, Q11 (6 marks)

Explain **one** benefit of the label below to the consumer.

It enables consumers to select appliances based on their energy efficiency, A–G scale. G is least energy efficient, A the most energy efficient.

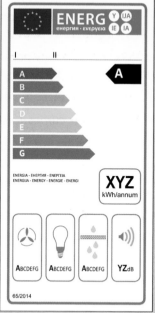

Higher Level 2012, Section A, Q12 (6 marks)

Explain energy labelling in relation to household appliances (see opposite).

Name **two** household appliances that carry an energy label.

1. *Washing machine*
2. *Refrigerator*

Higher Level 2014, Section B, Q4 (a)–(c)

'Kitchen appliances play a prominent role in enhancing the performance of modern kitchens.'

(a) Discuss the following factors that should be considered when selecting kitchen appliances for a family home.

(3 points × 4 marks each = 12 marks; 1 reference to each)

Sourcing consumer information: magazines, web sites, manufacturers' leaflets, advertisements.

Design: appliance should be durable, safe, easy to use and maintain.

Value for money: initial, running and servicing costs should be affordable, a guarantee, after-sales service.

(b) Set out details of a study you have undertaken on microwave ovens.

(20 marks)

Refer to **each** of the following:

(i) Construction and working principle (4 points × 2 marks = 8 marks)

Construction: metal-lined enamel steel box with a glass door, safety catch and seal, internal light, turntable, digital controls, a transformer, a magnetron, wave guide.

LINK

- Diagram of microwave oven (p. 243)

exam focus

Drawing a diagram of the microwave oven will help you describe the appliance.

(ii) Working principle   (3 points × 4 marks = 12 marks)

- Transformer increases standard domestic voltage.
- Magnetron converts electrical energy to electromagnetic energy.
- Wave guide directs microwaves into the oven to be reflected, transmitted and absorbed.
- Microwaves penetrate food, food molecules vibrate rapidly and produce high heat.
- Food defrosts, cooks or reheats.
- Water comes to the surface and prevents food browning.

(iii) Guidelines for use   (3 points × 2 marks = 6 marks)

- Use recommended cooking containers, never metal.
- Arrange food in a circle with the thickest part outwards.
- Allow recommended standing time.

(c) Explain how the consumer can protect the environment when choosing, using and disposing of electrical appliances.

(3 points × 4 marks; 1 reference to each)

1. **Choose** energy efficient appliances with a high energy rating
2. Only **use** dishwasher and washing machines with full loads
3. Follow the **WEEE directive**, use free in-store facility when buying a new appliance.

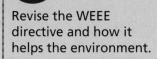

exam focus

Revise the WEEE directive and how it helps the environment.

Ordinary Level 2015, Section B, Q4 (a)–(c)

'John and Barry are 1st year college students living in rented accommodation and plan to cook their main meal each day.'

(a) Set out the results of a study you have carried out on small electrical household appliances which would assist John and Barry in carrying out food preparation tasks. Refer to:

(i) Type of appliance you would recommend and reason for choice   (8 marks)

Type: Food processor   (4 marks)

Reasons for choice: Speeds up the preparation of ingredients   (4 marks)

LINK

- Food processor (p. 236)

(ii) Factors to be considered when selecting the appliance   (3 factors × 3 marks = 9 marks)

1. Space available
2. Quality
3. Ease of cleaning

(iii) Guidelines for use   (3 guidelines × 3 marks = 9 marks)

 1. Follow the manufacturer's instructions.

 2. Follow all safety guidelines.

 3. Clean after each use and store in a ventilated cupboard.

(b) Suggest **one** method of payment which could be used to purchase the appliance and state why this method of payment would be suitable.

               (12 marks)

Method of payment: Cash

Reason why it is suitable: convenient, no risk of debt or overspending

(c) Describe the procedure to be followed should a problem occur with the new household appliance.   (3 points × 4 marks)

1. Return to the shop with the appliance, receipt and guarantee.

2. Speak to the manager and explain the problem with the appliance.

3. Explain what you require, e.g. refund, replacement, repair.

> **Practise the following Section B exam questions:**
> **Higher Level 2009** – Electrical appliances
> **Higher Level 2007** – Refrigerator
> **Ordinary Level 2010** – Washing machine
> **Ordinary Level 2009** – Machine with a motor

Textiles

Uses of textiles

- Household linen (bed, table and kitchen).
- Interior textiles (cushions, rugs, upholstery).
- Clothing (shirts, coats, etc.).

Functions of clothing

1. To enhance one's appearance and give confidence.
2. To protect against the weather, e.g. hats, coats.
3. To keep us safe from chemicals, disease, fire, injury.
4. To identify workers, e.g. gardaí, nurses, soldiers.
5. To express one's personality.

> **LINKS**
> - Management of household financial resources (p. 213)
> - Consumer choice (p. 254)

Functions of household textiles

1. To decorate our homes.
2. To create a comfortable atmosphere.
3. To provide warmth and insulation.
4. To absorb sounds, making the home more relaxing.
5. To provide privacy.

Be able to describe each function of textiles in more detail with specific examples.

Choosing household textiles (selection criteria)

When choosing textiles, consider the following factors:

1. Function of item: end use of textile.
2. Fitness for purpose: suitability, drape and weight.
3. Cost: buy the best you can afford.
4. Properties: check desirable/undesirable properties.
5. Care and maintenance: washable, dry cleanable, stain-resistant.
6. Personal taste: likes and dislikes.
7. Aesthetic appeal: colour, pattern, properties, appearance, drape, weight, lustre.
8. Safety: flame-retardant finishes for children's clothing, nightwear, upholstery.

Natural textiles are more expensive than synthetics.

Care of fabrics

Scientific principles

1. Use detergents to suit the fabric.
2. Choose the correct water temperature.
3. Agitate fabrics to loosen dirt and remove stains.
4. Add fabric conditioners to reduce static electricity.
5. Remove water using a method which will not damage the fabrics or their finishes.

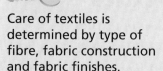

Care of textiles is determined by type of fibre, fabric construction and fabric finishes.

Detergent	Ingredients in detergents include bleach, enzymes, fluorescents, conditioner and surfactants
Water	Efficiency of wash is determined by type of water – hard or soft and lather produced
Temperature	Incorrect temperatures damage fabrics, e.g. fabric shrinks, loses shape
Agitation	Assists dislodging dirt, amount is determined by how dirty the fabric is and the type of fabric
Conditioners	Soften fabrics, reduce static and aid ironing

Textile care labelling codes

Symbol	Application
95°	White cotton and linen articles without special finishes.
60°	Cotton, linen or viscose articles without special finishes where colours are fast at 60°C.
50°	Nylon, polyester/cotton mixtures, polyester, cotton and viscose articles with special finishes, cotton/acrylic mixtures.
40°	Cotton, linen or viscose articles where colours are fast at 40°C but not at 60°C.
40°	Acrylics, acetate, triacetate (including mixtures with wool), polyester/wool blends.
40°	Wool (including blankets) and wool mixtures with cotton or viscose and silk.
✕	Do not wash
30°	Delicate fabrics

95° – cotton, linen, hot boil wash
60° – hot wash, cotton, linen or viscose
50° – nylon, polyester/cotton blends
40° – cotton, linen, viscose
40° – (one bar) acrylics, acetate, triacetate
40° – (two bars), wool, wool blends
30° – non-colour fast fabrics, silk

Ironing Symbols

Cool (120°C) acrylic, nylon, acetate, triacetate, polyester.

Warm (160°C) polyester mixtures, wool.

Hot (210°C) cotton, linen, viscose or modified viscose.

Do not iron.

Handwash

Articles which must not be machine washed.

Drying Symbols
Dry flat

 Fibres may stretch if line dried.

Drip dry

 Fibres may stretch or crease if wrung.

Line dry

Tumble drying beneficial

Do not tumble dry

Cleaning Symbols
Dry cleaning

(A) Normal goods dry cleanable in all solvents.

(P) Normal goods dry cleanable in perchloroethylene, white spirit, Solvent 113 and Solvent 11.

(F) Normal goods dry cleanable in white spirits and Solvent 113.

Some fabrics may be affected by different solvents, e.g. silk.

Chlorine bleach

 May be treated with chlorine bleach.

 Do not use chlorine bleach.

 Do not dry clean

Properties and care of fibres

1. Wool

Properties	Care required
● Absorbent and soft	● Hand wash or dry clean (read label)
● Damaged by bleach	● Medium machine wash at 40°C
● Shrinks	● Dry flat, avoid stretching
● Scorches easily	● Use a warm iron setting
● Weak when wet	● Do not use bleach
● Pills easily	● Do not tumble dry

2. Cotton

Properties	Care required
● Absorbent, dyes readily	● Hand wash with hot water *or* machine wash at 95°C (100% cotton) or at 40°C or 50°C (cotton blends)
● Strong	
● Burns/scorches easily	
● Creases easily	● Bleach can be used
● Cheap cotton becomes limp	● Iron when damp with a hot iron
● Shrinks	

3. Polyester (synthetic fibre)

Properties	Care required
● Resists creasing, mildew	● Machine wash in warm water
● Washes well, dries quickly	● Wash cotton/polyester blends at 50°C
● Non-absorbent, attracts dirt	● Cool iron
● Develops static build-up	

4. Viscose (regenerated fibre)

Properties	Care required
● Creases easily	● Medium machine wash at 50°C
● Weak when wet	● Must not be wrung out
● Shrinks at high temperatures	● Press/iron at low temperature
● Absorbent, drapes well	

LINK
● Consumer choice (p. 254)

exam focus

Revise the uses of different fibres/fabrics.

Fabric finishes include: anti-static, anti-pilling, crease-resistance, mercerising, shrink-resistant and stain-resistant finishes.

Household textiles – safety considerations

Only choose:

- Low-risk fabrics.
- Fabrics treated with flame-retardant finishes.
- CMHR foam filling in furniture.

Low-risk fabrics: wool, polyester.

High-risk fabrics: cotton, acrylic.

CMHR = combustion-modified high resilience foam.

Flame-retardant finishes

Fabrics with flame-retardant finishes will self-extinguish when the flames are removed.

Types of flame-retardant finish

1. Coated fabrics: not permanent, cheap.
2. Inherent flame-retardant finishes (fibres treated prior to weaving): durable, expensive.

Example: Proban – an expensive durable flame-retardant finish.

- A phosphorus/nitrogen layer is applied to fabric.
- Insoluble polymers form in the fabric.
- On lighting, fabrics do not melt or smoulder and flames will self-extinguish.

Effects of flame-retardant finishes

- Makes fabric more expensive.
- Care needed when cleaning.
- Reduces risk of igniting.
- Self-extinguishing when removed from flames.
- Allergic reaction in some people.

Fire Safety (Domestic Furniture) Order (1988, 1995)

Purpose is to reduce the risk of household fires from textiles.

The **Fire Safety Order** covers:

1. *Types of fillings and covers* used for upholstered domestic products, e.g. armchairs, beds, cushions, loose covers, pillows, sofas, children's cots and pushchairs.
2. *Labelling arrangements* for textile products.

Note: it *does not* cover bed linen, carpets, curtains, pillowcases and sleeping bags.

The regulations require that:

1. Manufacturers use CMHR.
2. Fabrics must pass a series of fire safety tests.
3. Permanent safety labels must be attached securely, be clearly legible and durable.
4. Products must have a swing or display safety label.

Types of safety label

1. **Red triangle:** filling meets the safety requirements, states that a fire-resistant interliner is present, states that outer fabric is not match-resistant.

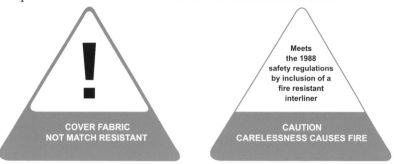

2. **Green square:** filling and covering fabric meet safety requirements for resistance to cigarettes and match ignition.

3. Permanent label: stitched permanently to fabric, provides a warning ('Carelessness causes fire') details about the manufacturer (name, address, identification number), description of filling and cover materials.

Exam questions and sample answers

Higher Level 2016, Section A, Q11 (6 marks)

List **two** desirable properties of fabrics used in upholstered furniture.

1. Durable and hardwearing

2. Flame-retardant

What information does the following label convey to the consumer?

Materials meet the requirements for resistance to cigarette and match ignition.

Higher Level 2013, Section A, Q11 (6 marks)

Explain the purpose of any **two** of the following fabric detergent components.

Surfactants:
Reduce surface tension in fabric, allow water to wet fabric, dirt seeps into the water.

Enzymes:
Remove protein-based stains, breaks them down to allow the detergent to work.

Fluorescents:
Reflect light and make fabrics appear whiter and cleaner.

Ordinary Level 2017, Section A, Q10 (6 marks)

Outline **two** points to be considered when selecting textiles for the home.
- *Suitability for purpose, e.g. hard-wearing, stain resistant, drapes well.*
- *Care: washable rather than dry-clean, drip-dry, easy-iron.*

Name **two** fabrics suitable for household textiles.
- *Wool*
- *Polyester cotton*

Ordinary Level 2015, Section A, Q9 (6 marks)

Using the words listed below, complete the following statements in relation to flame retardant finishes applied to textiles.

self-extinguish   Proban   flammability

Flame retardant finishes reduce the *flammability* of a fabric.

Proban is a flame retardant finish.

Flame retardant finishes cause fabric to *self-extinguish*.

Ordinary Level 2014, Section A, Q11 (6 marks)

(a) Name **one** natural fibre and one synthetic fibre.

Natural fibre	Synthetic fibre
Cotton	*Polyester*

(b) Explain why natural fibres are used in household textiles.

Natural fibres are absorbent, strong, easy to care for and resilient. Cotton can be dyed easily, treated with finishes to improve its properties and mixed with other fibres.

Consumer studies

What is a consumer?

A consumer is any person who buys or uses goods or services.

exam focus

Consumer studies is examined in both Sections A and B in Higher and Ordinary Level papers and is integrated across questions.

Consumer choice

Factors affecting consumer choice – key points:

1. *Household income:* single, dual, multiple sources.
2. *Personal values:* wants, needs and goals, likes/dislikes.
3. *Cost:* budget available, value for money.
4. *Family and friends:* their view of a product/service.
5. *Merchandising/advertising:* encourages spending.
6. *Salespeople*: persuade consumers of the value of a product/service.
7. *Packaging:* quality, eco-friendly, attractiveness.
8. *Labelling:* information on care, nutrition and safety.
9. Design, colour and functionality.

> **exam focus**
>
> Be able to explain in more detail and give specific examples for each factor affecting consumer choice.

> **LINKS**
> - Food commodities (p. 81)
> - Food processing (p. 147)
> - Food packaging (p. 153)
> - Management of household financial resources (p. 213)
> - Household technology (p. 234)

The purchasing process

HL ### Classification of retail outlets

Outlet	Examples	Features
Department stores	Arnotts, Brown Thomas, Debenhams, Shaws	<ul><li>Wide range of goods</li><li>Arranged in departments, e.g. shoes, electrical, cosmetics, furniture</li><li>Open plan for ease of movement</li><li>Variety of products to suit different budgets</li></ul>
Multiple chain stores	Dunnes Stores, Penneys, Elvery Sports	<ul><li>Same company, many branches</li><li>Same design and layout</li><li>Self-service</li><li>Shared advertising, marketing, etc.</li><li>Good value for money, shared bulk buying</li></ul>
Supermarkets	SuperValu, Dunnes Stores, Tesco, Aldi, Lidl	<ul><li>Self-service, open plan</li><li>Wide range of goods</li><li>Own brands are cheaper</li><li>Internet shopping offered</li><li>Some offer home delivery</li></ul>
Discount stores	Argos	<ul><li>High turnover</li><li>Lower prices</li><li>Order goods from catalogue</li><li>Limited pre-packed stock</li></ul>
Independent shops	Local butcher, jeweller, greengrocer	<ul><li>Local, often family-owned shops</li><li>Higher prices (higher overheads), limited stock</li></ul>

Voluntary supermarkets	Combined supermarket and independent shop e.g. Spar, Centra, Mace	• Good range of products • Local owner • Own brands as well as other popular brands

Other retail outlets/shopping systems:

- Mail order shopping
- Online shopping
- Television buying
- Street markets
- Farmers' markets
- Outlet shops
- Auctions

exam focus

Revise the advantages and disadvantages of online shopping.

Retail psychology

Retail psychology involves the study of human behaviour and decision-making when buying products and services. It influences research, advertising and marketing.

Techniques to encourage consumer spending

In-store stimuli	Background music, colours, aromas
Layout of store	• **Structured:** grid layout with aisles • **Unstructured:** free-flow layout
Product placement	• Luxury items placed at eye level • Essentials lower down or at back • Products grouped by association • Special offers at the end of aisles • Items, location and triangular balance
Product blocking	*'Blocking'* makes consumers notice products
Shelf position	Products with highest profit margins at eye level
Impulse goods	Magazines and sweets at checkout
Late-night opening	Accommodates workers and families
Loyalty schemes	Club card, tokens for other products
Merchandising	'Two for one' offers encourage spending
Size of decompression zones	Consumers adjust to shopping area
Home delivery service	Useful for people without transport or with physical disabilities
Car delivery service	Helping consumers take groceries to their car

key point

The entrance, or 'Dwell zone', located just inside the door, promotes specific items.

Shopping patterns

Factors that influence shopping patterns include:

1. Shopping traditions in the family.
2. Income, e.g. restrictive or non-restrictive.
3. Marketing and advertising strategies.
4. Environmental awareness.
5. Opening times of shopping outlets, e.g. 24-hour shopping.
6. Time available, e.g. if limited, use online shopping.
7. Dependence on others for transport.
8. Proximity to retail parks/shopping centres.

Consumers expect quality goods and services.

Consumer research

Consumer research involves collecting, analysing and processing information from consumers.

Research methods: surveys, interviews, customer panels and questionnaires.

Revise the changes in shopping patterns in the past 50 years.

Types of research

	Process	Advantages	Disadvantages
Desk research	• Data from state agencies, internet, trade associations, written/phone surveys • Useful for collecting data about trends and competitors	• Quick • Inexpensive	• Information is very general • Little detail • Risk of bias
Field research	• Data and information collected from the marketplace • Useful for examining consumer shopping habits • Data from surveys, questionnaires, interviews, observation, vox pop, panels	• Quick • Efficient method for collecting specific, accurate and detailed data	• Time-consuming • Expensive

Advantages of consumer research

1. Creates a consumer profile, e.g. age, gender, income.
2. Identifies consumers' likes and dislikes, needs and wants.
3. Highlights weaknesses in advertising and marketing strategies.
4. Identifies current and potential market sizes.
5. Identifies the competitors in the market.

6. Reduces retailer financial risks.

7. Allows development of new products and services.

Advertising

Functions of advertising

1. To sell goods and services.
2. To inform consumers of new products.
3. To improve the popularity/sales of old products.
4. To create an environmentally friendly image.
5. To promote a company as a consumer-friendly organisation.

Advantages of advertising

1. Provides consumers with information about a product.
2. Creates interest in new/old products, increases or maintains sales.
3. Encourages competition, may reduce prices.
4. Provides a range of employment opportunities.

Disadvantages of advertising

1. Increases cost of product/service.
2. Creates a desire in people to buy lifestyle products.
3. Encourages consumerism, buying of non-essentials.
4. Puts pressure on low-income groups.
5. Can reinforce stereotyping.

> **LINK**
> ● Food packaging (p. 153)

Consumer rights and responsibilities

Consumer rights

Consumers are entitled to the **right to**:

1. Honest information (labelling laws, instructions).
2. Redress (repair, replacement or refund).
3. High standards of safety (safety symbols, warning symbols).
4. Choice (competition is encouraged).
5. Value for money (never confuse cost and value).
6. High-quality services and goods (merchantable, fit for purpose).

> **key point**
>
> The 3 Rs: Repair, Replacement, Refund.

Consumer responsibilities

Consumers are expected to:

- Be informed when making decisions.
- Be familiar with consumer protection laws.
- Read the labels provided about goods and services.
- Examine products, investigate services before buying.

- Understand symbols and warnings on labels.
- Use the product as intended and follow the instructions.
- Keep receipts and guarantees.

Sources of consumer information

1. Points of sale, e.g. showrooms, salespeople.
2. Magazines, newspapers, brochures, leaflets.
3. TV, radio, Internet, billboards.
4. Friends and family.
5. Labelling information.
6. Official centres.

Consumer signs and symbols

Hazardous substances	
Harmful/irritant *Found on:* cleaning agents	
Toxic *Found on:* bleach, cleaning agents	
Highly flammable *Found on:* petrol, diesel	
Corrosive *Found on:* cleaning products	

Quality and safety	
Irish Standard mark/ Caighdeán Éireannach	
Guaranteed Irish	
Communauté Européenne	CE
BSI Kitemark	
Excellence Irish Quality Mark (awarded by EIQA)	Quality Certified
Double insulated	
Irish Mark of Electrical Conformity	

The consumer and the environment

Consumers have a responsibility to protect the environment by developing a waste management system in the home, and by re-using and/or recycling products.

Failure to protect the environment results in:

- Reduction in non-renewable resources (coal, oil).
- Global warming, climate change, pollution.
- Disappearance of tropical rain forests.
- Drought, flooding, famine, migration.

LINKS

- Food commodities (p. 81)
- Food processing (p. 147)
- Food packaging (p. 153)
- Household technology (p. 234)
- Textiles (p. 247)

Managing resources

Renewable resources come from naturally recurring resources, e.g. biomass, geothermal heat, hydropower, solar power, wind power, tidal power. Renewable resources:

- Can be used to generate electricity.
- Have little effect on the environment.
- Are clean and efficient – but set-up costs are high.

Non-renewable resources come from fossil fuels, e.g. coal, gas, oil, peat, uranium.

- They will run out.
- Release carbon dioxide and harmful pollutants into the air.
- Nuclear power produces hazardous waste.

key point

Ireland is committed to reduce greenhouse gas emissions under the Kyoto Protocol.

Waste management

Waste management involves prevention, minimisation, re-use, recycling, energy recovery and disposal. Consumers should refuse, re-use and recycle. **Sustainable development** promotes the use of renewable resources and ensures that the least possible amount of damage is done to the environment.

exam focus

Check out the Waste Management Pyramid (search the Internet) and central/local government Waste Management Plans.

Refuse, re-use and recycle

Responsible waste management involves:

1. Recycling organic and inorganic waste products.
2. Re-using products in the home, e.g. glass jars.
3. Bringing products to recycling centres/points.
4. Buying products with the EU Eco-label or the green dot.
5. Selecting biodegradable and phosphate-free products.
6. Disposing of freezers and fridges correctly.

key point

Buy only what you need, avoid over-packaged goods, harvest rainwater and dispose of waste liquids safely.

WEEE Directive (Waste Electrical and Electronic Equipment)

Producers must organise the collection and treatment of waste electrical and electronic equipment. A specific fee is charged at point of sale when buying electrical and electronic goods to cater for this waste management system.

Advantages of recycling

- Reduces costs of waste disposal.
- Reduces litter and pollution.

- Conserves non-renewable resources.
- Creates new businesses and employment.

Recycling symbols

Be able to name each symbol and state what it represents.

1. **Green dot**
   Companies are members of Repak, have made a contribution to cost of recycling products.

2. **Recycling symbol**
   Goods or packaging are made from recyclable materials or can be recycled.

3. **Eco-label**
   Little damage caused to the environment.

4. **PET label**
   Polyethylene terephthalate – certain plastics can be recycled.

Energy

Ireland supports a policy of sustainable energy.

SEAI (Sustainable Energy Authority of Ireland)

- Is a statutory authority.
- Aims to improve energy efficiency.

- Promotes the move to renewable energy resources.
- Aims to reduce the effects of energy production and use.
- Advises government on policies and measures.

Energy labelling – Energy rated A to G

See Household appliances (p. 235).

Sources of energy

Wind	Wind turbines produce energy, in coastal and hilly areas
Solar	Panels built into roofs, also used to power public devices, e.g. parking meters
Hydropower	Harnessing energy from fast-flowing rivers
Biomass	Sustainable energy source, e.g. wood, energy crops
Geothermal	Harnessing energy from heat in the earth

Energy consumption efficiency

Appliances	Use appliances with good energy ratings; use the 'half load' button on washing machines; unplug televisions and video machines when not in use; use Nightsaver electricity, etc.
Lighting	Use CFL bulbs; switch off lights when not in use
Insulation	Lag hot water cylinders; fix timers to immersion heaters; use draught-proofing; insulate the house, place timers and thermostats on central heating systems; turn down heating thermostats by a couple of degrees; replace old windows with double glazing
Others	Dry clothes in the fresh air; take a shower instead of a bath; use rechargeable batteries and a charger; add solar systems to new homes; replace fossil fuels with solar, wind or biomass energy

Air pollution

Causes:

- Chlorofluorocarbons (CFCs) from fridges and aerosols.
- Carbon monoxide from cars, buses, etc.
- Chemical sprays and cleaning agents.
- Burning fossil fuels.

Consequences/effects:

- Depletion of ozone layer, results in skin cancer and eye damage.
- Acid rain (damage to soil, buildings, plants).
- Global warming, climate change.
- Respiratory problems.

Preventing air pollution (preventative actions):

- Buy energy-efficient appliances.
- Choose renewable energy sources.
- Avoid products containing CFCs.
- Buy ozone-friendly aerosols.

Water pollution

Causes:

- Industrial and waste (chemicals).
- Farm waste (fertilisers, pesticides, slurry).
- Oil spillages on land and at sea.
- Illegal dumping of toxic waste.
- Detergents containing phosphates.

Consequences/effects:

- Destroys plants, animals and birds.
- Damages rivers.
- Damages fishing and tourist industry.
- Water becomes unsafe to drink.

Preventing water pollution (preventative actions):

- Opt for phosphate-free products.
- Reduce use of pesticides and fertilisers.
- Install effective sewage and water systems.
- Enforce legislation – impose penalties.

Noise pollution

Causes:

- Traffic (cars, buses, trains, aircraft).
- Equipment (household, garden).
- Noisy animals.
- House and car alarms.
- Loud music, e.g. discos.

Consequences/effects:

- Headaches.
- Lack of sleep.
- Tension, stress and ill-health.
- Rows between neighbours.

Preventing noise pollution (preventative actions):

- Good insulation (triple glazing).

- Live away from busy public roads.
- Turn down music systems, TVs and radios.

Consumer protection

Consumer rights are protected by legislation and the courts, statutory government agencies and voluntary agencies.

Sale of Goods and Supply of Services Act 1980

- Covers goods, services, guarantees and illegal signs.
- Legal responsibility lies with the supplier of a service or the retailer of a product.

The Act states that goods or services should:

- Be of merchantable quality.
- Be fit for purpose, suitable for use.
- As described on labels or brochures, or as described by salesperson.
- Correspond to sample on display.

Services:

- Must be supplied by qualified and skilled people.
- Must be provided with due care, following safety procedures.
- Materials used must be of merchantable quality.

Redress for consumers

Under the Act, if goods are faulty or services are unsatisfactory consumers may be entitled to a replacement, repair, refund or partial refund or repeat of a service.

Guarantees

A guarantee:

- Is covered by the Sale of Goods and Supply of Services Act 1980.
- Is a contract between the consumer and the manufacturer.
- Has a time limit, e.g. one year.
- Does not affect a consumer's rights.

Under the Act, guarantees should:

- Be legible and refer to specific goods.
- Name the product.
- Name the person/company offering the guarantee.
- Give the company address.
- Show the duration of guarantee from date of purchase.
- Outline procedures for making a claim.
- State what the manufacturer will do – what the customer should expect to receive in the event of a fault.
- Identify any extra charges claimant might pay, e.g. postage.

Signs

Signs that are illegal because they limit the rights of consumers:

- 'No cash refunds'.
- 'Credit notes only given'.
- 'No exchange of goods'.

Electronic Commerce Act 2000

- Established under the EU.
- Protects consumers when shopping online (e-bookings and agreements).

Consumer Protection Act 2007 (replaced Consumer Information Act 1978)

The Act protects consumers from misleading or false claims about goods, services and prices and prohibits misleading or false claims made:

- Verbally, e.g. sales assistants, in advertisements or in catalogues.
- About a service and those providing a service.
- About the price, previous price or recommended retail price.
- About extra costs (must be stated clearly on price tag).

Previous price must be true, e.g. from €10.99 to €4.99, and item must have been on sale at the original price for 28 consecutive days in the previous three months.

The current syllabus refers to the Consumer Information Act 1978. In exam answers refer to the Consumer Information Act 1978 and the Consumer Protection Act 2007.

Statutory and voluntary bodies protecting consumers

Statutory bodies	Voluntary bodies
• Competition and Consumer Protection Commission • Office of the Ombudsman • National Standards Authority of Ireland (NSAI) • Citizens Information Board • European Consumer Centre, Ireland	• Consumer Association of Ireland • Advertising Standards Authority of Ireland

Competition and Consumer Protection Commission

The Competition and Consumer Protection Commission took over the functions of the National Consumer Agency and the Competition Authority in 2014. It is an independent statutory body.

Functions

- Enforces consumer protection law and legislation.
- Informs consumers about their rights.
- Enforces product safety regulations.
- Enforces in Ireland EU and Irish competition law.
- Advises government, its agencies and public bodies.
- Encourages compliance with legislation.

Office of the Ombudsman, Ireland

The Ombudsman is appointed by the government. The role of the office is laid down in law by the Ombudsman Act 1980 and the service is independent and free. In 2013 the Ombudsman (Amendment) Act 2012 brought over 180 public bodies under the remit of the Ombudsman, e.g. CAO and SUSI.

Role of the Ombudsman

- To investigate unresolved complaints against public bodies: government departments, local authorities, the Health Service Executive, agencies that deliver health and social services on behalf of the HSE, An Post and all bodies covered by the Disability Act 2005.
- Valid complaints are reported by the Ombudsman to the department in question and recommendations are made to resolve the matter.

National Standards Authority of Ireland (NSAI)

The NSAI:

- Sets, monitors and develops standards of safety and quality in Ireland.
- Ensures that products meet EU and international safety and quality standards.
- Provides accredited certification, e.g. Food Hygiene and Safety.
- Formulates standards by consulting consumer groups, government agencies, environmental organisations and businesses.

Citizens Information Board

The board is a statutory body that provides the public with accurate information and advice on a range of public and social services areas, for example consumer rights, social welfare, health services, family law, housing, income tax, local services and redundancy. Information is provided through:

- A website (www.citizensinformation.ie).
- A phone service.
- Citizens Information Centres.

The Citizens Information Board funds and supports Money Advice and Budgeting Service (MABS).

European Consumer Centre, Ireland

- Located in Dublin (a walk-in centre).
- Provides free information on consumer rights in the EU.
- Participates in the European Consumer Centres Network (ECC-Net), research and surveys.
- Co-operates with national consumer organisations and enforcement agencies, e.g. National Consumer Agency.
- Co-financed by the European Commission and the Competition and Consumer Protection Commission.

Consumer Association of Ireland

- A non-profit-making, independent organisation.
- Publishes *Consumer Choice* magazine.
- Carries out independent research and surveys.
- Aims to improve consumer legislation.
- Represents consumers in state bodies, agencies and industry.
- Advises government on consumer issues.

Advertising Standards Authority of Ireland (ASAI)

- Independent, voluntary body.
- Ensures advertisements are legal, decent, honest and truthful.
- Investigates consumer complaints.

Making complaints – procedures to follow

- Do not use the product if you notice a fault.
- Stop using the product if it develops a fault.

Complaining in person

1. Return the product and the receipt to the retailer.
2. Ask to speak to the manager if the assistant is unable to help.
3. Explain the nature of the problem, produce the product and receipt.
4. Keep to the facts and calmly ask what the retailer will do to solve the problem.

Solution: might involve replacement, refund or repair.

Complaining in writing

Put the complaint in writing to the manager or director, outlining clearly:

1. Item purchased (manufacturer's name, make, model).
2. Date of purchase.
3. Copy of receipt of purchase and guarantee.

4. Nature of the problem.

5. Outline of return visit to the shop, name of the person spoken to.

6. Action you expect the company to take.

Keep a copy of the letter.

If your complaint fails, consider legal advice or the small claims procedure.

Small claims procedure

The Small Claims Court:

- Is a system within the local District Court.
- Is a cheap, fast and easy way of dealing with small claims.
- Can be used by consumers and businesses (since 11 January 2010).

A solicitor is not required.

Claims handled by Small Claims Court include:

- Faulty goods.
- Bad workmanship or minor damage to property.

Procedure for claimants

- Claimant completes an application form in writing or online using the court's online facility, and sends it to the local District Court Office with the fee.
- Information included on form:
  - Name and address of claimant (person making the claim).
  - Name and address of respondent (person/company against whom the claim is made).
  - Amount of claim.
  - Details of claim (set out simply and very clearly).
  - Date and signature of claimant.
- Application must be accompanied by the correct fee.
- Application is registered with the Small Claims Registrar.
- A copy of the claim and Notice of the Claim is sent to the Respondent.
- The respondent can accept the claim, dispute the claim, counterclaim or ignore it.
- Undisputed claims are settled, the Registrar will attempt to resolve disputed claims.
- If there is no resolution the case will be heard in the District Court.
- If the respondent does not reply within 15 days it is settled in favour of the claimant.
- A respondent has 28 days to comply with the judgement.

Exam questions and sample answers

 Higher Level 2016, Section A, Q9 (6 marks)

State the purpose of consumer research.

To identify consumer, needs, wants, likes, dislikes and expectations.

Name and describe **one** method of consumer research.

Desk research involves collecting data from state agencies, internet, trade associations, written/online surveys, phone surveys. It is a quick and inexpensive method of highlighting trends.

Ordinary Level 2015, Section A, Q12 (6 marks)

Outline **two** consumer rights.

- *Right to value for money*
- *Right to redress (repair, replace, refund, repeat of a service)*

> **LINK**
> - Consumer protection (p. 263)

State the functions of the Small Claims Court.

A system within the local District Court for dealing with consumer disputes/claims up to € 2,000 in an inexpensive, fast way.

> **LINK**
> - Making complaints (p. 266)

 Higher Level 2016, Section A, Q12 (6 marks)

Name **one** cause of air pollution and state the effect of this pollution on the environment.

Cause: gases released from burning fossil fuels, e.g. nitrogen, carbon dioxide, sulphur dioxide.
Effect: lowering of pH level of soil and water damaging plant and animal life.

Explain how air pollution can be reduced.

Use renewable or cleaner energy sources, e.g. solar energy, smokeless fuels, gas.

Ordinary Level 2017, Section A, Q12 (6 marks)

Give **one** example of the following types of pollution

Types of pollution	Examples
Air pollution	*Smoke from domestic fires*
Water pollution	*Farm fertilisers and pesticides*
Noise pollution	*Traffic*

Higher Level 2016, Section B, Q4 (a)–(c)

'While consumers are more optimistic about their financial outlook, they remain cautious, giving due consideration to all types of spend from grocery to big ticket items.'

(a) Discuss how consumer's shopping patterns have changed over the last 10 years and suggest reasons for such changes. **(5 points × 4 marks = 20 marks)**

> Elaborate on each change that has taken place and give examples.

- *Large shopping centres provide late 'one stop shopping'.*
- *Online and TV shopping is increasingly popular.*
- *Demand for convenience, quality services and products.*
- *Home delivery of groceries and other goods.*

Reasons: Convenience is a priority for time-limited and busy families, competition for consumer loyalty, increased consumer awareness.

(b) Give details of **four** merchandising techniques used by retailers to maximise consumer spending. **(4 techniques × 5 marks = 20 marks)**

1. *In-store stimuli: layout, background music, lighting, aroma, product placement.*
2. *Product placement: essentials are placed at the back or centre of stores, magazines at check-out desk, co-ordinated products together e.g. tea and biscuits, sauces and pasta.*
3. *Shelf-position: luxuries are placed at eye level, less expensive items are placed at higher or lower levels.*
4. *Blocking techniques: displays placed at entrance or on aisles ensure consumers see them.*

(c) Name and give details of **one** statutory agency that protects consumers. **(10 marks)**

Name: Competition and Consumer Protection Commission **(2 marks)**

Details: **(2 points × 4 marks = 8 marks)**

- *Enforces consumer protection law by investigating complaints.*
- *Provides consumer information.*

Ordinary Level 2013, Section B, Q4 (a)–(d)

'Jane bought Peter a jacket for his birthday. The jacket was a perfect fit for Peter but he did not like the style of it. Jane went back to the shop to return the jacket and get a refund but the retailer would only give her a credit note.'

> Revise the format of a case study.

(a) Was Jane entitled to her money back? Explain your answer. **(2 points × 5 marks = 10 marks)**

Jane is not entitled to her money back under the Sale of Goods and Supply of Services Act, 1980. The jacket was not faulty, or unfit for purpose, so the retailer was not obliged to return the money just because Peter did not like the style. You are not entitled to a refund when you change your mind.

(b) Outline the procedures to be followed when making a complaint when a problem occurs with a product or service. (3 points × 4 marks = 12 marks)

1. Stop using the product when the fault is identified.

2. Return to the shop with the receipt and guarantee (if it is an appliance)

3. Explain the complaint and what you expect to happen (redress).

4. If not satisfied, put the complaint in writing giving all the details.

5. If unable to resolve the matter take action through the Small Claims Court.

(c) Name and explain **four** rights of the consumer.
  (4 rights × 4 marks = 16 marks)

1. Right to choice

2. Right to honest and truthful information

3. Right to safety

4. Right to redress

exam focus

Elaborate on each point in detail and give examples.

(d) Discuss **three** ways by which the consumer can help protect the environment. (3 ways × 4 marks = 12 marks)

- Check energy rating on appliances. Rating A is more energy efficient than Rating G.
- Choose products in biodegradable packaging. Avoid excess packaging.
- Use full loads in dishwashers and washing machines or choose the half-load button.

5 Social Studies: The Family in Society

aims To learn and revise:
- The family
- Marriage
- Family law

exam focus

The topics in this section are examined in Section B of the exam. In the exam, be able to elaborate on the points given and back up your answers with **factual, up-to-date information**. Use bullet points when answering questions, keep to the facts or the point, elaborate on the information you give, do not give personal opinions and avoid essay-style answers.

Sociological terms

Sociology: The systematic scientific study of the organisation and functioning of human society.

Society: A group of people who share a similar way of life.

Social groups: Groups of people linked by a common purpose. Social groups may be primary or secondary.

- **Primary social groups**: Small groups whose relationships are seen as permanent, e.g. family and close friends.
- **Secondary social groups**: Larger groups of people whose relationships are more impersonal and less permanent, e.g. school community, voluntary groups and work groups.

Culture: The beliefs, customs, language, norms, mores, values, roles, knowledge and skills passed on from one generation to another.

Norms: Accepted established patterns of behaviour that guide society, e.g. going to school.

Mores: Accepted customs, norms and values that are considered important by a society, e.g. being respectful.

Values: The principles and beliefs held by a society about what is 'right' and 'wrong'.

Role: The expected pattern of behaviour of an individual according to their status or position.

Status (ascribed or achieved): The position held by people relative to others within the society and the respect or prestige given to that position by others.

Socio-economic grouping: The classification of people according to occupation, income level and education.

Social mobility: The movement of people between socio-economic groupings due to changes in education, income, occupation and social circumstances.

Kinship: Relationships based on blood relations, marriage, adoption and other connections.

Socialisation: The lifelong process of learning how to become members of society and learning acceptable attitudes, social skills and behaviours. There are two types:

- Primary socialisation: in the family.
- Secondary socialisation: in school, workplace, community.

Social change: Changes that take place in a society due to events (national or global) or scientific and technological developments.

Social institutions: The organised social arrangements in a society, e.g. marriage.

The family

The Irish Constitution defines the family as the 'natural, primary and fundamental group of society'.

The family is:

- A group of people related to each other through blood, marriage or adoption.
- 'The basic unit of society which acts as a support for its members and transmits values from one generation to the next'.

The family exists in all societies in different forms. The **family of origin** is the family in which we grow up. The **family of procreation** is the family we form as adults when we have our own children. The **family of affinity** (family of choice) is formed by those who form bonds with or without legal or blood ties.

Family structures

Types of family structure

- Nuclear (parents and children)
- Extended (parents, children, grandparents, other relatives)
- Blended/reconstituted (partners and children from previous relationships)
- Lone-parent (one parent and his/her children)
- Same-sex families (two parents of same sex with or without children)

Nuclear family – based on modern family structures

1. Small in size, consists of parents and children.
2. Mobile, moves for a variety of reasons, e.g. career.

3. Democratic – shared decision-making.
4. Egalitarian – roles are shared. *believing in that all ppl are = and deserve = rights and opportunities*
5. Economically dependent on a small number of people.
6. Often both parents work outside the home (dual-income).
7. Accepts change more easily than an extended family.
8. Less reliable and more isolated in a crisis.
9. Short lived: death, divorce, children move away.

Extended family – based on traditional family structures

1. Large family group living close to each other, e.g. in the same house or area
2. Frequently economically interdependent, e.g. sharing a farm or other business
3. Authoritarian and generally patriarchal.
4. Segregated roles, gender-specific in nature.
5. Family is immobile because it is large.
6. Long lasting, several generations interdependent.
7. Good network of support in a crisis.
8. Less accepting of change than a nuclear family.

Blended family (step-family, reconstituted family)

1. A family unit formed by two adults and their children from previous relationships/marriages.
2. May result from separation, divorce or death.
3. Family size changes, number of children may increase.
4. Changes in placement of children according to age.
5. Discipline may be a source of conflict between parents.
6. Links with multiple sets of grandparents/family groups.
7. Relationship with non-resident parent may be difficult.
8. Can be more isolated than nuclear or extended family.
9. Balancing finances across two families is difficult.

exam focus

Revise the range of difficulties or problems lone parents might experience.

Lone-parent family

1. Consists of one parent and her/his children.
2. Results from death, divorce, separation, unplanned pregnancy, spouse in prison, or personal choice.
3. Increased workload, parent may be isolated.
4. Reduced ability/opportunities to work outside home.
5. Financial difficulties due to high cost of childcare.
6. Greater risk of poverty and unemployment.
7. Increased dependence on state benefits.
8. Emotional difficulties, depression and stress.

LINK
- Management of household financial resources (p. 213)

HL Social, economic and technological changes affecting the family

Social changes

1. Decline in the extended family and traditional roles.
2. Increase in new family forms and more egalitarian roles.
3. Decrease in family size due to family planning.
4. Acceptance of divorce, separation and co-habitation.
5. Decrease in religious influence; a more secular society.
6. Education and career achievements are priorities.
7. Focus on individualisation and personal choice.
8. Improved educational and work opportunities for women.
9. Increased influence from social media and television.
10. Social problems impacting on family life (violence, alcohol, drug abuse, online bullying).
11. Greater cultural and religious diversity.

Relevant legislation:

- Family Law (Divorce) Act 1996
- Civil Partnership (2010), Children and Family Relationship Act 2015
- Marriage Act 2015
- Employment Equality Acts 1998–2015

Economic changes

1. Food, housing and childcare are expensive.
2. Dual-incomes required to meet financial commitments.
3. Economic recession increased unemployment, debt, etc.
4. Increased demand/reliance on state benefits and allowances.
5. Economic recovery since 2015 reducing unemployment.
6. Increased property prices impacting on limited rental market.
7. Family homes in negative equity, so unable to move house easily.

exam focus

Be able to develop each point associated with changes affecting the family.

Technological changes

1. Time and energy-saving appliances for home and work.
2. TV, films, social media changing family values and expectations.
3. Entertainment technology influencing how family members spend time.
4. Internet, email, smart phones have improved global communication.
5. Communication is instant, some people work from home.
6. Online shopping and banking allow access from home 24/7.
7. Mass production reduces costs, farming is more mechanised.
8. Increased employment in the IT and related areas.

LINK

- Household technology (p. 234)

Development of the family in Ireland

Before industrialisation (1900–1960)

Family form	Extended family was the usual structure.
Family size	Large: children viewed as an economic asset, worked from an early age, high child mortality rates.
Economic status	Households functioned as residential and work units. The father controlled the finance (breadwinner). Differences between poor and rich families with regard to income, home ownership.
Roles	Household tasks were organised along segregated roles. Authority was gender-related, vested in the father (patriarchal). Sons had higher status than daughters.
Position of women	Women considered inferior to men legally and socially. Marriages were often arranged for females and dowries offered.
Employment	Limited work opportunities: badly paid and determined by level of education. Limited access to education without finance. Emigration was common. The mechanisation of farming resulted in unemployment; emigration increased.
Religion	Strict religious upbringing.
At home	<ul><li>Introduction of *rural electrification* (1946) and *water schemes* (1960s) improved home life for women and children.</li><li>1950s: improvements in standards of living, women's health and decrease in child mortality rates.</li></ul>
Education	Most education took place in the home. Literacy levels were low, and few attended secondary school.

After industrialisation (1960–1990)

Family form 1970s.	Nuclear families emerged, urban-based, decline in extended family. People married younger. Romantic love the basis for marriage, decrease in arranged marriages. Couples interdependent emotionally and financially.
Family size	Smaller in size, lower child mortality rates. Children not viewed as economic assets. Regulations were put in place to reduce child labour.
Economic status	Men viewed as the main income earners, some married women worked outside the home. Emergence of the dual-income family. Improved standard of living. Increase in life expectancy, with improved nutrition and healthcare.
Education	Increased educational initiatives and opportunities for all. Education viewed as important. Children able to attend both primary and secondary school. Literacy increased, free education introduced.
Roles	Husband viewed as the breadwinner, wife as the homemaker and carer, focus was on children, their development and family life. Decline in status and role of older family members. More egalitarian roles emerged mid-1970s.

Position of women	Women working in the home had a greater say on parenting, finance and discipline. Improved life expectancy and family planning.
Employment	More married women in the workforce from the mid-1970s. Higher wages and more leisure time. Reduction in working hours.
Developments	Improved heating, electricity and sanitation. Availability of mortgages.

Contemporary Irish families (1990s–present day)

Family form stressed.	More lone-parent, blended and same-sex families. Introduction of divorce (1996), increased rates of separation and co-habitation.
Family size	Smaller family size, more reliable methods of family planning.
Economic status	Increase in costs of childcare, mortgages and rents. Homelessness an issue. Vastly different standards of living within communities.
Employment	Increase in employment, decrease in youth unemployment, increase in retired population (Census 2016). More dual-income families.
Roles	Integrated, egalitarian roles, shared responsibility. Men or women may be homemaker or main earner, shared childcare.
Religion	Decline in religious influence. Society is more secular.
State support	State supporting family functions, e.g. financial, education and socialisation.
Technology	Benefits in the home, work and education. Increased influence on family life (social media, internet, mobile phones).

Functions of the family

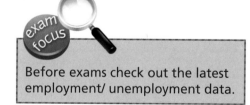

exam focus

Before exams check out the latest employment/ unemployment data.

Protection	• Family protects vulnerable members (babies, disabled people) • Provides a safe environment for all
Reproductive function	• Ensures the survival of the human race • Regulates adult sexual behaviour • Unregulated sexual behaviour results in unwanted pregnancies, STDs and AIDS
Nurturing and rearing function	• Provides basic physical needs (food, clothing, shelter) • Child develops a well-balanced personality in a safe, secure and loving environment
Emotional function	Meets the emotional and psychological needs of the child by providing reassurance, encouragement, love and security

Economic function	Adults in the family work to earn money to provide for the needs of the family, families contribute to the economy (taxes, buying goods/services)
Education function	• Primary centre of early learning • Family supports the state in the education of children by supervising homework, praising and encouraging the child and by providing a stimulating home environment
Socialisation function	• The primary centre of socialisation • Introduces children to the traditions, norms, and values of society • Acts as an agent of social control by showing children what is acceptable and unacceptable behaviour

LINKS
- Dietary and food requirements (p. 54)
- Family resource management (p. 207)
- Management of household financial resources (p. 213)
- Housing finance (p. 228)

State interventions in family functions

1. Protective
- May place children at risk in foster care.
- Cares for the elderly and those suffering from long-term illness through home help, public health nurse, sheltered accommodation, sheltered working environments.
- Provides Child Benefit monthly.
- Developmental health checks at local health centre.

2. Educational/intellectual
- Provides full-time free education from 5 to 18 years.
- Provides Early Childhood Care and Education Scheme.
- Provides assessments to identify learning difficulties.
- Provides learning support, resource teachers and special needs assistants (SNAs).

3. Nurturing
Assisted by pre-schools, primary and secondary schools.

4. Economic
Provides social welfare payments, state services, e.g. Medical Card Scheme, Housing Assistance Payment (HAP), Housing (new council/government mortgage scheme 2018).

exam focus

Revise the current state intervention schemes that support family functions.

5. Socialisation
- Provision of pre-schools, primary and secondary schools.
- Official agencies support families unable to fulfill their social functions.

6. Caring
- Parenting skills courses, e.g. the Parents Plus programme.
- Parent and toddler groups.

Exam questions and sample answers

Higher Level 2016, Section B, Q5 (a), (b)

(a) Analyse the social **and** the economic changes that affect contemporary families

(5 points × 4 marks = 20 marks)

> Make **two** references to social, **two** to economic, plus **one** other.

Social:

1. *Decline in traditional family, increase in new family types.*
2. *Smaller family size due to effective family planning.*
3. *Changing family roles, more egalitarian, less segregated.*

Economic:

1. *Increased cost of living, childcare, mortgages/rent.*
2. *Dual incomes required to pay bills.*
3. *Unemployed dependent on state supports.*

LINK

- Changes affecting the family (p. 274)

(b) Explain how the family can meet the physical and psychological needs of children so that they can contribute to and succeed in a rapidly changing society.   (6 points × 3 marks = 18 marks)

Physical (a summary):

1. *Provide a safe and comfortable home in which to develop.*
2. *Provide a healthy balanced diet to ensure good health.*
3. *Protect vulnerable members of the family, e.g. elderly.*

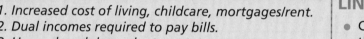

> Give **two** points on physical, **two** on psychological plus **two** others. Elaborate on points given.

Psychological (a summary):

1. *Provide a stable loving atmosphere as a basis for future relationships.*
2. *Encourage and praise children to develop self-esteem and confidence.*
3. *Create a trusting environment for children to express themselves.*

Ordinary Level 2017, Section B, Q5 (a), (b)

(a) Describe each of the following family structures:

(3 types × 6 marks = 18 marks)

Nuclear family:

Independent small family, mobile, can move easily from place to place, parent/parents and their children live in the same house, household tasks are shared, parents work outside the home, short-lived, isolated in a crisis.

Extended family:

Parents, children, grandparents, aunts, uncles and cousins all living close to each other in the same area, may be financially interdependent (farming), segregated roles for women, men and children, immobile, long lasting, good support in a crisis.

Blended family:
One or both adults have been in a relationship previously, children come from different relationships, may occur due to death, divorce, etc.

(b) Discuss **three** ways in which gender roles have changed in the modern family.
(3 ways × 5 marks = 15 marks)

1. *Egalitarian roles, shared household tasks and financial management.*
2. *Dual-incomes, improved living standards.*
3. *Either parent might stay at home to care for children.*

Higher Level 2014, Section B Q5 (b) (i), (ii)

(i) Give an account of **each** of the following functions of the family. (15 marks)

Economic   **Socialisation**   **Educational**

> **LINK**
> • Family functions (p. 276)

(ii) Explain how state interventions assist the family in carrying out these functions.
(2 points × 5 marks = 10 marks)

1. *Allowances: Child benefit, carer's allowance, job seekers allowance.*
2. *Socialisation: pre-school, primary and secondary schools through subjects, activities and the hidden curriculum.*

> **LINK**
> • State interventions (p. 277)

Higher Level 2013, Section B, Q5 (a)

(a) Explain the following sociological terms: (4 points × 3 marks = 12 marks)

Culture: *Behaviour patterns, norms, values, language, music, mores and customs of a society, passed on from one generation to the next generation.*

Norms: *Acceptable ways of behaving in a society, e.g. queueing, greetings.*

Values: *Attitudes and beliefs of what is considered to be right and wrong.*

Role: *Patterns of behaviour considered acceptable for individuals based on position in society or family.*

Marriage

In Ireland, marriage is 'a voluntary, legally binding union between persons without distinction as to their sex, to the exclusion of all others'. It involves rights, obligations and protections. (See Civil Partnership Act 2010, Civil Registration (Amendment) Act 2014, Marriage Act 2015.)

Cultural variations

1. **Choice of a partner:** mutual consent of couple, marrying someone of the same background, arranged marriages, e.g. Hindus, Sikhs, Muslims, endogamy (particular race, religion, social class).

2. **Number of partners:**

Monogamy	
	• One partner
	• Serial monogamy: marries and divorces many times
	• Legally binding until death or divorce
	• Most common type of marriage for Christians and western societies
Polygamy	• More than one partner at the same time
	• More acceptable outside western societies
	Polyandry:
	• One woman and two or more husbands
	• Prevents the division of land (scarce resource)
	• Practised in some Tibetan families
	• Forms of polyandry:
	– Fraternal (husbands are brothers)
	– Non-fraternal (husbands are not related)
	Polygyny:
	• One man and two or more wives
	• Practised in Islamic countries and some African countries
	• Patriarchal in nature and a way of displaying wealth

key point

Bigamy occurs when a person who is legally married to one person enters another marriage.

3. **Locality:** patrilocal, matrilocal and neolocal.

4. **Transfer of inheritance:** eldest son, between spouse and all offspring, inheritance to children born outside marriage – varies across the world.

5. **Minimum age for marriage:** 18 years in Ireland. Some countries do not have a minimum age.

Legal requirements for marriage in Ireland

- Both partners must be over 18 years of age.
- Under 18s need the Court's permission to marry.
- Both partners must freely consent to the marriage.
- Persons may marry without distinction as to their sex.
- They must be free to marry, i.e. be single, divorced or widowed.
- They must not be closely related by blood (consanguinity) or marriage (affinity).
- They must give three months' written notice to the Registrar of Civil Marriages (and the relevant authorities if a religious or secular ceremony is planned).
- The ceremony is held in a registered location, in the presence of a registered Solemniser.

LINKS
- Family structures (p. 272)
- Functions of the family (p. 276)

key point

1st January 2011 – The Civil Partnership and Cohabitation Act 2010 came into effect.

LINK
- Family law (p. 296)

Rights and responsibilities in marriage

- The married couple are obliged to live together (cohabit).
- They have a right to each other's company.
- They are expected to be faithful and loyal to each other.
- They must consummate the marriage, i.e. have sexual relations.
- They must provide financial support for each other and their children.
- They have joint guardianship/custody of children born within the marriage.
- Couples are each responsible for having a Will.

LINK
- Making a Will (p. 297)

key point

Relevant legislation:
- Domestic Violence Act 1996
- Family Home Protection Act 1976
- Succession Act 1965

Preparation for marriage

In the home

- Ideas on marriage are based on experiences in the home.
- Parents are the first role models for married life.
- A supportive and contented relationship between parents provides a positive image of marriage for their children.
- A caring and loving home environment, where good communication, honesty and trustworthiness are evident, helps the development of positive, stable relationships.

At school

- Marriage is studied in a variety of subjects: SPHE, RSE, Health Education, Religion and Home Economics.
- Students discuss topics related to relationships and marriage.

Pre-marriage courses

- Provide opportunities for couples to discuss the realities and expectations of marriage.
- Pre-marriage courses are offered by Accord, Relationships Ireland, etc.

exam focus

Revise the benefits of attending a pre-marriage course.

- Areas discussed include: relationships, roles and responsibilities, children, family planning, finance, marriage and family law, setting up home, problems such as alcoholism, drug abuse, gambling and domestic abuse.
- Financial experts, lawyers, doctors, marriage counsellors and home economists act as facilitators.

Marriage breakdown

Reasons for marriage breakdown include:

1. Marrying for the wrong reason, e.g. pregnancy.
2. Getting married at too young an age.
3. Background differences (social, cultural or religious).

exam focus

Revise the factors that have an impact on marriage stability.

4. Unrealistic expectations associated with romantic love.

5. Social problems (alcoholism, violence, gambling, drug abuse).

6. Infidelity, loss of trust.

7. Changing attitudes towards marriage.

Choices available when a marriage breaks down

Marriage counselling

- Couples look for help to avoid marriage break-up.
- Counselling is provided by relationship counselling services.
- Both spouses must attend.
- Trained professionals help couples to communicate difficulties in a non-threatening environment and to reach resolutions through discussion.
- Referrals to other relevant services may result, e.g. MABS (financial difficulties), bereavement counselling.

Family Mediation Service

- A free, confidential, state-run service.
- Provided for couples who have agreed to separate or divorce.
- A mediator supports couples in a co-operative, non-threatening, confidential atmosphere.
- Couples reach agreement about:
  - Arrangements for children (parenting and custody).
  - The family home and property.
  - Financial matters.
- A written document records the details of the agreement between the couple and this can be taken to a solicitor to formalise the agreement.

Legal/civil nullity

- The marriage never existed, and is declared null and void by a court.
- A marriage is **void** if one of the following was the case prior to or on the day of marriage.
  1. Either party was already married (bigamy).
  2. A legal requirement was not met.
  3. Lack of consent of one of the parties.
  4. Non-consummation due to physical or psychological problems.
  5. Either party is unable to form and sustain a normal marital relationship.
- **Effects of legal nullity**: Partners are free to marry, they have no legal right to share in the estate of the other party, the rights of dependent children are not affected.

Church annulments

- The marriage never existed in the eyes of the Church.

- Church annulments have no legal standing.
- For either spouse to remarry legally, a decree of nullity or divorce is required.

Separation

Types of separation:

1. Deed of Separation or legal separation
2. Judicial Separation.

Deed of Separation or legal separation

Reminder – check for any amendments to family law before your exam.

- Arranged through mediation.
- A written legal agreement between a couple.
- Outlines the terms of the separation relating to their future rights, and their obligations to each other and their children.
- Both partners must agree to all terms.
- A solicitor draws up the Deed of Separation.
- The written contract is signed in front of witnesses.

Judicial Separation Act 1989

- This was amended by the Family Law Act 1995.
- It is implemented when a couple fail to agree on the terms of a separation.
- It involves a court judgment under the Act.
- Grounds for a Judicial Separation include:
    1. One spouse committed adultery.
    2. Couple have been living apart for one year by agreement **or** for three years without consent.
    3. One spouse deserted for more than one year.
    4. Absence of normal marital relationship for one year prior to application.
- Case is heard in court if application meets one of the grounds above.
- Additional order may be made by a judge relating to children, maintenance payments, property, barring and safety orders and succession rights.

Divorce

- Introduced into Ireland in 1996.
- Governed by the Family Law (Divorce) Act 1996.
- A divorce may be granted when:

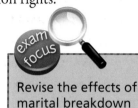

Revise the effects of marital breakdown on spouses, children and society.

    1. The parties have lived apart for four of the five previous years.
    2. There is no prospect of reconciliation.
    3. Provisions have been made for spouse, children and other dependents.
- The divorce hearing is held in the Family Court.
- Direction is provided on maintenance, child custody and access, property and pension adjustment.

Exam questions and sample answers

Higher Level 2017, Section B, Q5 (a)–(c)

'Marriage is still very popular in Ireland. In 2015, religious ceremonies accounted for the highest proportion of marriages (63.3%). Civil ceremonies were the most popular choice for non-religious marriage ceremonies (28%). In recent times the Humanist Association has also risen in popularity with 5.7% of marriages.' (Central Statistics Office, 2016)

(a) Outline the variations that exist in marriages today.

(4 points × 4 marks = 16 marks)

1. *Cultural variations: minimum age, 18 in Ireland, younger ages in other countries.*
2. *Number of partners: monogamy, polygamy (polyandry, polygyny).*
3. *Type of ceremony: Civil ceremony, religious ceremony, etc.*
4. *Second marriages: due to bereavement or divorce, blended/constituted families.*

Elaborate on each variation and give examples.

(b) Discuss the benefits of pre-marriage courses for couples preparing for marriage. (4 benefits × 4 marks = 16 marks)

1. *Provides an opportunity for couples to discuss their expectations.*
2. *Couples can explore their views on relationships, children and family planning.*
3. *Experts provide information on buying a home, mortgages and financial planning.*
4. *Discussions on problems that might occur, conflict resolution and communication.*

> **LINK**
> - Pre-marriage courses (p. 281)

> **LINK**
> - Marriage breakdown (p. 281)

(c) Evaluate **each** of the following options available to couples experiencing difficulties in their marriage.

Marriage counselling: (2 points × 3 marks = 6 marks)

1. *Helps couples to resolve disputes before grounds for separation or divorce emerge.*
2. *Counsellors may refer couples on for specialised help, e.g. MABS, bereavement counselling.*

Family mediation: (2 points × 3 marks = 6 marks)

1. *Provides a confidential service for separating couples to meet with an impartial mediator to negotiate acceptable arrangements for parenting of children, financial support, family home and property.*

Elaborate on each point, giving examples.

2. If negotiations are successful a written document sets out the details which can be drawn into a Legal Deed of Separation by a solicitor.

Legal separation: (2 points × 3 marks = 6 marks)

1. A Separation Agreement/Deed of Separation is a legally binding written contract drawn up by a solicitor, establishes the future rights and duties of both parties to each other and to their children. It may be agreed through mediation.

2. A Judicial Separation/Decree of Separation is made under the Judicial Separation and Family Law Reform Act 1989. The solicitor must advise their client about counselling and mediation services. The application is based on adultery, unreasonable behaviour, desertion or absence of marital relations. It involves a court judgement and may include additional orders.

Ordinary Level 2016, Section B, Q5 (a)–(c)

(a) Discuss why marriage is a popular option for couples in Ireland today.

(3 points × 5 marks = 15 marks)

1. More options of marriage ceremonies are available, e.g. civil, religious, secular.

2. Legal protection for spouses and children in events of difficulties.

3. Provides a safe and protective relationship in which to have children.

(b) Discuss (i) the rights and (ii) the responsibilities within the marriage relationships. (4 points × 5 marks = 20 marks)

(i) Rights:

1. To live together as partners

2. To consummate the marriage

(ii) Responsibilities:

1. To financially support each other and children

2. To provide for children's physical, emotional, moral, social and educational needs

exam focus

Discuss each point in more detail.

(c) Name and give an account of **one** option available to couples experiencing difficulties in their marriage.

exam focus

Name = 5 marks, account = 2 points × 5 marks total = 15 marks.

exam focus

Choose from the following: marriage/relationship counselling, family mediation, legal separation, judicial separation.

LINK

• Marriage breakdown (p. 281)

Family as a caring unit

Family roles

- Each family member plays a role.
- Each individual fulfils many roles.

Roles and responsibilities of children

1. To learn how to behave in an acceptable manner.
2. To be role models for younger siblings.
3. To follow the rules set down by parents, to show respect.
4. To help out with basic tasks, e.g. making their beds.
5. To learn about responsibility, to follow rules.
6. To become socially competent, be happy and secure.

key point

A role is the expected pattern of behaviour of an individual, determined by society's expectations.

LINK
- Family resource management (p. 207)

Roles and responsibilities of adolescents

Adolescence is a period of transition from childhood to adulthood. Role expectations are difficult as adolescents try to:

- Become more responsible for themselves.
- Help out in the home in preparation for life.
- Learn from role conflicts that may arise.
- Use independence and freedom wisely.
- Study hard and achieve their potential.

key point

Compromise and trust are important in the adolescent and parent relationship. Peer pressure is frequently an area of conflict for adolescents.

Roles and responsibilities of parents

1. To provide for children's physical, psychological and social needs.
2. To act in a respectful, loving and caring manner.
3. To show what is right and wrong, to set clear limits.
4. To act as good role models for their children.
5. To balance discipline with encouragement and love.
6. To provide a stimulating and safe environment.
7. To care for older family members, e.g. grandparents.
8. To modify the role as children get older, demonstrate compromise.

exam focus

Answer exam questions in point/bullet form and expand on each point. Keep to the facts.

Older person's roles and responsibilities

1. To live active and healthy lives.
2. To plan for retirement and to maintain independence.
3. To develop new, active roles on retirement.
4. To provide active support to younger family members.
5. To share knowledge and wisdom with younger generations.
6. To continue to be involved in family and community life.

Gender roles

- **Gender** refers to being male or female.
- **Gender role** refers to the pattern of behaviour expected from a man or woman.
- **Gender equity** means treating all individuals equally at home, at school and in the workplace.

Gender and modern family roles

Gender in relation to modern family roles:

- Now more egalitarian due to improved education and awareness.
- Changes in equality legislation, family structures and employment.
- Less defined roles for parents, roles are integrated and shared.
- Stereotyping occurs early in childhood, e.g. toys, colour, tasks.
- Encouraging all children to be independent, ambitious and strong.
- Encouraging all children to consider STEM subjects.
- Encouraging all children to participate in a variety of activities.

Factors affecting changing roles in families

Social factors

Type of family	<ul><li>Fewer extended families</li><li>More nuclear, blended, lone-parent families</li></ul>
Family size	<ul><li>Smaller families, more child-centered</li><li>More resources spent on children</li></ul>
Roles	<ul><li>More egalitarian roles; both parents involved in family life</li><li>Shared decision-making, childcare and housekeeping</li><li>Changing role of women in the home</li><li>Women better educated and financially independent</li></ul>
Employment	<ul><li>Shorter working week, more leisure time spent with children</li><li>Increase in women working outside the home, fathers may be at home</li><li>Increased employment levels since 2015</li></ul>
Grandparents	<ul><li>Frequently provide child care and financial help</li><li>Independent, physically active and healthy, improvements in healthcare, nutrition and finance</li><li>Increased life expectancy</li></ul>
Education	<ul><li>Emphasis on education, school completion and life-long learning</li><li>Skilled workforce has emerged</li><li>More adults seeking places on training courses due to unemployment</li></ul>
Adolescence	Recognition of adolescence as a period of transition, more involved in decision-making at home and school

Economic factors

1. Increase in standard of living, dual-income families.
2. Couples are unable to get mortgages due to reduced income, unemployment and inability to repay loans.
3. High cost of childcare, grandparents are more involved.
4. Young adults have become more financially dependent on parents.
5. Adolescents may choose to work part time, but opportunities are limited.
6. Families experiencing financial difficulties are supported by state welfare system.

> **LINK**
> ● Family resource management (p. 207)

Role conflict

- Occurs when roles are not clearly defined and when one role interferes with another.
- Arises when there is a clash between role expectations.
- Arises when expectations of individuals are to be met at the same time.
- Role conflict creates stress for adolescents, siblings, parents and grandparents.

Examples:

1. Individuals may experience role conflict when a family role interferes with the demands of a work role.
2. For men a role conflict might arise when they are no longer the breadwinner in the family, e.g. because the mother has a better-paid job or because they have become unemployed.

Relationships in the family

Examples:

- Child/parent relationship.
- Adolescent/parent relationship.
- Sibling relationships.
- Grandparent/grandchild relationship.
- Relationships across the extended family.

Child/parent relationship

A good child/parent relationship:

1. Provides for the child's physical, emotional, psychological and social needs.
2. Is the most important first relationship for children.
3. Enables children to learn self-discipline in order to meet social norms.
4. Emphasises and develops honesty, justice, a sense of responsibility and maturity in a secure and safe environment.
5. Provides opportunities for children to experience praise, security, approval and acceptance.
6. Develops self-esteem and confidence in children so that they are capable of forming healthy relationships.

> **LINK**
> ● Importance of good communication in a family (p. 290)

Rights of children within the family

Under the **UN Convention on the Rights of the Child**, children are entitled to:

- Life, a name and a nationality.
- Protection from physical, emotional and sexual abuse.
- Develop physically, spiritually, emotionally, morally and socially.
- Love, understanding, freedom and dignity.
- Education within the family.
- Free primary and secondary education.
- Freedom from discrimination, exploitation and cruelty.
- Provision for special physical or emotional needs.

> **LINK**
> - Child Care Act 1991, 1997 (p. 297)

Adolescent/parent relationship

- Adolescence is a time of rapid transition from childhood to adulthood.
- Adolescents expect privacy, more freedom and responsibility.
- Opportunity for paid part-time work depending on age.
- Conflict may emerge between adolescents and their parents.
- Adolescents more attached to peers and social media, e.g. Facebook, etc.
- Adolescents may adopt a new personal value system.

Causes of adolescent/parent conflict

- Demand for more freedom, independence and responsibility.
- Questioning of parental authority, being more outspoken.
- Peer expectations clashing with parental expectations.
- Educational expectations creating undue stress.
- Parental concerns about alcohol, drugs and relationships.
- Lack of parental awareness of teenagers and social networks.
- Parental worries about safety, e.g. bullying or predators.

Dealing with adolescent/parent conflict

- Establishing respectful, open, honest communication.
- Remaining calm, avoiding confrontation.
- Talking with and listening to each other.
- Trying to understand both points of view.
- Compromising to find an acceptable solution.

> **key point**
> **Key words** in resolving conflict are listening, showing interest, openness, honesty and compromise.

Generational conflict

Causes of generational conflict

- Different norms, mores, values and expectations.
- Young people feeling misunderstood.
- Older people feeling undervalued and unwanted.
- Perceived lack of respect for family members.

- Grandparents questioning parenting skills of adult children.
- Grandparents trying to control their adult children.
- Experiencing ageism, prejudice, discrimination.
- Adults making negative statements about younger people.
- Lack of space and privacy in busy family homes.

Dealing with generational conflict

- Open system of communication in a secure atmosphere.
- Listening, understanding, consideration, respect for all viewpoints.
- Appreciation of experiences of different generations.
- Keeping up-to-date with the latest developments.
- Fair, consistent systems of discipline.
- Consider the issues and possible solutions.
- Negotiate compromises in a calm atmosphere.

Importance of good communication in a family

1. Determines the quality of the relationships between family members, develops respect for others.
2. Ensures that all family members can express their ideas, feelings and thoughts in a safe environment where their views are valued.
3. Requires the development of good listening skills.
4. Supports a positive approach to solving disagreements.
5. Enables all involved to reach agreed solutions together.
6. Prevents misunderstandings.

key point

Communication is a two-way process.

Role of older people in the family

Older people in families play an important role by:

- Passing on norms, mores and values to the next generation
- Enriching society through sharing knowledge and life experiences
- Spending free time with grandchildren, helping their social development
- Providing a childcare option for their adult children
- Offering financial assistance to younger family members.

Grandparent/grandchild relationships

- Tend to be less formal, more relaxed with fewer rules.
- Are very special relationships.
- Grandparents teach grandchildren how to respect others.
- Grandchildren learn how to communicate/negotiate.

Independence of older people in the family

To maintain quality of life and independence, **older people need:**

- An acceptable level of privacy.

- An independent lifestyle to maintain self-esteem.
- Respect and freedom to make their own choices.
- Recognition of their role within family and society.
- Clarification in relation to role expectations.
- Protection and care if unable to look after themselves.
- Involvement in family life, not excluded or ignored.

Economic supports

- State or private pensions allow financial independence.
- State supports may include free TV licence, free fuel, etc.
- Free travel in Ireland for all people aged 66 and over.
- Medical cards if allocated reduce costs of health care.
- Mobility Aids Scheme, Warmer Homes Schemes.
- Home Care Package (under HSE) supports independent living.

Problems associated with ageing

Problems associated with getting older include deterioration of eyesight, hearing, memory and mobility; loneliness; change in status; change in roles; and reduced income.

Accommodation options for older people

- Living at home alone (with family close by).
- Living with family (own section within the house).
- Home care in their own home.
- Sheltered housing scheme in the local community.
- Residential care (private or public nursing home).

Community supports in action

- Meals-on-wheels provide nutritious and balanced meals.
- Family/friends help with shopping, cleaning, home maintenance.
- Sheltered housing schemes provide support and independence.
- Groups in the community prevent isolation, e.g. Age Action etc.
- Senior Alert Scheme grants for monitored personal alarms/pendants.

Exam questions and sample answers

Higher Level 2014, Section B Q5 (c)

(c) Assess the role of grandparents in modern family life.   (3 points × 3 marks = 9 marks)

exam focus

Elaborate and explain **each** of these points to give a complete answer.

1. *Provide practical support for adult children through child-minding.*
2. *Provide emotional support to parents and children during difficult times.*
3. *Act as positive role models for parents and children (directly and indirectly).*

HL

Higher Level 2011, Section B, Q5 (b)

(b) Discuss roles **and** responsibilities of family members **and** explain how these roles change through the life cycle of the family.

(6 points × 4 marks = 24 marks)

exam focus

Make sure to include all family members. Answer using bullet points and elaborate.

Summary of points presented in a chart format:

	Role	Responsibility	Change
Child	*Sibling, son or daughter, grandchild*	*Show respect, behave in an acceptable manner, gain knowledge formally and informally*	*Gradual independence, more responsibility, learn at school, treat everyone with respect, etc.*
Adolescent	*Sibling, son or daughter, grandchild*	*Extra responsibilities, e.g. household tasks, baby sitting siblings, homework*	*Contribute to household decision-making, gain adult independence*
Parent	*Mother/father, spouse/partner*	*Reproduction, nurturing, socialisation, financial, caring for all family members*	*Caring for older parents or relatives*
Grandparent	*Spouse, parent, grandparent*	*Maintain good health, keep active, emotional support for other family members, passing on values, knowledge*	*Spending time with grandchildren and adult children, financial support to adult children*

Ordinary Level 2013, Section B, Q5 (b) (i), (ii), (c)

(b) Comment on:

(i) The importance of independence for elderly people in the family.

(2 points × 5 marks = 10 marks)

   1. *Providing childcare (for grandchildren) maintains sense of self-esteem and being valued.*

   2. *More time for participating in local communities to reduce risk of isolation, e.g. Active Age.*

(ii) How the state supports the independence of elderly people.

(2 points × 5 marks = 10 marks)

   1. *Pensions, free travel and medical cards supports financial independence, keeping active and healthy.*

   2. *Sheltered housing options or modification of family home in cases of physical disability.*

(c) Explain what you understand by generational conflict **and** state **two** ways of dealing with conflict.

Explanation:

Opinions or interests of two generations crash into each other, e.g. views of parents on parenting not the same as their parents (grandparents), conflict between adolescent and parents on friendships and use of social media.

Dealing with conflict:

1. *Do not ignore conflict, create opportunities to negotiate, compromise and resolve it.*

2. *Listen to all points of view in a calm atmosphere where people feel safe talking.*

exam focus

Elaborate on **each** of these points.

Ordinary Level 2015, Section B Q5 (b), (c)

(b) Describe **two** ways of dealing with conflict within the family.

(2 ways × 6 marks = 12 marks)

1. *Avoid confrontation and listen to all views to understand the issues.*
2. *Negotiate and compromise on issues helps reduce conflict.*

(c) Explain why good communication is important between family members.

(2 points × 5 marks = 10 marks)

1. *Open discussion allows all parties to hear the views of others.*
2. *Allows conflict to be resolved in a safe and respectful manner.*

Caring for family members with special needs

Types of special needs – some examples

Types	Examples
Physical disabilities	Visual impairment, hearing impairment, speech disorders, wheelchair use
Intellectual disabilities	Down syndrome
Mental health disorders	Addictions, depression, obsessive compulsive disorder, schizophrenia
Emotional/cognitive impairments	Autism spectrum disorders, attention deficit hyperactivity disorder (ADHD)
Emotional traumas	Abuse, bereavement

Problems, examples of responses

Difficulties and problems	Responses: family, voluntary, state
Quality of life	
• Lack of mobility, isolation	• Early assessment, diagnosis, intervention
• Dependence on others	• Carer's Allowance/Benefit
• Isolated parents	• HSE Respite Care
• Exhausted parents who are the carers	• Extended school year

• Reduced income when one parent stays at home, increase in expenditure • Experience of guilt by parents trying to care for all family members	• Voluntary camps/programmes • Equipment grants • Support groups, e.g. Irish Wheelchair Association. National Council for the Blind, DeafHear

Special emotional needs

Attitudes and inclusion	
• Prejudice experienced by families • Lack of understanding • Exclusion and isolation	• Awareness promoted by organisations, e.g. Down Syndrome Ireland, Irish Autism, Special Olympics Ireland, Schizophrenia Ireland, Aware
Accessibility	
• Homes and buildings prove challenging for those with physical disabilities	• National Disability Authority (NDA) • Social assistance and grants available for modifications to the family home
Education	
• Right to free education to 18 years • EPSEN Act 2004 (Education for Persons with Special Needs) states education should take place as far as is possible in a mainstream setting • Lack of educational resources, facilities and inadequate access may limit education, employment opportunities	• Early assessment and diagnosis allows for early educational intervention • Resource teachers, learning support and special needs assistants (SNAs) • Early Childhood Care and Education Scheme (pre-school education) • Sheltered workshops and community work and care programmes for adults, e.g. Rehab, National Learning Network
Lack of financial support	
• Limited employment opportunities	• State benefits, entitlements and tax credits available, age dependent and means tested
Independence	
• Some individuals may need life-long support	• Encouragement to set goals, develop life skills and interests • Become involved in support groups • Setting up of trust funds for future care and financial support

Other support groups: Al-Anon, Alateen, Irish Society for Autism, Mental Health Ireland.

Statutory services available

Special schools

- Schools catering for specific types of special needs, e.g. visual and hearing difficulties.

The National Disability Authority (NDA)

- Informs and advises government on policy and practice.
- Undertakes and commissions research to maintain standards.
- Develops and monitors implementation of codes of practice.
- Promotes universal design of buildings, products, services and IT.

Voluntary service available

Rehab

- Independent, non-profit making organisations.
- National Learning Network provides training courses.
- Supports social and economic inclusion of people with disabilities.
- Rehab employs people with disabilities.
- Provides health and social care services.

Check out the following before your exam:

- The Irish Human Rights and Equality Commission (www.ihrec.ie)
- Citizens' Information Board (www.citizensinformationboard.ie)
- The Health Service Executive (www.hse.ie)
- Enable Ireland (www.enableireland.ie)

Exam questions and sample answers

Higher Level 2016, Section B, Q5 (c)

(c) Discuss the challenges that may be experienced by the parents of a child with special needs. (3 points × 4 marks = 12 marks)

Financial: Lack of financial support may put extra pressure on family as one parent stays at home and family income may be inadequate to provide for the needs of the individual.

> **LINK**
> - Family members with special needs (p. 293)

Mobility: Individual may lack mobility and have difficulty accessing public transport systems and facilities. They may be dependent on family members or the state to provide transport. The home may need to be modified in cases of physical disability.

Emotional and physical: Isolation, exhaustion, stress and guilt on the part of parents.

Higher Level 2012, Section B, Q5 (a), (b)

(a) Outline **four** rights of children within the family.

(4 points × 3 marks = 12 marks)

1. *Right to life, a name and a nationality.*
2. *To develop physically, mentally, socially, morally and spiritually.*
3. *To be protected from neglect, abuse and discriminations.*
4. *To special care, education and training if disabled.*

(b) Discuss **each** of the following:

- Difficulties that the family unit may experience when a child has special needs; and

Refer to both child **and** parent.

- The difficulties that the family unit may experience when a parent has special needs.　　(3 points × 4 marks = 12 marks)

Child with special needs:

1. *Reduced income if parent stays at home to care for child.*
2. *Inadequate state financial support and medical facilities, family try to provide these.*
3. *Shortage of home help available, parent depends on family and friends for support.*

Parent with special needs:

1. *Emotional and social isolation for the parent with special needs.*
2. *Reduced mobility reduces access to public transport, may need access to a driver or modified car.*
3. *Reduced or limited employment opportunities for parent with special needs and carer.*

Family law

Family Law (Maintenance of Spouse and Children) Act 1976

- Entitles a dependent spouse and children to financial support from his/her partner.
- A child is dependent if aged under 18 years or under 23 years and in full-time education or has a disability.
- Maintenance is requested following a separation or divorce, even if both spouses live in the same home.
- If the parties cannot reach an agreement an Attachment of Earnings Order can be granted and paid directly to the spouse.
- An 1987 amendment allows for a maintenance application for a child even if parents were never married.

LINK
- Family Law (Divorce) Act 1996 (p. 283)

key point

The Children and Family Relationships Act 2015 has amended the Family Law (Maintenance of Spouses and Children) Act 1976.

Domestic Violence Act 1996

- Covers the protection of individuals who are threatened by physical, mental or sexual abuse.
- The Act states that a spouse/partner may apply to the courts for a:
  1. **Protection Order:** temporary order while waiting for a Safety or Barring Order
  2. **Safety Order:** Prevents abuser using violent behaviour towards spouse/partner/children; may extend to five years.
  3. **Barring Order:** Abuser must leave the home, order can last for up to three years.

> **exam focus**
>
> Higher Level: revise Judicial Separation Act 1989 (p. 283).

Family Home Protection Act 1976 (amended 1995)

- Act states that neither spouse can mortgage, sell, lease or transfer the family home without the written consent of the other.
- Applies regardless of whose name is on the title deeds – family homes are generally in joint ownership today.

Child Care Act 1991 (amended under Children and Family Act 2013)

> **LINK**
> - Housing finance (p. 228)

- Outlines a range of regulations providing for the protection of children who are at risk and is enforced by the Gardai and Tusla.
- If concerned about the child's safety, the Gardai or Tusla can intervene and apply for a Care Order or a Supervision Order.
- **An Emergency Care Order** permits the HSE to remove a child from their home for up to eight days. A Standard Care order may last until a child is 18 years of age.
- **A Supervision Order** is granted where it is necessary to monitor a child.

Making a Will

Reasons for making a Will:

1. Your wishes are carried out by an executor.
2. Money and property go to those you choose as beneficiaries.
3. Eliminates family stress and disagreements.
4. Parents ensure that children are cared for by appointing a guardian.
5. If no Will is made the estate is distributed according to the Succession Act 1965.

The **Succession Act 1965** outlines what should happen in the case of an individual dying without leaving a Will in the following cases:

- A spouse and no children
- A spouse and children
- No spouse but children
- Without a spouse or children
- No parents
- No siblings.

Procedures for making a Will

1. Employ a solicitor.
2. Make a list of assets, current value and location.
3. Compile a list of beneficiaries to include names, dates of birth and contact details.
4. Appoint two executors. Nominate guardian/trustee if there are children.
5. Divide the estate (cash and specific property) between the beneficiaries.
6. Outline your wishes regarding funeral arrangements and burial place.
7. Draw up the Will in a written form.
8. Sign the Will in the presence of two witnesses (witnesses do not need to know contents).
9. Keep in a safe place (bank or solicitor's office).
10. Ensure relevant people know where the Will is kept.

Features of a valid Will

- The **testator** must:
  - Be aged 18 years or over.
  - Act of his/her own free will.
  - Be of sound mind and understanding.
- The Will must be in writing (an oral Will is not acceptable).
- The Will must be signed by testator in the presence of two witnesses.
- Witnesses must sign the document in the presence of the testator. A Will can be drawn up by a solicitor or independently by an individual.

> **key point**
>
> **Key words:** testator, beneficiary, executor, guardian, trustee.

Exam question and sample answer

Ordinary Level, 2017, Section B, Q5 (c)

Give **one** reason why it is important to make a Will. Outline three important features of a valid Will.

Reason: (5 marks)

A person formally sets out his/her wishes for the distribution of their estate after death and may also include funeral arrangements. It can also prevent family disagreements.

Features of a valid Will: (3 points × 4 marks = 12 marks)

1. *The person making the will must be over 18 years of age and of sound mind.*
2. *The Will must be written down. A verbal Will is not acceptable.*
3. *The Will must be signed and dated in the presence of two witnesses.*

Higher Level 2010, Section B, Q5 (c)

(c) Explain the importance of parents making a Will and the procedures involved. (14 marks)

LINK
- Wills (p. 297)